Poetics of Emptiness

POETICS OF EMPTINESS

Transformations of Asian Thought
in American Poetry

JONATHAN STALLING

Fordham University Press

NEW YORK   2010

© 2010 Fordham University Press

Library of Congress Cataloging-in-Publication Data

Stalling, Jonathan.
    Poetics of emptiness : transformations of Asian thought in American poetry / Jonathan Stalling. — 1st ed.
       p.   cm.
    Includes bibliographical references and index.
    ISBN 978-0-8232-3144-7 (cloth : alk. paper)
       1. American poetry—Chinese influences.   2. Emptiness (Philosophy)
3. Philosophy—East Asia.   4. Poetics.   I. Title.
PS159.C5S73 2010
811.009'384—dc22

                                                          2010005596

Printed in the United States of America

12 11 10   5 4 3 2 1

First edition

THE
AMERICAN
LITERATURES
INITIATIVE

A book in the American Literatures Initiative (ALI), a collaborative publishing project of NYU Press, Fordham University Press, Rutgers University Press, Temple University Press, and the University of Virginia Press. The Initiative is supported by The Andrew W. Mellon Foundation. For more information, please visit www.americanliteratures.org.

For Amy Noél Stalling

If we take an instantaneous photograph of the sea in motion, we may fix the momentary form of a wave, and call it a thing; yet it was only an incessant vibration of water. So other things, more things, apparently more stable, are only large vibrations of living substance; and when we trace them to their origin and decay, they are seen to be only parts of something else. And these essential processes of nature are not simple; there are waves upon waves, process below processes, systems within systems;—and apparently so on forever.

—ERNEST FENOLLOSA, "THEORY OF LITERATURE"

CONTENTS

Figures and Tables

Figures

Table

ACKNOWLEDGMENTS

In the end, I will not be able to gather the names of everyone who has contributed to this project (all my relations throughout America, China, Korea, and the UK), for its gestation has been nourished from middle school, when I first began studying Chinese and poetry. To be sure, I am grateful to my mother for holding us all together through many familial transformations and permutations and for allowing me to transform our home in the Ozarks into my own transpacific imaginary; and to my father, whose philosophical inquiry into the nature of self (and art) has formed the basis of a lifelong dialogue; and to my childhood stepfather, who made Chinese internal martial arts (*bagua, xingyi, taiji*), with their attendant imaginative universe, a central part of my upbringing. I owe a debt of gratitude to my sister for her steadfast support, and to the companionship of my brothers.

I would like to thank so many of my teachers, from my first Chinese instructor, Li Qinqmin, and her husband, Wang Yunlong, to my Chinese philosophy and religion professors at the University of Hawaii and UC Berkeley—especially Dr. Michael Saso, Dr. Fransicus Verellen, and Dr. Patricia Berger. I owe a great debt to the late June Jordan, who instilled in me the belief that poetry can and does impact the world around us. I am also grateful to John Frow, who facilitated my transition to cultural theory at the University of Edinburgh, and to my professors in the Poetics Program at SUNY Buffalo, Charles Bernstein, Myung Mi Kim, Ma Mingqian, and Dennis Tedlock. Their rigorous and generous support of this project cannot be overstated. I am also very grateful for the help given to me by friendly staff at both Yale's Beinecke Library and Harvard's Houghton Library, where I spent many hours poring over Fenollosa's papers. I also want to thank Haun Saussy, whose support of my Fenollosa research has been unbounded and whose scholarly rigor continually inspires me, and Lucas Klein, who has been another partner in my effort to have Fenollosa's important unknown work acknowledged. There have also been numerous people who have read portions or all of this book in various stages, but I would like to single out John Whalen-Bridge for his helpful comments, as well as my colleagues at the University of Oklahoma, Ron Schliefer and Daniel Cottom, who both painstakingly commented on this work, as well as Charles Alexander and Linda Russo, who have also provided helpful suggestions and comments along the way. I also want to acknowledge my students at OU, and students and colleagues at Beijing Normal University, who have in one way or another helped me formulate the ideas that inform this work. I must stress my sincere gratitude to the anonymous readers at Fordham University Press, whose helpful suggestions and comments have improved this book greatly, and to Thomas C. Lay whose steadfast editorial attention kept the project moving forward at all points, and Helen Tartar, whose unwavering support of my work began with the acceptance of *The Chinese Written Character as a Medium for Poetry: A Critical Edition* and continues unabated through to the present. I am especially grateful to the careful attention provided by the editors of the American Literatures Initiative, Tim Roberts and my copy editor, Ruth Steinberg, who painstankingly overturned every word to look for (the many) elements that needed a firm editorial hand.

Material support for the present volume came from grants from the McNulty Fellowship in Ethnopoetics, which supported my research at SUNY Buffalo; and from two Junior Faculty Research Fellowships and a Presidential Travel Fellowship (to China) at the University of Oklahoma. I would also like to thank the Andrew W. Mellon American Literatures Initiative, without which the present volume would likely not have been possible. I would also like to thank Wang Yahui, a Calligraphy PhD student at Capital Normal University in Beijing and student of Zhongshi Ouyang for the calligraphy that adorns the opening of each chapter. I would also like to thank the University of California Press and New Directions Press for permission to reprint various images, SUNY Press for permission to publish a much expanded and updated version of a chapter published in *The Emergence of Buddhist American Literature* (ed. John

Whalen-Bridge and Gary Storhoff, 2009), and especially Brice Marden for granting me permission to use his painting for the cover.

Finally, I want to thank my wife and children, who reward me daily with the tremendously rich texture of a life lived among them. This project would simply not exist were it not for my wife, Amy, who has for years kept us all on the right side of the road when my mind would wander off into the complex architecture of the present volume. More importantly, the warm and full life she made available outside of this work enabled me to return to it time and again with restored energy and interest. Proximity, the simple fact of being close to them everyday, is the most rewarding aspect of being alive.

In the end, many have contributed to the aggregate of causes and conditions that have become this work, but any and all errors are mine alone: a textbook case of karma in action. I offer this work, with all its imperfections, in the hope that it may stimulate more ways—better ways—to explore the always-shifting planes of the poetics of emptiness.

Jonathan Stalling
Norman, Oklahoma, November, 2009

Poetics of Emptiness

Prologue: Transformations of a Transpacific Imaginary

江雪
千山鳥飛絕
萬徑人蹤滅
孤舟簑笠翁
獨釣寒江雪

In his essay "The Poem behind the Poem," the translator/anthologist Tony Barnstone offers an extended discussion of his experience translating the poem reproduced above, by the Tang poet Liu Zongyuan (柳宗元, b. 773–d. 819). Before offering his translation, Barnstone leads his readers in what appears to be a guided meditation: "Let us take a minute to read it aloud, slowly. Empty our minds. Visualize each word." His translation follows:

> A thousand mountains. Flying birds vanish.
> Ten thousand paths. Human traces erased
> One boat, bamboo hat, bark cape—an old man
> Alone with his hook. Cold river. Snow.[1]

Barnstone then comments: "Snow is the white page on which the old man is marked, through which an ink river flows. Snow is the mind of the reader, on which these pristine signs are registered, only to be covered with more snow and erased. . . . I like to *imagine* each character in 'River Snow' sketched on the page: a brushstroke against the emptiness of a Chinese painting—like the figure of the old man himself surrounded by all that snow."[2]

Barnstone asserts that each line of the translation "should drop into a meditative silence, should be a new line of vision, a revelation. The poem must be empty, pure perception; the words of the poem should be like flowers, one by one opening, then silently falling."[3] Michelle Yeh, a well-known scholar of modern Chinese poetry, might notice, as I would, that

Barnstone's poetic diction offers a particular lens through which we are invited to view the "poem behind the poem." As Yeh has pointed out, the poem can as easily be read as an expression of possible class tensions (an old man unbearably cold in a bitter landscape).[4] Furthermore, we are not to look at how the poetic form may conform to state-sponsored aesthetics, or how, as Lucas Klien has argued, the poem's prosodic effects might undermine its outward appearance of quietude.[5] Instead, Barnstone chooses to emphasize a loosely philosophical language that is hard to pin down: What does it mean that a poem must be "empty"? How are we to imagine this so-called "pure perception"?

According to Michelle Yeh, Barnstone likes to imagine things. In her short essay, "The Chinese Poem: The Visible and the Invisible in Chinese Poetry," she argues that, "implicit in the Anglo-American perception of the Chinese poem is a particular kind of correlation between stylistics and epistemology (namely Buddho-Daoist)." And it is this correlation that she finds questionable.[6] For Yeh, Barnstone not only imagines the snowy scene, he also imagines that classical Chinese poetry is the embodiment of a loosely Buddho-Daoist worldview and that the translator's task is to channel this worldview, to transfer its epistemological and ontological orientation to the reader, not through a discursive "explanation" but through English verse which enacts it. Yeh finds this reductive reading of classical Chinese poetry problematic because it limits other possible meanings and reading frames, and while I share Yeh's point of view, I think that one cannot dismiss these "Buddho-Daoist" claims. Instead, we need to focus on these claims, as a specific domain of heterocultural poetics conditioned by a history of transpacific intertextual travels. Reductive—yes—but important nonetheless.[7]

Of course, Barnstone is only one of a host of American translators, poets, and critics who naturally assume a particular correlation between East Asian philosophy and poetry—what in shorthand I am dubbing a "poetics of emptiness." Clearly, the generations of American poets who have turned to Chinese poetry have also turned to this imagined geography—a "transpacific imaginary," or nexus, of intertextual engagements with classical East Asian philosophical and poetic discourses.

By using the term "imaginary," I do not want to imply a dichotomy between imagination and reality. I do not want to imply that these poets have simply "imagined," that is, made up, or projected, an "Asian fantasy" into their poetic practices (although this may be also applicable at times). Instead, I want to present their ability to bring into view what are, prior to their imaging, merely potential heterocultural configurations.

In other words, I want to privilege and yet complicate the positive denotation of "imagination" as the ability to deal with reality through "an innovative use of resources"—as in, *she handled the problems with great imagination.* Yet I will not be using the term "imaginary" as a romantic expression of the creative individual either. Instead, I prefer to follow Rob Wilson, who defines an "imaginary" as a "situated and contested social fantasy." As he writes, "In our era of transnational and postcolonial conjunction [. . .] the very act of imagining (place, nation, region, globe) is constrained by discourse and contorted by geopolitical struggles for power, status, recognition, and control."[8] I embrace this more complicated view of imagination because the generation and proliferation of competing forms of the poetics of emptiness explored in this work cannot escape the geopolitical contexts in which they arise. Therefore, I want not only to chart the catalytic role that concepts of emptiness have come to play in the creation (imagining) of new poetic discourses and aesthetics in twentieth-century American literature, but also to show how these discourses draw upon and contribute to distortions of East Asian poetics and philosophy generated from within historically and politically specific social contexts. While sorting through these situated distortions comprises much of the work performed in the following chapters, I want to foreground how each of the poets examined here transforms both East Asian philosophy and American poetics through their explicit attempts to fuse distinct discourses into new, heterocultural productions. And while this book will show how notions or images of "emptiness" displace multiple other (and often very important) elements of Chinese poetry and poetics in the American poetic consciousness, it will also show how these "transpacific imaginaries" are valuable and worthy of our careful attention.

While the term "transatlantic" has found a prominent place in American and British literary criticism, the term "transpacific" has only recently been introduced as a category or region of interest to contemporary literary critics. One must be careful with such concepts since they can become subsumed within the conceptual networks that undergird existing geopolitical discourses, like those which imagine a space of neoliberal transnational corporate exchange that collapses difference, thus creating a smoothed over region across which cultural and capital exchanges freely and "neutrally" take place. Rob Wilson problematizes the idea of a "Pacific Rim," or "Asia Pacific," when he argues that "the commonplace and taken-for-granted assumption of 'region' implied by a signifying category like 'Asia-Pacific' entails an act of social imagining," which, he continues, "had to be shaped into coherence and consensus in ways that could call attention to the power politics of such unstable representations."[9] So I would like to cautiously employ the term "transpacific" to demarcate the historically specific cultural and textual pathways across which various philosophical, literary, and aesthetic discourses travel, specifically from China (often by way of Japan) to America.

In this sense, my usage of the term follows that of Yunte Huang, who uses "transpacific" in conjunction with "displacement" to describe "a historical process of textual migration of cultural meanings, meanings that include linguistic traits, poetics, philosophical ideas, myths, stories, and so on." Such displacement, continues Huang, "is driven in particular by the writers' desire to appropriate, capture, mimic, parody, or revise the Other's signifying practices in an effort to describe the Other."[10] As a way of distinguishing his notion of "displacement" from Stephen Greenblatt's concept of "appropriative mimesis," which Greenblatt defines as "imitation in the interest of acquisition," Huang emphasizes that the "appropriative mimesis" of American poets could not avoid making "images of the Other." This "imaging," or ethnographic impulse, lies at the heart of what Huang calls "displacement," insofar as the "ethnographic vision," or "image," of the Other displaces "multiple readings of the 'original'" into "a version that foregrounds the translator's [or ethnographer's] own agenda."[11] Following this definition, the various ways in which American poets and critics have imagined classical Chinese poetry as a "poetics of emptiness" can be considered a "displacement" of other readings of the same body of literature and poetics.

I would like to pause for a moment to clarify my preference for the prefix "hetero-" (which I use to emphasize "heterogeneity," "mixture," "unevenness," not "heterosexuality") over the more commonly used prefixes "cross-," "inter-," or "trans-," to describe the cultural works in this book. Wai-lim Yip (葉維廉, Ye Wei-lien), a prominent transpacific poet and critic who has published more than forty books, conceives of his work as a "cross-cultural poetics," understood through the somewhat dated ideas of what can be called Whorfian linguistic determinism. Yip draws parallels between the lack of tense conjugation in Chinese and the different concepts of time in the Hopi language, which undergirds the Whorf-Sapir thesis.[12] Yip quotes Whorf at some length: "I find it gratuitous to assume that a Hopi who knows only the Hopi language and the cultural ideas of his own society has the same notions, often supposed to be intuitions, of time and space that we have, and that are generally assumed to be universal."[13] Yip agrees, and he further endorses Whorf's

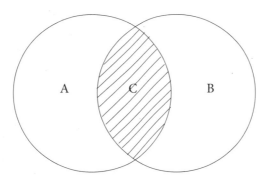

FIGURE P.1. Wai-lim Yip's cross-cultural interpretation diagram. From Wai-Lim Yip, *Diffusion of Distance: Dialogues between Chinese and Western Poetics*, 18. © 1993 Regents of the University of California. Published by the University of California Press.

belief that there are no adequate words in Western languages to define Hopi metaphysics: "Whorf has demonstrated excellently that to arrive at a universal basis for discussion and understanding it is dangerous to proceed from only one model; we must begin simultaneously with two or three models, comparing and contrasting them with full respect and attention to indigenous 'peculiarities' and cultural 'anomalies.'"[14]

Having affirmed Whorf's ideas, Yip then offers up a diagram to clarify his own idea of a "cross-cultural poetics" (see Figure P.1). Yip argues that circle *A* and circle *B* represent two distinct cultural models, and that the shaded area *C*, where the two circles overlap, "represents resemblances between the two models" that can serve as "the basis for establishing a fundamental model."[15] To produce such a model, Yip argues, the poetics of culture *A* must not be subjected to the terms of circle *B*, or vice versa. In Chapter 4, I explore Yip's formulation of this discourse on models as an extension of the Daoist concepts of *wuwei* and *ziran,* but for now it is sufficient to point out the general conceptual horizons of his cross-cultural poetics. Yip's term, "cross-cultural," could equally be replaced by the term "intercultural," since he envisions cultures as distinct spheres (represented by circles). Like the cognate term, "interpersonal," which refers to contact between two distinct bodies, "intercultural" does not refer to heterogeneity, but to autonomous spheres that can be compared. The shaded area *C* in Yip's diagram does not represent a place of cross-fertilization, or cultural heterogeneity, but simply an area of cultural similarity which comparative literature scholars find and map. Both prefixes, "cross-" and "inter-," imply purely distinct cultural worlds between which comparisons can be made but does not make room for actual heterocultural admixture.

The sinologist Zong-qi Cai praises Yip for his emphasis on "the basis of equality for any truly 'cross-cultural' dialogue." But Cai also questions the adequacy of Yip's model: "In it [Yip's diagram] we can find no clues as to from which point of view we should look at the similarities and differences shown. We are left to conceive of three possible points of view: from A, B, or C. If we look at the similarities and differences solely from either A or B, we will be seeing two cultural traditions through the vistas of one, and hence become susceptible to the two polemics. On the other hand, if we focus our attention solely on C, we will be tempted to overemphasize the similarities to the point of essentializing them as 'universals,' and consequently neglect the examination of differences."[16] Cai then offers his own model, as shown in Figure P.2. Cai's diagram has improved upon Yip's insofar as all of the lines constituting boundaries are represented as porous and dynamic rather than autonomous and static. For Cai, however, the main change between the two is his establishment of a "transcultural perspective" from which he attempts to locate his own work. Cai argues that this perspective "is born of an effort to rise above the limitations and prejudices of any single tradition to a transcultural vantage point, from which one can assess similarities and differences without privileging, overtly or covertly, one tradition over another."[17] While I applaud Cai's perforation of the boundaries, his attempt to establish such a "transcultural vantage point" reveals a certain non-self-reflexivity toward the cultural conditions of his own thinking. To be fair, Cai offers this transcultural vision as a goal rather than as a description of scholarship directed at such a goal, but the transcultural position, like the cross- and intercultural concepts would fail to acknowledge the already heterocultural nature of the transpacific imaginary. In a sense, the prefixes "inter-," "cross-," and "trans-" are circumscribed by the limitations of strictly comparative scholarship and as a result remain unable to address the fact that the cultural productions they name are almost always heterocultural productions themselves.

In short, there is a problem with using the diagrams, as well as these comparative prefixes, as conceptual aids for visualizing heterocultural productions. Diagrams are devices largely developed and deployed in the social sciences to map complex cultural phenomena. As visual aids, they can be helpful but also harmful. What would a diagram presenting the different configurations of a poetics of emptiness as discussed in this book look like? Would the multiple circles drawn circumscribe cul-

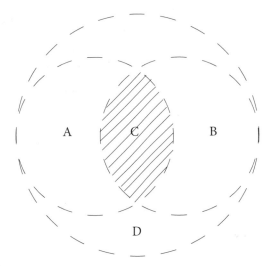

FIGURE P.2. Based on material in Zong-qi Cai's *Configurations of Comparative Poetics*, 16.

tural phenomena associated with individual nation-states, ethnicities, cultures, races, time periods, or some other conceptual grouping? Such circles would be wrong from the start. Take China, for example (but you could just as easily take America, Europe, or Russia). China conceived of as a nation-state, a unified culture, or a "race" is an illusion—or, to be more specific, an ideological formation. These terms are and have been deployed to consolidate power over a heterogeneous population, and drawing a circle around China reinforces this ideology. The visual representation of boundaries, common in mapmaking, and even seen in the Chinese character for nation-state, 國, traffics in the language of siege warfare, and I believe it cannot be relied upon to explore the intricacies of heterocultural literary productions.

This term, "heterocultural," avoids the pitfalls of "cross-," "inter-," and "trans"-cultural, since it does not posit two pure, autonomous cultures between which transmissions or crossings can occur, nor a transcendent position beyond culture itself, but instead complicates the very conceptual integrity of monolithic concepts of culture altogether. Yet I do not believe that this term can be applied equally to all cultural productions; instead, I want to reserve its use for those texts that are clearly working from within multiple cultural idioms.

Heterocultural texts offer an opportunity to expand literary criticism's interpretive frames—make them subtler, add new registers, and tune new antennae. If we want to move beyond Greenblatt's metacritical notion of "appropriative mimesis" to engage the heterocultural theories of language and perception animating such texts, it is my belief that literary critics must formulate interpretive frames as hybrid as the texts being read. This entails a heterocultural criticism that forms itself dialogically with the texts being interpreted. Instead of assuming that a given theoretical frame is sufficient to respond to the heterocultural discourses animating a text being read, the critic acknowledges when additional study is required and pursues these leads. Trying to explicate the term "emptiness" even within its most explicitly "Buddhist" occurrences, as in the work of Gary Snyder, might require a critic to trace the term through at least three distinct Japanese schools of Buddhism (Soto and Rinzai Zen and Kegon) before it further bifurcates into Chinese and Indian schools. Such intertextual travels reveal "emptiness" to be a heterogeneous nexus of potential meanings every bit as contentious as, say, "truth" or "beauty" in Western philosophy and literature (a point I will pursue further in the Introduction). Tracing the term's use value in Zen poetics offers still more pathways and sinkholes. Of course, we know such semiotic caverns are infinite, just as we know that the need for spelunking is also absolutely necessary.

Introduction: The Poetics of Emptiness, or a Cult of Nothingness

Just the idea of nothingness makes us shudder; but there are minds that, far from being frightened, are charmed by it. They love nothingness because they detest life; we, on the other hand adore life and abhor nothingness.

—JULES BARTHÉLEMY SAINT-HILAIRE

Poetry makes nothing happen.

—W. H. AUDEN

I have nothing to say and I am saying it and that is poetry as I need it.

—JOHN CAGE, "LECTURE ON NOTHING"

For much of the nineteenth century, Buddhism, with its emphasis on the enigmatic concept of "emptiness," was reduced to what Roger-Pol Droit has called the "cult of nothingness." According to Droit, Buddhism, for its early-nineteenth-century Western commentators, appeared to be an inconceivable worship of nothingness, a delusional and impossible religion based upon "the annihilation of any thinking principle . . . a daze where consciousness is dissolved . . . a negation of the will . . . a desire for a death without return."[1] From this viewpoint, Buddhism was a threatening inversion of the West's core beliefs. At best, it was a fetishization of nonexistence, and at worst, a worship of annihilation—an institutionalized desire for the world and all we hold dear to disappear, leaving only a cold, gaping absence, a negation of everything, without end.

Yet the "cult of nothingness" invented by Western commentators can be seen as a predictable reaction to the Buddhist concept of "emptiness," which is difficult if not impossible to understand vis-à-vis binary (or dualistic/dichotomous) constructs like being/non-being, existence/nonexistence, or even the more intuitive binary of fullness/emptiness.[2] In a very real sense, the poetics of emptiness discussed in this work is a response to the Western idea of (and fear of the idea of) nothingness (of nihilism), which one might consider an unstable attachment to various binary constructs privileging notions of "somethingness."[3] The poets discussed in this work attempt to bring into American letters new languages adapted from two distinct and yet heterogeneous philosophical systems (Buddhism and Daoism) to expand thought beyond the horizon of these inherited binaries. Before exploring the different ways Buddhist and Daoist discourses disrupt Western something/nothing dichotomies,[4] it may be helpful to look more carefully at this fundamental dualism in Western metaphysics and philosophy.

In a well-known passage in his 1862 novel, *Les miserables,* Victor Hugo writes: "Nihilism has no substance. There is no such thing as nothingness, and zero does not exist. Everything is something. Nothing is nothing. Man lives more by affirmation than by bread."[5] What Hugo fails to take into account are the conceptual constraints of traditional Western categories of existence themselves. At the base of each concept we find an *a priori* category called "thing" or "thingness." "Things" are existents that take up space, time, or both, and "something" posits the existence of at least one "thing." Accepting this solid definition of a "thing," "nothing" would simply be the state of "no things," and under these conceptual constraints, it would seem "nothing" cannot be "something" and "something" cannot be "nothing." The relationship that binds the binary together is mutual and irreconcilable difference, a difference nonetheless traversed each time a "something" ceases to be anything at all. In this black-and-white dualism, annihilation haunts all being with total extinction. This is no doubt why so many nineteenth-century Westerners found the prospect of a religion grounded in "nothing" so frightening. It is no doubt why "nothing" remains so frightening to this day.

Following the logic of this binary, Western philosophy and metaphysics have been and continue to be largely grounded in ontological "being," not "nothingness." And even in the cases where nothing is posited, such as with the classical atomists (for whom nothingness was needed to conceive of discrete entities and account for their motions), such voids were no more than conceptual supplements to systems of thought grounded in various notions of "somethingness." In Christian theology, for instance, God creates the universe (as the first cause) from nothing (*creatio ex nihilo*), and we might say that the dark pockets of God's absence accounts for the possibility of evil (as in the phrase "God forsaken").[6] Looking back on Western philosophy and metaphysics, therefore, "nothing" takes shape generally from the standpoint of being, against being's presupposed and universal presence. Ironically, when understood as the subordinated supplement of being, "nothingness" must first be transfigured into a "something" in order for it to be dismissed as a mere shadow or absence of the real. While philosophers still debate questions like "Why should there be something and not nothing?" (articulated by Leibniz)—which Heidegger called the only metaphysical question—with a few notable exceptions (clearly Heidegger would be the prime example but only after his encounter with the *Daodejing*[7]), the dialectic has not moved beyond the conceptual restraints of the binary itself, even when "nothingness" has been exalted.[8]

Given the entrenched nature of this dualism, it should not be a surprise that early encounters with Buddhist "emptiness" would result in nearly complete incomprehensibility. Yet the early reception in the West of Buddhist notions of emptiness as a "nothingism," or nihilism, could not have been more misguided, since, unlike Western philosophy and metaphysics, Buddhism does not make use of the concept of "nothing," its primary philosophical argument being the rejection of the category of "somethingness" (and therefore its binary supplement). Nevertheless, the fear of "nothing" in the Western psyche presaged by a misinterpretation of Buddhism would blossom into full-blown cultural fixation in the twentieth century. When Yeats writes in his paradigmatic modernist poem, "The Second Coming," that "Things fall apart; the center cannot hold," he makes available this fear of "nothing," a fear of an absent center, dislocated, among other things, by Darwin's displacement of theological teleology with evolution, by Freud's displacement of reason with the unconscious (and the irrational causes and outcomes of World War I), by Nietzsche's pronouncement of God's death, and, only a few decades later, by Saussure's liguistics (which asserts the relation between words and their referents as not governed by positive entities but only by differences).[9] While Yeats's relationship with the concept of "nothingness" cannot be subsumed under this reading of "The Second Coming," the reception of the poem serves as an indication of a great, if sometimes ambivalent, fear of nothingness.

To be more precise, one might go so far as to say that elements central to modernist poetics arose as a realization of and a general reaction against seeing Western philosophy, politics, religion, and culture as the spinning accretion disc circumnavigating the absence of an autonomous, enduring identity. When in *The Genealogy of Morals*, Nietzsche writes that "man would sooner have the void for his purpose than be void of purpose,"[10] he has in his crosshairs the possibility that religion generally, and Christianity specifically, is itself the realization of nihilism, since religion, for him, has at its center a profound absence, or "the absence." For Yeats, such a "nothingness" may offer a resource for a negative theology capable of absorbing one into its undifferentiated "sphere,"[11] but for Nietzsche and the later existentialists following him, the *nihil* (Latin for "nothing") at the heart of the Western mind was something that had to be faced and overcome (hence the catharsis of "God Is Dead" and of the "Eternal Return of the Same"), a pathos informed by faith in an indomitable will to power inherited by modernist poetics, which at least in part accounts for its heroic attempt to "shore up the fragmentation" of Western civilization.

Modernism may have signaled a break with the signature themes and poetic forms of Romanticism's organicist, idealistic, and unified epistemological vision; nevertheless, vestiges of earlier heroic visions (even if Nietzsche's and Yeats's visions were self-consciously so) continued to permeate modernist poetics. So while Modernism may have inaugurated a dissolution of epistemic coherence through what Marjorie Perloff later came to call its "poetics of indeterminacy," the aesthetic fragmentation of Ezra Pound's *Cantos* still required readers to create or reconstruct ontological wholes through complex yet eventually coherent images (the "concrete image" may well be the primary device—or trope—of the metaphysics of "somethingness").[12]

In this context, we might read W. H. Auden's prophetic line, "Poetry makes nothing happen" (which, for Auden, may have been intended as a movement toward the depoliticization of poetry—or at least an aesthetics of experience against direct political engagements),[13] or certainly the Buddhist-inspired anti-teleological indeterminacy of John Cage's "Lecture on Nothing," as a break with the belief in ontological stability itself, and furthermore as a move toward releasing the teleological ends of many core American values. As Stephan Fredman writes, "If American culture bases so many of its ideals upon the furtherance of individual self-interests—lauding the person who can 'take charge' and promoting the 'pursuit of happiness' and the American Dream of getting ahead—Buddhism stresses letting-be, nonattachment, the cessation of desire, and the illusory nature of the 'self.'"[14] Most of these challenges to Western values privilege various kinds of "nothing" (or doing nothing) over a "something" (or doing something) by way of challenging the *a priori* acceptance of the ontological values placed on various guises of "somethingness." Here, "no-self" is privileged over self/soul/spirit, process (procedure) is valued over product, mindfulness (loose awareness of the mind itself) over directed cognition and analysis, et cetera—and of course, many poets interested in integrating these Buddhist ideas into American poetry look to existing Asian poetic techniques already used to communicate or enact Buddhist (and Daoist) philosophical insights. The present study is interested in exploring this last vector of transmission, which brings to mind an important question: what did American poets find in existing Asian textual practices that could be integrated into American cultural productions to enable or enact new cultural values undergirded by non-Western notions of emptiness?

It is this question that brings to mind Tony Barnstone's Buddho-Daoist reading of "River Snow," discussed in the Prologue, and the attendant cultural arguments that read classical Chinese poetry as a praxis that enables "emptiness" to enter language in ways we have not seen in the Western literary tradition. Ernest Fenollosa synthesizes his poetics of emptiness based upon his understanding of the aggregative nature of Chinese characters, the indeterminacies of Chinese grammar, and the correlative cosmology of Chinese prosody. Gary Snyder and Wai-lim Yip both ground their poetics of emptiness on different doctrinal interpretations of classical Chinese poetry, and Theresa Hak Kyung Cha blends the conceptual textuality of Daoist alchemy and Korean shamanism to enact her own unique poetics of emptiness.[15] While each of the figures in this study comes to his or her notions of emptiness by way of various concepts of Chinese poetic and philosophical textuality, their notions of emptiness are radically different from one another because each draws upon historically specific configurations of different Buddhist and Daoist discourses.

Buddhism Changes Everything—Daoism Changes Nothing: The Many Sides of Emptiness

BUDDHISM

The American poet/critics discussed in this book work from several distinct Buddhist notions of emptiness that can be largely broken down between positive (affirmative) notions of emptiness as a variety of distinct monisms, and negative notions of emptiness (more a dehypostatizing method than a notion in itself). But we can get an even more specific introduction to different forms of Buddhist emptiness, and a sense of how they overlap and interlock, by briefly looking at how they appear in the work of the poets included in this study. In this section, I offer a brief genealogy of some of the most influential Buddhist concepts and schools: Tiantai (via Nāgārjuna), Huayan, and Yogācāra/*tathāgatagarbha* (central to Zen). As we do this, it might be useful to return for a moment to

Hugo's dismissal of nihilism (by way of affirmation), but this time modify his ideas to reflect a very different idea of "nothingness," one more in line with the late-nineteenth-century thinker Ernest Fenollosa's poetics of emptiness, for instance. Instead of Hugo's assertion that "There is no nothing," Fenollosa would counsel us by asserting that "There is no something," by which he would mean that every "thing" is not existent as a "thing" nor nonexistent as a "nothing," but exists by way of being an aggregate of "things," which in themselves are aggregates of nearly infinite other "things," and that to speak of these ultimately arbitrary categories (or, as Fenollosa will call them, "bundles") as cut-off, autonomous, self-generated, and sustained "things" is to misunderstand the nature of the phenomenon itself. And to speculate about existence and nonexistence based upon ultimately unstable, impermanent, and arbitrary aggregates simply misses the point. From his Tendai Buddhist perspective (a school of Buddhism that will be discussed in more detail shortly), the only "thing" or "phenomenon" that exists in a stable form is not a given "thing" at all but the manner in which "things" exist (as "emptiness," or *śūnatā*). Of course, for Hugo there can be no "nothing" since there cannot be a "zero," but it is instructive to note that the term "zero" came via the Italian *zefiro*, from the Arabic *çifr*, meaning "empty, void," which is in turn the Arabic translation of the Sanskrit term *śūnatā*.[16]

The term *śūnatā* is often translated into English as "emptiness" and into Chinese as 空 (*kong*), but can be better understood in the sense that nothing possesses essential, autonomous, enduring identity, which is also often called *anattā*, or "not-self." Fenollosa encountered this foundational concept during his study and conversion to a specific form of Japanese Buddhism (Tendai Buddhism), which traces its roots to the Chinese Buddhist school 天台 (Tiantai) and espouses a notion of emptiness derived from the second-century Indian philosopher Nāgārjuna. Emptiness, for Nāgārjuna, simply means that all phenomena lack a "self-nature," or "autonomous essence." In other words, all things are contingent, and "dependent [on] their causes and conditions," or *pratītya-samutpāda*. Nāgārjuna relentlessly dehypostatizes (that is to say, reverses the process whereby individual things are "hypostatized," or regarded as concrete or fixed realities) phenomena that appear to exist independently, by arguing that they cannot self-exist (exist independent of contingency—have a non-relational complete meaning), and are, therefore, "empty of self-autonomy." Yet even though these phenomena are understood as lacking inherent existence, Nāgārjuna argues that they are not nonexistent either—but are simply "conventionally real." It is this dual thesis that gives rise to Nāgārjuna's doctrine of the Two Truths—a conventional truth (things appear to exist autonomously) and an ultimate truth (nothing is ultimately autonomous).[17] This idea will become important in an altered form in Ernest Fenollosa's own poetics of emptiness (via Tendai) as he applies this theory to the common misperception that "words" are, or point to, "cut-off" or "autonomous things" rather than "conventional (arbitrary) meeting points" of "complex relations."

So while Hugo, like others within the Western metaphysical/philosophical tradition, looks to affirmation as a defense against the specter of nihilism, Nāgārjuna's negative emptiness would open another route entirely. Before moving on to other Buddhist notions of emptiness, we might revisit this "negative" notion of emptiness one more time by imagining a debate between practitioners of this view:

> Speaker 1: Nothing is autonomous.
> Speaker 2: No it's not!
> Speaker 1 (*realizing his/her mistake*): Oh, of course, not even nothing is![18]

The speakers are first and foremost concerned with uprooting attachment to any notion of autonomous "somethings," for which of course the concept of "nothing" is merely another example. By recognizing the hypostatized nature of "nothing," negative emptiness counters it by undermining its ontological autonomy by way of negating "somethingness" more generally.

Yet Fenollosa also deploys another concept of emptiness, derived from the Kegon school of Japanese Buddhism, which can be traced back to the Chinese Huayan school (華嚴), and ultimately to its central sutra, the *Avatamsaka Sutra* (Ch: *Huayan jing*, 華嚴經). The *Avatamsaka Sutra* describes the historical Buddha's moment of awakening itself, and therefore offers a nirvanic perspective of emptiness, where "things" are not simply "dependent upon prior causes and conventions" we see in the concept 空 (*kong*), but where there is a complete unobstructed interpenetration of all things (*shishi wu'ai*, 事事無礙), where every-thing (*shi*) is interrelated to every other thing (*shi*). This vast web of interpenetration is known as "Indra's net," 因陀羅網 (Ja: インタラモウ; Ch: *yintuo luowang*) and is envisaged as a vast web or net of interconnections where a jewel lies at every point of convergence and reflects every other jewel in the net.[19] By moving beyond the dehypostatizing method of Nāgārjuna's "dependent arising" to posit the positive existence of this interconnected totality, the Huayan school established a new ontological foundation for

emptiness: the net itself. In other words, Nāgārjuna, who was particular-
ly concerned with undermining a philosophical reification of emptiness,
denied the ultimate self-existence of anything (including any concept
of emptiness), while Kegon asserts that while every "jewel in the net"
is empty of self-existence, the "net" fundamentally exists as a monism.
This monistic emptiness granted Fenollosa a more aesthetic theory of
emptiness capable of embodying more ontological possibilities and what
we will come to see as his aesthetic concerns. Again, an imagined (and
simplified) dialogue between Kegon Buddhists may be helpful.

> Speaker 1: Are you a self?
> Speaker 2: I am conventionally a self, but the ultimate nature of this
> self is dependent upon every other self in existence. So strictly
> speaking there is no autonomous "I," just the web.

While Fenollosa's Buddhism has remained submerged beneath his editor
Ezra Pound's "anti-Buddhist" interpretation (and editorial decisions),[20]
by the mid-twentieth century American poetry had experienced a broad
spectrum of transpacific cultural and philosophical migrations. Of the
many American poets who engage Buddhist (and to a lesser extent Dao-
ist) notions of emptiness, few can claim to be more influential than Gary
Snyder.

While Snyder, following Fenollosa, drew inspiration from the Huayan
(Kegon) concept of "Indra's net," this is but one aspect of the founda-
tion of his Buddhist metaphysics (which arises principally in relation
to his ecological commitments). While Fenollosa's Buddhism has re-
mained largely unexplored because of its complicated historical con-
text, it should not be surprising that America's most well-known (and
celebrated) Buddhist poet's ideas of emptiness reflect the mainstream
views of Mahayana Buddhism more generally. Snyder might also argue
that all "somethings" are empty (of autonomy)—although for him they
are empty largely because of their dependency upon the mind of the
perceiver—and furthermore that this perceiving mind is not a singu-
lar mind, but the very essence that gives rise to all phenomena. Snyder's
poetry and poetics derived from his Zen studies can be traced back to
yet another school of Indian Buddhism, called Yogācāra (法相宗—Law
Character school or *citta-mātra*, or 唯識—Conciousness Only school),
and to Tathāgatagarbha notions of "Buddha Nature." While the founders
of the Yogācāra school, Vasubandhu and Asaṅga (4th cent.), agreed with
the Nāgārjuna that there are no ultimately "real" things, the Yogācāra
school argues that the mind (which perceives things) is ultimately "real"

or "self-existent."[21] While in some ways distinct from classical Indian Yogācāra, its principal notion of a generative monistic "Mind" entered China through a set of sutra collectively labeled *tathāgatagarbha*, or "Buddha Nature."[22] Imaged as a vast, deep ocean, "thusness," or "suchness," is a *gharba*, or "womb/locus," that all transient phenomena arise from (like waves) and recede back into. Since everything arises as just an aspect of this monistic mind/consciousness/sea, all phenomenal existence (including one's sense of "self") is not truly autonomous (real), but its "true self" is its nature as an aspect of ontological Oneness/Mind. Some Buddhologists argue that Yogācāran and Tathāgatagarbha thinkers brought Brahmanism back into Buddhism through the back door to replace the often hard-to-swallow notion of "no-self," or *anātman*, with more ontologically stable "positive" notions.[23] I will discuss this possibility in more detail in Chapter 3 when I discuss Snyder's poetry in greater detail. For now, it is important to simply note that this set of ideas came into Snyder's Buddhism through the Zen tradition's adoption of the Tathāgatagarbha teachings (which entered by way of key texts like the *Nirvana Sutra* (涅槃經)[24] and the *Lankavatara Sutra* (楞伽經).[25]

Another short dialogue may be illustrative of Yogācāran and Tathāgatagarbha ideas of emptiness:

Speaker 1: Are you a self?
Speaker 2: No, my notion of self is a construct [illusion] of mind.
Speaker 1: Are you not the mind that constructs this self?
Speaker 2: Yes, I am only this Mind, but since there is only One Mind, how can it be mine and yours? From the perspective of ultimate reality, there is no me or you (no-duality), just this "thusness," just "Buddha Nature itself," pure awareness.

While these different Buddhist notions of emptiness are radically distinct, they each aim at "emptying" all "somethings" of their assumed autonomous "thingness" through admitting some degree of contingency. Daoism, on the other hand, offers a very different way beyond the "something/nothing" binary.

DAOISM CHANGES NOTHING

Sinologists like Isabelle Robinet point out that the idea of "Daoism" as a coherent unified tradition is problematic at best, given the radically heterogeneous texts, practices, and institutions that are grouped under this term. Yet I will be speaking of "Daoism" as largely a particular configuration of the transpacific imaginary, one conditioned by a proliferation of translations and interpretations of a limited number of texts tied to this tradition. Qualified in this way, I will continue to use the term "Daoism" to indicate that which is made available through the history of this intertextual travel (but I will also gesture toward a broader, more inclusive definition as well). The heading of this section playfully suggests that "Buddhism changes everything—Daoism changes nothing" so that I can draw attention to the way that Daoist notions of emptiness are less directed toward the dehypostatization of "thingness" and instead move toward a "positive" ontological understanding of nothingness. As I pointed out earlier, "nothingness" has remained the "other" of "being" in the West and, as such, is usually relegated to the status of a supplement, not a concept developed in its own right. Outside the formal domain of mathematics (where zeros and negative numbers play a significant role), the main exception to this rule in Western discourses is astrophysics, which may be useful to look at for a moment before moving on to specifically Daoist discourses.

Due to the nearly infinite nature of detectable "somethings" surrounding us on our planet (after all, terrestrial nature abhors a vacuum, right?), it should not come as a great surprise that "nothing" has been a far greater concern for astronomers (and astrophysicists) than for those in other fields of study. Historically, "nothing" remained a concept of little use for figures in mechanical science, like Galileo, who relied on the notion of "ethers" to explain, among other things, the effect of gravity on celestial objects. Light, too, was a cause of concern, for how could there be a wave without a medium? Today, however, after several decades studying the bizarre behavior of black holes, and the recent return of Einstein's "cosmological constant" in the past decade's discovery of "dark energy," voids are taking on a newer, more active role. "Nothing" (or, to be more precise, "nothing directly detectable"), as it turns out, not only exerts energy, it appears to be the prime mover behind the increasingly expanding universe, so science may be on the threshold of new ways of thinking and theorizing the undetectable ("nothing") as other than an inert inverse of something's mass and energy. The criteria of detectability, which after the advent of gravitational lensing (the arch-like distortion of light imaged through the "lens" of gravitational fields), exposes the limitations of the human senses, and has been further challenged by evidence of energy and mass wholly undetectable outside its effects upon observable phenomena. Nevertheless, even as science begins to develop new languages from these findings, the existential residues of an abject and frightening nihilism still permeate "nothingness," even, or especially, "nothings" that appear to have non-detectible (directly) yet overwhelming mass and energy (and are physically "there"). Perhaps these findings will help destabilize the binary of something/nothing, or perhaps simply exasperate the terror of nothingness envisioned as "being's other" driving life (even all matter) at ever increasing speeds toward complete darkness.

It is here, in cosmology and, more specifically, cosmogony,[26] that Daoist notions of nothingness are often formulated. In the Buddhist discourses just discussed, we can see that the concept of "nothing" is wrong from the start, since according to either negative or positive forms of Buddhist emptiness, "nothingness" would be a dependently arisen (and therefore empty) "no-thing." There is no need for cosmogonic narratives here, but in Daoism "nothing" and "emptiness" are aspects of a strange concept that we might be forced to call a "thing," from the standpoint of most forms of Buddhist analysis, but certainly behave differently than most "things" in Western philosophy or metaphysics. Imagine for a minute (Daoist cosmogony often utilizes this faculty) the moment before the birth of the universe. Of course, we are in trouble right away: do we not need space and time in order to describe anything at all? Therefore, we are forced to adopt a strict apophatic language. This state of not-yet a universe is described in the *Daodejing via negativa*:

> Searching but not seeing, we call it dim.
> Listening but not hearing, we call it faint.
> Groping but not touching, we call it subtle.
>
> These three cannot be fully grasped.
> Therefore they became one.
>
> Rising it is not bright; setting it is not dark.
> It moves all things back to where there is nothing.[27]

Nameless, formless, and without substance, this strange non- or not-yet-beingness is beyond perception and the language of perceptibility. Perhaps we could describe this as a state of undetectable uniformity, for without manifested edges there is nothing to name, no differentia to see against the backdrop of "nothingness." This state of infinite sameness is referred to as "the One" and is treated as a fecund condition, which according to Daoist cosmogony may not have a shape but does have an angle—it leans toward time, toward becoming manifest and distinct. While always already replenishing itself (having no end or beginning, it cannot be exhausted), it is continually giving rise to difference. Chapter 42 of the *Daodejing* states:

> Tao engenders One;
> One engenders Two;
> Two engenders Three;
> Three engenders the ten thousand things.[28]

The undifferentiated whole (One) gives rise to the correlative phases of *yin* and *yang*, which become manifest in all phenomena as the expression of temporally unstable configurations of these correlative energies (and therefore are transient from the perspective of the undifferentiated One, variously called *taiji, taiyi, hundun, qiantian*, etc.). While I will discuss this progression in more detail in the chapters that follow, it should be sufficient here to point to the re-oriented pathos of the generative "nothingness" of the One. While the general Western view of "nothingness-as-zero" requires a first cause or God to fill absence with presence by way of creation, "nothingess-as-One" has no supplement, contrastant, shape, or edge. Without differentia, there is nothing one can say or see, as there are no differences that can be used to contextualize, orient, or triangulate identities. Thus "nothing" as the "One" is not envisioned as absence, but infinite fecundity, one that continually spills over itself into the realm of becoming "somethingness" by way of correlative cosmology (*yin* and *yang*, five element theory). By recasting nothingness as the womb of being(s), rather than that which threatens being with its extinction or annihilation, Daoism offers a very different pathos through which to view, among other things, the nothingness threatening Western modernity from within. While helpful, Daoist cosmogony, invested in the language of origins, is incomplete and problematic if taken as the whole. Of course, Daoism is not called "Taiji-ism," or any other term used to stand in for the undifferentiated One. Instead, "Dao-ism's" central term can be translated as "way," and refers to the "way" in which the One pours into or becomes in time, and even the "way" in which change takes place within time. The Dao is the "way" of the One, and like the primoridial void/womb, can only be discussed *via negativa*:

> Tao called Tao is not Tao
> Names can name no lasting names.
> Nameless: the origin of heaven and earth.[29]

In chapter 40, we get, "All things originate from being [*you*]; Being [*you*] originates from non-being [*wu*]."[30] In both of these chapters, *wu* appears as a point of origin, but it is important to note that *wu* is not only the origin of existence but also the "way" things become existent. For emptiness is closely linked to the "way" (Dao) things exist. In this sense, emptiness is linked to the central concept of the "Dao" itself, which according to the first chapter of the *Daodejing*, cannot be named, cannot be brought into language. This is because the Dao, as it is conceived in Lao-Zhuang thought (discourses centered on two texts, *Daodejing* and *Zhuangzi*) is empty of any dependence upon a structuring principle. One can say that the Dao is not 他然 (other so), dependent on others for its existence, but instead, that it arises of its self, naturally自然 (*ziran*, self-so).[31] This distinction points to a fundamental difference between Daoist and Buddhist notions of ultimate reality.

As you will recall, most forms of Buddhist emptiness point precisely to the dependent origination (non-self-arising) of phenomena 因緣生的 (all things are caused), whereas Doaist emptiness springs from a belief that everything arises naturally from itself, "empty" of intellectual artifice, or of what the transpacific poet/critic Wai-lim Yip calls "epistemological elaborations." To perceive the Dao, therefore, requires a special form of consciousness that does not intervene upon the mysterious "self-so" nature of becoming. This state of un-impeding attendance to the *ziran* of all becoming is called *wuwei* 無為.[32] This state, often translated as "non-interference," requires one to empty the mind of preconceived notions that would impede upon the un-mapped becoming of the Dao. This notion of self-emptying is often connected to a key line from the other principal Daoist text, the *Zhuangzi*, where the author offers the phrase 心齋坐忘 (*xinzhai zuowang*, "to fast the mind-heart and sit in forgetfulness") as a way of perceiving the Dao.[33] The *Daodejing* places a great emphasis on striving to reach such an experience of emptiness figured as a void: "Attain complete emptiness [void], Hold fast to stillness."[34]

One may have noticed a subtle shift in the function of the term "empty" throughout the previous paragraph. In the beginning of the paragraph, I used the term in its more Buddhist sense "empty of," as in the Dao is "empty of dependence on other things." By the end of the paragraph, however, a new meaning of the term arose; emptying starts to behave in a manner not unlike its more typical English sense: empty your plate, pockets, or glass. So, "fasting the mind" refers to the attempt to empty it of thoughts, for instance. This notion of emptiness is coupled with another specifically Daoist notion. As noted in the cosmogonic narrative, where the universe of existents arises from the womb of empty/nothingness, things that find value in their "emptiness" are prized for being more in accord with the

Dao. For instance, the emptiness within bowls or cups, between spokes of a wheel, inside the enclosed space of caves, and so on, is accorded a special status in Daoist discourses. But perhaps the most important "empty" place is imagined within the human body/mind. For as the sinologist Kristofer Schipper writes in his classic book, *The Taoist Body*, the body is figured as a vast geography inhabited by numerous deities and energies, but is ultimately viewed as a grotto or a chamber in which adepts undergo a pregnancy to give birth to the One, the nameless, ultimate Dao incarnated as infinite potential no longer subject to time or decay—an immortal.[35] The vast number of texts about references to this emptying and/or self-cultivation of body-mind-heart as chambers, vessels, or caverns are clearly different than the nexus of Buddhist notions of emptiness discussed earlier. To distinguish this overarching valuation of "emptiness" in Daoist discourses from those associated with Buddhist discourse, I am going to refer to them as *housed emptiness*.

Two of the four poets discussed in this book draw upon notions of a housed emptiness, yet it is hard to imagine two poetic paradigms more distinct than those of Wai-lim Yip and Theresa Hak Kyung Cha. Yip is particularly interested in terms that embody the constitutive negation at the heart of his wider cultural project: 無言 (*wuyan*, empty/non-language), 無我 (*wuwo*, empty/non-self), 無知 (*wuzhi*, empty/non-knowledge), and the like. In each case, the first term 無 (*wu*) of the binome transforms the function of the second term without destroying its existence in space. There is a language, but it is empty of grammar/syntax; there is a self, but it is empty of ego; there is knowledge, but it is empty of cognizable information, etc. (each of these terms share this notion of a housed emptiness). Yet for Yip, Daoist notions of emptiness free language from the confines of representation and the mind from what he terms "epistemological elaborations," granting poets and readers direct access to what he (in a nearly Platonic fashion) terms the "real-life world." By positing classical Chinese language as a natural empty/non-langauge 無言 (*wuyan*), Yip uses translation as the means through which to empty English poetry of linguistic mediation, and the Western mind of its egoic impositions. While problematic (in very interesting ways), Yip's poetics offers a unique heterocultural vision of American modernist poetics that continues to be very influential today.

Also drawing upon notions of a housed emptiness, Theresa Hak Kyung Cha's book, *Dictée*, offers a very different interpretation, informed by the folk-Daoism-infused matrilineal tradition of Korean shamanism and the "Daoist Imaginaries" circulating both in American poetry/poetics and around Roland Barthes and the Paris avant-garde (the Tel Quel writers). Cha's turn toward mediums, alchemy, and Daoist soteriology is simply not a part of the line of poetic and philosophical thought inherited by Yip. Furthermore, she rearticulates poststructuralist concepts like "the death of the author" and arguments surrounding passive and active reading practices in distinctly Daoist language, which differs greatly from Yip's modernist commitments.

The catalogue of Buddhist principles or assumptions I have presented here, as well as the complications of the Daoist tradition, offer a striking counterpoint to ideas that have governed Western poetry since the Renaissance. The poetics of emptiness, as I am calling it, that springs forth from these assumptions and complications as they were encountered in twentieth-century American poetry, offers an umbrella under which various poetic responses to transpacific encounters have taken place. These encounters have inflected and enriched American poetry even when they were not clearly perceived—the history of Poundian poetics gives evidence of this—and have allowed remarkably fecund poetics to thrive in the twentieth century.

The Chapters

While Daoist and Buddhist epistemological notions claim to open ways of "seeing" without preconceiving or reifying any*thing,* the status of "thingness" to which this non-self relates differs significantly. Daoist ontology emphasizes the absolute autonomy of things (*ziran*), which cannot be objectively cognized but must be related to through *housing* their mysterious unfolding within the emptied chamber of the fasted mind. While Buddhist discourses generally agree that things cannot be objectified, they often place more emphasis on the inherent dependency of all "things" (*taran*) as a way of understanding emptiness generally and the emptiness of self specifically. In this sense, it is difficult to imagine two more radically divergent approaches to the proper view of phenomena. Nevertheless, through Chinese (and later Japanese and Korean) history, Buddhism and Daoism (and Confucianism) have informed and conditioned all three "teachings" (*sanjiao:* Daoism, Confucianism, and Buddhism). Read in the context of Western popular literature (including poetics), however, the three teachings (but specifically Buddhism and Daoism, in the American case) are often difficult to differentiate. I must try to be clear here: the object of the present study is not to cleanse American poetry of its heterocultural, muddied, transpacific estuaries, or to pine for more authentic and pure interpretations of these philosophical traditions; nevertheless, I believe the first step toward acknowledging the particular force and weight of their presence within American poetics is to attempt to trace their multiple migratory pathways and tributaries, and attempt to point out their non-Eastern aggregates so that more meanings might be made available from their mixtures.

As for this mixture, even a cursory glance at American poetry and poetics would turn up an impressive number of figures and movements that have looked eastward for inspiration. Just to name a few that are not discussed at length in this study, for instance, would bring to mind the transcendentalists (though this group's access to even intertextual tributaries was quite limited); important modernist figures like Lafcadio Hearn, Laurence Binyon, or Wallace Stevens; most of the so-called Beat poets, ranging from Kenneth Rexroth, Joanne Kyger, Jack Kerouac, and Phillip Whalen, to Michael McClure, Albert Saijo, Diane DiPrima, and Lew Welch, among other Naropa-based writers like the later Allen Ginsberg, Anne Waldman, and Andrew Schelling; figures associated with the so-called LANGUAGE-oriented writers like Leslie Scalapino, Tenney Nathanson, Mei-mei Berssenbrugge, Beverly Dahlen, John Caley, and Norman Fischer, and their predecessors, John Cage and Jackson Mac Low; writers who presence diasporic Buddhist experience like Garrett Kaoru Hongo, Lawson Inada, Tsering Wangmo Dhompa, Shin Yu Pai, or Russell Leong (who often overlap culturally and intertextually with convert Buddhists); and finally, there are more mainstream, principally lyric poets like Sam Hamill and Jane Hirschfield, among still many others who are difficult to place (Aafa Weaver and Arthur Sze, for instance). There is truly an embarrassment of riches here, and, luckily, recent anthologies of Buddhist American poetry (*Beneath a Single Moon*; *What Book?!*; *American Zen: A Gathering of Poets*; and *The Wisdom Anthology of North American Buddhist Poetry*), which draw attention to this diverse family of work, offer not only collections of Buddhist-oriented poetry for easier classroom access, but helpful statements on poetics by poets, and, often, helpful introductions that offer different ways of conceiving and categorizing the heterogeneous nature of this work. Building on Michael Davidson's book *The San Francisco Renaissance*, a growing number of books, like Tony Trigilio's *Allen Ginsberg's Buddhist Poetics*, and new Snyder criticism by Timothy Gray, Anthony Hunt, and John Whalen Bridge, among others, are moving beyond Beat hagiography to critically engage aspects of Buddhism in more direct and useful ways. A new series of books, entitled Buddhism and American Culture, in production at SUNY Press and edited by John Whalen-Bridge and Gary Storhoff,[36] will also help establish this new subfield of American literature and criticism. So while it is beyond the scope of *Poetics of Emptiness* to explore the work of all American poets who work with Buddhist philosophy or aesthetics (not to mention Daoist), I have high hopes that the next few years will see many more publications to bring attention to this important and largely unexplored territory of American literature.

To keep the size of this work manageable, I have chosen to focus on different transformations of the single, if polyvalent, English term *emptiness* derived from various interpretations of principally Chinese poetics/philosophy (discourses, it is important to note, that were themselves born in India and further transformed by Japan). In other words, many of the poets listed above access Buddhist discourses through different (yet equally interesting) avenues from the ones I have chosen to include. Even so, there are other poets, like Jackson Mac Low, whose work would still fit into the present project's scope, if I could continue to add chapters indefinitely.[37] Nevertheless, it is my hope that by limiting this project to the present constellation of writers, I will be able to offer more than a taxonomy of Buddhist- or Daoist-inflected American poetics; I hope to offer a sustained exploration of a few of the most original and/or influential varieties of the poetics of emptiness developed inside the transpacific imaginaries of American poetry, while leaving still others for future scholarship. Given the differences between these distinct configurations of transpacific poetics, even within this specific group of poet/translators, it may be helpful to discuss the work of each chapter more specifically.

In his introduction to the newly published critical edition of Ernest Fenollosa's original essay, "The Chinese Written Character as a Medium for Poetry: An Ars Poetica," Haun Saussy succinctly argues, "Partial, blinkered, or to put it less censoriously, strategic: the reading of Fenollosa's essay mirrors the scatter among its contents under tension. It seems to have to be doled out in slices rather than whole."[38] Given the many entry and exit points through which readings of Fenollosa's infamous essay may travel, I have conceived *Poetics of Emptiness* as a supplement, or companion, to the *The Chinese Written Character as a Medium for Poetry: A Critical Edition*, by focusing on the heterocultural "slices" of this important text that have not previously been addressed by critics.[39] Chapter 1, "Emptiness in Flux: The Buddhist Poetics of Ernest Fenollosa's 'The Chinese Written Character as a Medium for Poetry,'" fundamentally challenges both Ezra Pound's representation of the text and

American literary criticism's reduction of Fenollosa to a naïve positivist by revealing the essay's function in Fenollosa's peculiar Buddhist mission. The current misconceived trajectory of Fenollosa criticism relies on two faulty assumptions: first, that Fenollosa's idiosyncratic theories of Chinese language and poetry (and to a lesser extent visual arts and philosophy) are the result of his limited knowledge of these subjects rather than the result of the peculiar historical and cultural context in which he came to East Asian philosophy and poetics; and second, that Fenollosa believed Chinese characters are but "pictures of the things they name." This charge is misplaced: this was Pound's view, never Fenollosa's. Only by reading Fenollosa's essay within the context of his wider Buddhist project, which sought to integrate Buddhist metaphysical ideas into all aspects of Western thought (philosophical, poetic, artistic, even economic and political) can we see that Chinese characters, for Fenollosa, actually prevent their users from mistaking words for "autonomous things," since each character is clearly an aggregate of its causes and conditions (dependently arisen). Far from an abstract "Buddhist reading" of Fenollosa's poetics, this chapter, grounded in the details of his specific historical and cultural engagements, reveals a poetics tied closely to an unusual school of Japanese Buddhism known simply as "New Buddhism" (the hybrid Hegelian Tendai Buddhism I have already mentioned), which Fenollosa himself had a role in founding. In short, this chapter will fundamentally redirect the principal manifesto of American Modernism against the grain of Pound's modernist desire for ontological coherence to reveal a heterocultural deconstructive poetics that was articulated over a half century before the rise of postmodern poetics.

In Chapter 2, "Patterned Harmony: Buddhism, Sound, and Ernest Fenollosa's Poetics of Correlative Cosmology," I look into another related yet distinct set of cultural engagements within Fenollosa's transpacific imaginary, which surface in the lost half of Fenollosa's "The Chinese Written Character as a Medium for Poetry." When Ezra Pound published Fenollosa's short essay in 1936, he revised and published only one half of Fenollosa's original essay. The second half (which has never been cited or mentioned until the present work and its previously mentioned sister text, *The Critical Edition*) deals largely with the sounds of Chinese formal prosody and theories of how to translate and transliterate these sounds into English poetry. This finding is important because critics have long censured Fenollosa for his choice to ignore sound in his discussion of Chinese poetry. This chapter, therefore, will explore Fenollosa's ideas of Chinese prosody and, by extension, examine how his theories of translation and transliteration extend from his understanding and triangulation of Western Romanticism, traditional Chinese philosophy, poetics, and his Japanese Buddhist investments (the elements of Fenollosa's hybrid Hegelian Tendai Buddhism).

The chapter begins by exploring the elements of Fenollosa's poetics that draw upon the classical Chinese concept 文 (wen, "pattern"). Not only does such a discussion reveal the reasons behind his desire to translate classical Chinese verse into existing forms of English prosody, but why he believed the West must import the metaphysical structures from East Asia to connect poetry and prosody to the rest of the human and natural world. He refers to this set of beliefs as a "universal theory of literature": "synthetic harmony," 文章 (Ja: bunsho, Ch: wenzhang, which is usually translated as "essay" or "literary work"). The chapter will reveal how Fenollosa's peculiar system of representing Chinese poetry (and names, etc.) as an alphabetized Japanese transliteration of the original characters is merely an extension of the Japanese Buddhist claim that the kana (Japanese phonetic script) not only preserves the original Sanskrit sounds of Buddhist mantras but also the Tang and Song dynasties' pronunciation of China's golden period of poetry, and that furthermore, such sounds, far from being arbitrary, are as significant as the semantic elements themselves. Taken as a whole, the metaphysical elements that support Fenollosa's thinking about Chinese aurality are stunningly complex, and an interesting element of his transpacific imaginary.

Chapter 3, "Teaching the Law: Gary Snyder's Poetics of Emptiness," explores the didactic and soteriological function of classical Chinese poetics that take shape in Snyder's desire to transmit the Buddhist dharma (法), so that I may shed some light on how different notions of emptiness produce radically different poetic praxis. But by chasing the intertextual tail of emptiness through Snyder's work and theories of translation, I hope to show how he transforms concepts of emptiness drawn from Zen and Yogācāran Buddhist discourses into a unique unifying grammar in his own poetic productions. Using Snyder's explicitly Buddhist body of work, I argue that his writing reflects and reframes Zennist (a term I use to distinguish practitioners or advocates of Zen, rather than the family of discourses and traditions that make up Zen per se[40]) readings of classical Chinese poetry found in Dogen's Shōbōgenzō, the Zenrin kushu ("Zen Forest," a Koan-like anthology of Chinese poetry), along with Snyder's own Zennist reading of the Tang poet Han Shan. Lastly, I map the ways in which Snyder's Zen reading of classical Chinese poetry draws upon and further codifies specific (and in that sense limited) Zennist (doctrinal) interpretive habits, which have come to infuse American poetry and poetics through his own poetry.

Chapter 4, "Language of Emptiness: Wai-lim Yip's Daoist Project," begins Part Two of this book by exploring another influential poetics of emptiness, this time drawn from a historically specific transpacific "Daoist" poetics. In many ways similar to Snyder's Zennist poetics, Yip postulates a transpacific imaginary in which Chinese poetry, infused with the Daoist worldview, allows (through linguistic *wuwei*) phenomena to represent itself "as it is" without distortion (*ziran*), and so can be adopted as a methodological solution to cross-cultural misinterpretation. In this chapter, I explore Yip's use of translation to support his heterocultural vision, as well as the theoretical and poetic precedents for Yip's poetics in both Daoist and Western discourses. While shedding light on the central importance of Yip's work to the transpacific Daoist imaginary, this chapter also takes Yip to task for his transhistorical/cultural reading of Chinese poetry as an image-laden, syntax-free (or paratactic), pure reflection of the natural world "emptied of obfuscating subjectivity," or a "language of emptiness" (無言, *wuyan*), in order to move beyond latent elements of cultural essentialism in Yip's work and to open pathways beyond the received tradition of "Daoism" in the West.

Continuing the discussion in Chapter 4 of (transpacific) Daoist poetics, Chapter 5, "Pacing the Void: Theresa Hak Kyung Cha's *Dictée*," shows how Cha's novel/poem *Dictée,* unquestionably the most important transpacific document of American Postmodernism (Cha's *Dictée* is the subject of numerous essays, book chapters, and a full-length scholarly collection, *Writing Self, Writing Nation*) has, like Fenollosa's essay, not been adequately contextualized within the explicit East Asian philosophical discourses running through it. While one can trace Cha's interest in Daoism to, for example, her daily practice of *taiji chuan* during her years at UC Berkeley, or to the numerous Daoist concepts and references to "inner alchemy" (內丹, *neidan*) in her MFA thesis "Paths," the depth of her Daoism is clearly attributable to a fusion that has taken place between the poststructuralism of Roland Barthes and the Daoist desire to enter the "void" (虛, *xu*), the undifferentiated/infinite/potentiality, from which, according to Daoist cosmogony, all things emerge and, according to Daoist soteriology, one can (through alchemical practices) return. While it is clear that this fusion takes place in Barthes's own thinking, Cha is able to take these concepts much further by enacting them in the living cultural practices of Korean shamanism, an indigenous matrilineal discourse infused with folk Daoist practices. Here the philosophical discourses surrounding "self-emptying" are embodied literally in the figure of mediums channeling otherness. The heterocultural aggregate of this poetics of emptiness re-imagines "active reading practices" and "writerly texts" as a gateway through which to empty (or liberate) the subject of its ideologically constructed "expressive voice." Acts of channeling voices and dictation release the subject further, making room to house "otherness," while at the same time offering ways to transform the abject void that follows colonialization, forced assimilation, indoctrination and interpellation into "the void" of Barthes's "infinity of languages," which "baffles the idiom" and resists ideological reification and commodification—in short, the void for Cha becomes not another ideological refuge, but a refuge from ideology.

A poetics of emptiness, or a cult of nothingness? I hope it is clear that the concepts arriving cramped and crowded in the nearly insufferably confined quarters of the signifier *emptiness* are quite distinct from one another and from meanings referenced by the idea of *nothingness*, both when it is exalted and when it is abhorred. So when Emerson places "nothingness" on high as the name of the transcendent ego—"I become a transparent eyeball; I am nothing; I see all"[41]—one is interacting with notions distinct from (if influenced and altered by) the emptiness discourses entering American poetics through the intertextual streams traced in this work. One of the principal tasks of this book, therefore, is to decouple these concepts (*emptiness* and *nothingness*), not by continually "comparing" Eastern and Western concepts as if they have remained distinct and pure, but by releasing and tracking a few of these heterogeneous discourses of "emptiness" as they not only transform, but are in turn transformed by, twentieth-century American poetry.

PART ONE

BUDDHIST IMAGINARIES

1 / 空 Emptiness in Flux: The Buddhist Poetics of Ernest Fenollosa's "The Chinese Written Character as a Medium for Poetry"

On Friday, December 24, 1920, the front-page headline of the *Boston Evening Transcript* announced "Japan's Tribute to Fenollosa." Below, an image of a stone monument depicting a young Ernest Fenollosa fills more than half of the front page. The article begins: "On September 21, 1920, in the ninth month of the ninth year of Taisho—Japan in a memorial service formally honored the late Professor Ernest Fenollosa by the unveiling of a monument to him and his work for Japan—his interpretation of Japan to the non-Asiatic world, and its corollary, expounding the Western world to Nippon." The image and accompanying text present Fenollosa as a towering influence within the history of transpacific (specifically Buddhist East-West) cultural migrations. As reported by the *Evening Transcript*, the monument reads: "Professor Fenollosa was a great believer in the Buddhist religion. After long study he became a convert to it, and he received baptism from the abbot Sakurai Keitoku [桜井敬徳] of Enjo-ji. His Buddhist name is Tei-Shin."[1]

Tei-Shin was the first Euro-American poet to receive a Buddhist name, but he would soon be joined by a *sangha* (Buddhist community) of American poets ranging from Zenshin Ryufu (Phillip Whalen) to Ho-Ka (Armand Schwerner). Even though Ernest Fenollosa was one of the first Westerners to become a lay-ordained Buddhist, his work in poetics has never been read in relation to his Buddhist studies or practice. This is, of course, not to say that Fenollosa's essay, "The Chinese Written Character as a Medium for Poetry" (henceforth abbreviated in text and notes as CWC), has been ignored with regard to the study of Modernism's transpacific origins. Ernest Fenollosa's essay not only stands at the center of East-West studies of American poetry,[2] it remains one of the most important prose works in twentieth-century American poetry and poetics more generally. In the eyes of Ezra Pound, the essay's editor and its greatest supporter, it is "a study of the fundamentals of all aesthetics."[3] The English critic Donald Davie considered the essay "perhaps the only English document of our time fit to rank with Sidney's *Apologia*, and the Preface to *Lyrical Ballads*, and Shelley's *Defense*."[4] Other giants of American literature, including Charles Olson, also reserved a special place for it.[5] Fenollosa's essay appears at the beginning of Donald Allen's seminal anthology, *The Poetics of the New American Poetry*, and it has remained available in a small-bound edition published in 1964 by City Lights Books to the present day. The editorial blurb on the back of the City Lights edition gives contemporary readers a glimpse into the essay's controversial past and, I would argue, offers a clear indication as to why its Buddhist orientation has remained obscure through to the present:

> This important and much-disputed essay edited by Ezra Pound from the manuscript of Ernest Fenollosa (and published in Instigations, London, 1920) has since gone through several editions, despite the ridicule of such sinologists as Professor George Kennedy of Yale, who called it "a small mass of confusion."
>
> The old theory as to the nature of the Chinese written character (which Pound and Fenollosa followed) is that the written character is ideogrammic—a stylized picture of the thing or concept it represents. The opposing theory (which prevails today among scholars) is that the character may have had pictorial origins in prehistoric times but that these origins have been obscured in all but a few very simple cases, and that in any case native writers don't have the original pictorial meaning in mind as they write.
>
> Whether Pound proceeded on false premises remains an academic question. Let the pedants rave. An important extension of imagist technique in poetry was gained by Pound's perception of the essentially poetic nature of the Chinese character as it is still written.

In this short blurb we are told that scholars object to the essay's support of the "old idea" that Chinese characters are "a stylized picture of the thing or concept it represents," but that "whether Pound proceeded on false premises remains an academic question." The blurb, therefore, offers readers what appears to be a live debate between Pound's support-ers (poets) and detractors (academics), who take different sides in a con-tinuing debate over the nature of the "ideogram." But the editors' use of phrases like "an academic question" or "let the pedants rave" reveals that the detractors stand in the unenviable position of being "square," or too narrowly focused on unimportant technical distinctions—not so dissimilar from "Trekkies" (or "Trekkers," as I understand they prefer to be called) unhappy with misspelled "Klingon." In short, poets appear to have offered Fenollosa a pardon, and in many cases appear to legitimize the incorrect belief in ideogrammic pictures. This understanding of the text and its influence on a wide reading public has made Fenollosa into a dirty word in sinology.

With tongue partly in cheek, Haun Saussy highlights the danger the text poses to sinologists who even mention Fenollosa in their writing:

> WARNING. The following section contains passages from the writ-ings of Ernest Fenollosa that may be objectionable to some readers. The reproduction of these statements does not indicate endorse-ment or approval of their content by the author or the Press, or the President and Fellows of Harvard College, who decline all respon-sibility for any damages, direct or incidental, that may result from the reading of them. . . .

Saussy continues: "Having a professional interest in Chinese literature, I know I expose myself to trouble simply for having mentioned Fenollosa's name. As we learn very early in our training, Fenollosa was an enthusi-ast: in his wonderment at the Chinese language, he vastly overestimated the number of primary pictograms in the writing system. . . . The profes-sion has never forgotten his error."[6] While it is perfectly understandable that Chinese linguists like Peter Bodburge and George Kennedy take Fenollosa to task for his linguistic errors, literary critics have become just as harsh, but for different, and I would argue, less legitimate reasons. Most contemporary literary critics follow the reading of Fenollosa pre-sented in Hugh Kenner's critical juggernaut *The Pound Era,* in which he paints Fenollosa's poetics as a derivative transcendentalist hallucination. By juxtaposing quotes from Fenollosa's CWC next to Emerson's essays "The Poet" (1844) and "The Method of Nature" (1841), Kenner unjustly claims that "we can collect without trouble a body of propositions indis-tinguishable in import from the statements about reality out of which Fenollosa's great Ars Poetica is educed."[7]

In an even more dismissive tone, Kenner rejects the originality of Fenollosa's work by quoting Emerson (who is himself quoting a proverb), "He that would bring home the wealth of the Indies . . . must carry out the wealth of the Indies," and then comments, "Ernest Francisco Fenollosa (1853–1908), born in Salem and educated at Harvard, took with him to Japan in 1878 as Professor of Philosophy (Hegel, Herbert Spencer) the treasures of Transcendentalism, and brought with him from Japan on his last journey in 1901 the same Transcendentalism, seen anew in the Chinese Written Character."[8]

While Kenner is right to note the influence of Emerson's thinking on the CWC (and one would need to include William James here as well), his idea that Fenollosa's work never moved past his Harvard education even after two decades of intensive study and immersion in East Asian art, politics, literature, and philosophy is unconvincing. By taking Kenner's convenient dismissal to heart, however, scholars of American Modernism (and even East-West studies) have relieved themselves of the burden of exploring Fenollosa's rich heterocultural poetics, and in the end they ignore the complex cultural and historical conditions that give rise to what Yunte Huang calls the "transpacific displacement" at the very foundation of American Modernism.[9]

The most recent interpretive angle on Fenollosa's "ideogrammic error" comes from literary critics like Robert Kern, who has pointed to Fenollosa's reading of Chinese characters as an Orientalist imposition (à la Edward Said). In Kern's trendsetting work, *Orientalism, Modernism, and the American Poem*, he argues that Fenollosa's CWC continues to represent "the recurrent nature of the role that Chinese seems to play in Western linguistic projects." He continues, "What I have in mind here specifically is the 'Adamic' doctrine that language, in poetry and other modes of discourse as well, can achieve a penetration to the truth or essences of things."[10] Therefore, Kern argues that Fenollosa's idealization of Chinese reflects the uniquely Western search (grounded in a certain reading of Emersonian transcendentalism inherited by American poetics) for the Adamic language of absolute mimesis. Kern concludes that Fenollosa, "regardless of [his] knowledge (or lack of it) of Chinese, [is] motivated by a concept of linguistic possibility that is entirely Western."[11]

Yet there is an important interpretive error at the very foundation of both Fenollosa's detractors and supporters: namely, that he, like Pound, says that characters are "stylized pictures of things." Pound believed this—Feanollosa did not. In fact, what he does assert is that characters, unlike alphabetic writing, make it impossible (or much less likely) to mistakenly assume that words or the things they signify "exist autonomously," because it is clear that they arise "dependently" as aggregates of their causes and conditions. The argument that Fenollosa pursues an Adamic language or that his thinking is derivative wholly from transcendentalism can only be arrived at if his writing remains cut off from its historical and heterocultural (Buddhist) contexts. The present chapter, therefore, will challenge the "monocultural" reading of the text by situating Fenollosa's work within his peculiar historical context to reveal a startlingly rich heterocultural poetics characterized by a complex weave of Western philosophy and Buddhist epistemology (as unique then as today).

Why have literary critics (even sinologists) rarely if ever addressed Fenollosa's Asian religious/philosophical study and practice? The answer is complex. I have already pointed to one of the most obvious reasons: Buddhism is not principally interested in finding an "Adamic language," and as long as Fenollosa's readers believe that he was ultimately seeking a language of perfect mimesis, then his project appears to be fueled by an "entirely Western" desire. Yet another reason can be attributed to the relationship between Fenollosa's writing and his principal editor and supporter, Ezra Pound. It is only natural that Fenollosa's essay would be largely read through the prism of Pound's own reading, since Pound edited, published, popularized, and continually defended the essay throughout his long career. Nor is it surprising that Pound, who aligned himself with (his positivist reading of) Confucianism,[12] reserved a special distaste for Buddhists, whom he derogated to as "Bhud-foés." Pound writes in Canto 98, "And as for these Bhud-foés / They provide no mental means for / Running an empire, nor do Taoists / With their internal and external pills—is it external? The gold pill?—to preserve them from physical death."[13]

While leaving the essay's basic Eastern-philosophy–inspired poetics intact, Pound actively deletes the original essay's more Buddhistic rhetoric, including Kegon-inspired (華嚴, Huayan) figurative language suggesting aesthetics similar to "Indra's net"[14] where "prismatic tints" reflect off of one another, creating "ethereal fabric" woven together from infinite "intermingling tones," and so on.[15] Pound regularly deleted the more verbose sentences or passages marked by what Fenollosa would call "Buddhist colour," since he and other Modernists wanted to break away from the "infinities" and "vibrations" that preoccupied nineteenth-century transcendental Romanticism. He cut sections where Fenollosa expounds on things "vibrant with the thousand affinities of nature and of man,"[16] or the blending of "colours of sympathetic tones of orchestral instruments, lost in the harmony of their chord,"[17] as well as passages such as, "In painting, great colour beauty springs not from the main colour masses, but from the refined modifications or overtones which each throws into the other, just as tints are etherealized in a flower by reflection from petal to petal."[18] Such passages, for Pound, belonged in flowery "Bhud-foé" sutras, not Modernist manifestos seeking to "make it new."[19]

Fenollosa's Buddhism

In addition to Pound's heavy editorial presence, the second and perhaps equally important reason that scholars have not addressed Fenollosa's Buddhism rests within the complex historical conditions of the "Buddhism" at play in Fenollosa's work. Unlike later poets like Gary Snyder or Phillip Whalen, who studied forms of Zen still popular today, Fenollosa became deeply engaged in a historically specific Japanese revival and reconstruction of Buddhism known as Shin Bukkyô (Ch: 新佛教, xinfojiao), or "New Buddhism," a nationalistic Buddhist movement deeply influenced by Social Darwinism and Hegelian philosophy. Simply put, Fenollosa's Buddhism was a product of his unique time and place and could not be easily recognized or reconstructed.

Fenollosa arrived in Japan in 1878 to teach philosophy and sociology at the Imperial University of Tokyo only two years after he finished his BA at Harvard (in philosophy). He lectured mainly on Hegel and Herbert Spencer and quickly found himself a prominent intellectual, due to the extreme interest in Westernization prevalent during the Meiji (明治時代) period (1868–1912).[20] Able to capitalize on this rush to Westernize, Fenollosa gained access to the greatest authorities in Japanese art and philosophy. In addition to studying Tendai Buddhism under the direction of Sakurai Keitoku 桜井敬徳, the abbot of the Tendai monastery of Miidera 三井寺, he studied traditional Japanese painting with Kanô Hôgai 狩野芳崖, the last remaining painter of the Kanô school.[21] This period of incredible intellectual access to Japanese elite culture culminated, in 1886, in the creation of the Mombushô (Imperial Commissioner of Fine Arts in the Ministry of Culture), through which Fenollosa had the unparalleled opportunity to travel around Japan to compile a list of Japan's artistic and architectural treasures.[22] Later, in 1889, along with a group of his students and associates, he helped found the Tokyo Academy of Fine Arts (Tôkyô bijutsu gakkai, 東京美術學會), in which they sought to integrate New Buddhist ideas with Western art theory, practice, and pedagogy.[23] The work of the Tokyo Academy of Fine Arts would come to play a central role at the 1893 World Parliament of Religions, where Fenollosa's student Okakura Kakuzô (Tenshin), building upon work in part initiated by Fenollosa, presented a view of Japanese culture strategically rearticulated in the Social Darwinist language that framed the parliament's Eurocentric agenda.

The World Parliament of Religions—held in Chicago and organized at the beginning of America's romance with eugenic thought only a decade before America would expand its empire to overseas territories—is an excellent context in which to understand Fenollosa's Buddhism more generally. The parliament was to be "'an object lesson' in Social Darwinism, displaying the rightful place of the people of the world in the hierarchy of race and civilization."[24] The Japanese delegates attending the parliament arrived from a nation already subordinated to the new American economic and military power in the Pacific Rim. While Commodore Perry's "gunboat diplomacy" had helped usher in the Meiji's rush to Westernize, it also set up a series of "unequal trade treaties," similar to those forced upon China from the most powerful European nations. Presuming that the equalization of these treaties would only come about after "proving" the equality of Japanese and Western cultures, the Japanese delegates, under the tutelage of Fenollosa (among others), redirected the very Darwinist discourses that the parliament's organizers were deploying to degrade Japan toward their own nationalistic purposes.

Okakura, by the time of the parliament, was the director of the Tokyo Fine Arts Academy and was placed in charge of the centerpiece of Japan's contribution to the World's Fair and Parliament, the *Hooden*, or Phoenix Hall. In his essay "Contemporary Japanese Art," Fenollosa describes the *Hooden* as an "architectural casket" consisting of a series of traditional Japanese structures meant to represent the different "epochs" of Japanese architecture.[25] The *Hooden* exhibit had two missions. First, the ornate structures themselves were meant to send a message to Americans about the evolved state of Japanese civilization at the time of Columbus's discovery of the Americas.[26] But in Social Darwinist terms, age does not equal vitality, and it can signal stagnation. Thus, Okakura strategically designed the interior spaces of the exhibit to deliver a different cultural argument: each structure housed contemporary Japanese art, created under the auspices of the Tokyo Fine Art Academy, which demonstrated Japan's contemporary vitality and a dynamic synthesis between traditional Asian and modern Western art theories.[27] There is little doubt that this strategy was meant to signal to the rest of the world that Japanese art could not be reduced to historical artifacts (and therefore controlled as an "object" of knowledge within Western Orientalism), but rather that the cultural streams that produced the artifacts collected by Fenollosa and Okakura a decade earlier still animated contemporary Japanese art. To quote the historian Judith Snodgrass, "Because cultural achievements were indications of evolutionary development, Japan's message was that it had reached great heights long before Europeans arrived in the Americas."[28]

The Buddhist delegates to the parliament had a similar task confronting them. If the *Hooden* "was evidence of Japan's 'highly evolved' material culture," argues Snodgrass, then "Japanese Buddhism demonstrated concomitant intellectual achievement."[29] In short, the New Buddhist delegates to the parliament not only argued that Japanese Buddhism was superior to other forms of Buddhism, but that it was superior to Western religions and philosophy, and was, therefore, "Japan's gift to the world."

The principal architect of the New Buddhism presented at the parliament was one of Fenollosa's earliest students, Enryō Inoue 井上圓了, who had studied Hegel and also Spenser's "evolutionary sociology" under him at Tokyo University. Inoue's study of philosophy with Fenollosa, and his later public break with organized Buddhism, granted him the title of "philosopher," which allowed him more flexibility to synthesize Western and Japanese ideas. Inoue often used this background as the basis for his claim to an "unbiased" treatment of both Buddhism and Christianity, a claim central to his 1887 manifesto *Bukkyô katsuron joron* (佛教活論 序論, "Preliminaries to the Revitalization of Buddhism"). In this work, Inoue recounts his initial dissatisfaction and break from institutionalized Buddhism, his study and later dissatisfaction with both Christianity and Confucianism, and his study of Western philosophy, which led him back to Japanese Buddhism with new eyes: "Having discovered the truth within the world of philosophy, when I made one more review of the various religions of the past . . . only Buddhist religion is largely in accord with philosophical principles. . . . Who would have thought that the truth that was the product of a thousand years of study in Europe already existed three thousand years ago in the East."[30] Inoue's manifesto, and its slogan *Gokoku airi* (Defend the nation and love the truth), not only asserted that Japanese Buddhism contained the highest forms of philosophical insight, but it claimed that the Japanese had preserved the highest forms of Buddhist practice and thought long after these had been lost to the rest of Asia. It was this particular form of nationalistic Buddhism that became the blueprint for the presentation of Japanese

Buddhism to the West at the parliament, and the form of Buddhism to which Fenollosa himself largely ascribed.

One need not look further than the introduction of Fenollosa's CWC to see his own conversion to the New Buddhist paradigm, which embodied several notions: Japan's fear of the encroachments of the Western colonial powers; the claim that Japan was the cultural repository of the highest forms of Asian philosophy and religion (the central argument being that Japan was the storehouse of Tang and Song dynasties' Chinese Buddhism); and that Japanese Buddhism offered the West higher truths than those available in Western philosophy or religion.[31] Fenollosa, however, who was, in his own words, "in this incarnation a man of Western race," geared each of these arguments to an American audience with its own national interests and biases. He begins his essay by stating, "This twentieth century not only turns a new page in the Book of the World, but opens another and a startling Chapter."[32] For Fenollosa, this "startling chapter" promised a coming fusion between the East and West. However, he argues that such a fusion could only take place between equals, and since "the people of Continental Europe fear the possibilities of selfhood in the East" and will try to "crush her, before her best powers shall have time to ripen,"[33] much of his writing (including the CWC) argues that America should join forces with Imperial Japan to intervene on "China's behalf." It was Fenollosa's belief (and a central belief of many in the New Buddhist movement, including his two most prominent students, Inoue and Okakura) that China should submit to the "protection" and "guidance" of Japan, since Japan's relative isolation had "preserved" the most "evolved" form of Chinese philosophy, while China's move toward increasingly "bureaucratic Confucianism" had led to "cultural stagnation" and "degeneracy."

According to Fenollosa and his Meiji circle, if China was to find her "selfhood" again, she would have to be both reinvigorated and protected by her Eastern neighbor, for not only was Japan's (Buddhist) culture the entelechy of Chinese civilization, but Japan had acquired the military and economic power necessary to fight off European encroachments that were attempting to "chain" China "in slavery to some Western form of Despotism."[34] For Fenollosa, then, the European "spheres of influence" were the primary stumbling blocks to the coming era of "East-West fusion," since these threatened to permanently partition China into separate colonies similar to those established in Africa.[35]

The introduction to the CWC is not really a plea for sympathy, but a warning to the West, for "strange as it may seem," Fenollosa says, "the future of Anglo Saxon supremacy in the world" is tied to "the future of that East." He continues, "The Chinese Problem, alone, is so vast that it dominates the world and forces that supreme historical crisis which has been waiting for centuries. No nation can afford to ignore it; we in America least of all. We must face it across the Pacific, and master it—or it will master us."[36] This talk of "mastery" may appear to contradict Fenollosa's own plea, in his essay "The Coming Fusion of East and West," to "fuse with" rather than "oppress" China (after all, "Anglo-Saxon Mastery" was not a fringe concern of a few white supremacists at the time, but a topic of great public concern and debate in America at the turn of the century).[37] Yet one must be careful not to misidentify the antecedent to the pronoun "it" (which must be mastered) found in this last line. This "it" does not refer back to "Chinese Culture" or even "China" itself, but to the "historical crisis," the "problem" resulting from European colonialism.

Read in the wider context of Fenollosa's writing, this warning is twofold. First, in a move that preempts current concerns about the "rise of China,"[38] Fenollosa argues that the combination of China's natural resources and industrial potential will transform it into the world's largest industrial power by the end of the twentieth century, and if America wants to be China's partner in the coming Pacific era, it must join with Japan and integrate itself with China politically, economically, and culturally before this takes place.[39] The second warning comes later in the CWC (and can be found elsewhere in Fenollosa's writing),[40] where Fenollosa tells his readers that the "thin," "stagnant" formalism of "medieval logic" has weakened Western languages (and, by extension, thought) and is leading the West down a path of cultural degeneracy. Cultural evolution for both China and the West can only come, according to Fenollosa, through the integration of Eastern philosophy and Western science.[41] Of course, this is not a thesis of Fenollosa's own invention, but the party line of the New Buddhists more generally. For Fenollosa, the coming synthesis, prophesied in his epic poem *East and West*, appeared shockingly real at the turn of the century, with the annexation of the Philippines at the end of the Spanish American War and with political reforms in China that hinted, however briefly, at a period of Westernization and reconstruction similar to the Meiji.[42] For Fenollosa, the annexation of the Philippines was the first step toward America's permanent entrance into China, ushering in a peaceful era of East-West cultural fusion.[43] Fenollosa's essay "The Coming Fusion of East and West," like the CWC, addressed an American audience bitterly divided by the annexation of the Philippines. Most of the public debate was dominated by white supremacist fears of "swarms" of "Asiatic races" threatening to "engulf" America and lead to "racial degeneration."[44] Fenollosa, on the other hand, entered this debate from the opposite pole, as he regarded the annexation as "a drama more sudden and mighty than the Macedonian's transport of Greece to India. And if that former contact of East and West resulted in a union of cultures, from which sprang modern Europe, so must this latter-day meeting issue in a world-wide fusion, from which shall arise a broader manhood."[45] In effect, Fenollosa uses Social Darwinist terms but inverts their normative use-values by arguing for amalgamation rather than against it, so that humanity "will be wonderfully enlarged."[46] And unlike President McKinley, who felt, along the lines of Kipling's now infamous "White Man's Burden," that it was America's "Christian burden" to govern "those incapable of self governance,"[47] Fenollosa's desire for fusion did not spring from a "Christian burden," but was decidedly aligned with the New Buddhist rhetoric deployed at the World Parliament of Religions. It was this particular late-Meiji admixture of Social Darwinism and Buddhism that gave birth to the geopolitical orientation of Fenollosa's prophetic calling.

While one wonders what Fenollosa might have thought about Japan's ability to lead Asia toward a Buddhist rebirth after the "rape of Nanking," or of Japan's brutal colonial legacy in Korea and elsewhere (not to mention U.S. fitness for stewardship after firebombing residential Tokyo and the atomic bombings of Nagasaki and Hiroshima), it would be unfair to confront him with atrocities committed thirty to forty years after his death (although it is never unfair to presence and criticize the logic that leads to such eventualities). After all, even during the height of World War II, Nishida Kitarō, the father of the Kyoto School of Hegelian Buddhism (in many ways Shin Bukkyô's heir) still spoke of Japanese domination in terms of the Japanese ability to synthesize Eastern and Western epistemology and "go straight to things."[48] It is not difficult to find examples of philosophical agendas taking precedence over historical events. Recently, the generation of Japanese Buddhists that succeeded Shin Bukkyô has been taken to task by scholars associated with the "Critical Buddhism movement" for their support of wartime policies, and some scholars have even suggested that it was the nationalist and imperialist forms of Buddhism practiced by the Japanese at the time that facilitated these atrocities.[49] But a fair treatment of this issue must include the ways in which the militarism of the late 1920s and 1930s imbued religion and culture with new and more jingoistic meanings. Again, these could not have been predicted before Fenollosa's death in 1908. Nevertheless, I believe it is clear that Fenollosa's prophetic (if imperialist) cultural project was, in part, a manifestation of a "Bodhisattva Burden"[50] ideologically forged in the historically specific rhetoric of Fenollosa's New Buddhist circle. A *bodhisattva*, the paragon of Buddhist ethics, refers to a being who, having reached enlightenment, has postponed entering *nirvana* until he/she has helped all other beings reach enlightenment first. So if Kipling justified his imperialism by arguing that it was the duty of every white Christian to "civilize" the heathen Filipinos (the so-called White Man's Burden), then we can see Fenollosa's and the New Buddhist desire to "re-civilize" China as a cognate form of "compassionate imperialism," couched not in the rhetoric of Christian, but Buddhist, ethics. Not only did Fenollosa advocate Japan's mission to revitalize China, but he saw himself as a principal player in bringing enlightenment to the West as well.

Shortly after returning from Meiji Japan, where he had risen to the rank of "Imperial Commissioner of Fine Arts," Fenollosa took up residency as the curator of the East Asian wing of the Boston Museum of Fine Art. His papers contain a personal note, written at about this time, entitled "My Position in America; a Manifest of Mission,"[51] which helps flesh out his personal vision of this "Bodhisattva Burden" by outlining his role in the coming convergence of East and West. "First," he writes, "I must remember that, however much I may sympathize with the past civilizations of the East, I am in this incarnation a man of Western race, and bound to do my part toward the development of Western civilization." Fenollosa sees this role not as "the narrow one of a mere scholar or antiquarian, or a historian who burrows in the past for mere accuracy of fact . . . nor a merely philosophical writer." Rather, his aim is "to mould the future," by utilizing "his historical and theoretical knowledge of Buddhism, and of Eastern ideality in general." Furthermore, Fenollosa states that we should "above all develope [*sic*] in our ideals the Bodhisattva spirit. Let us depict it in its lofty impersonal forms, as well as in its contemporary human incarnations."[52] For Fenollosa, the Bodhisattva spirit requires that art and poetry bring respite to the suffering masses:

> For we cannot ignore the great economical questions of the day,
> nor the terrific problem of the world's suffering, sin, and disease.
> Any undue art developement [*sic*] which turns away the mind from
> sympathy with these must be a failure. But this function of art must

be so used as to brighten and gladden the lot of the poor, social re-arrangement giving them leisure to cultivate taste, like the Japanese peasant.[53]

For Fenollosa, then, art and poetry (infused with the epistemological and aesthetic foundations that will be discussed in a moment) are "skillful means" for helping alleviate the suffering masses through broad cultural change. It is clear that Fenollosa's cultural project attempts to capture both the wisdom and compassion of the *bodhisattva* vows he took under the Abbot Sakurai Keitoku of the Tendai monastery of Miidera:

> However innumerable the sentient beings, I vow to save them all.
> However inexhaustible the passions [*klesas*], I vow to extinguish them all.
> However immeasurable the *dharmas*, I vow to master them all.
> However incomparable the truth of the Buddha, I vow to attain it.

For Fenollosa, this "development" of the "Bodhisattva spirit" would entail both mastering "dharmas" (Asian religious and philosophical discourses) and then "saving" the Western world (the charge of his present incarnation as a Westerner) by integrating these ideals into the very fabric of Western lives.[54] To accomplish his new role as the "prophet of the coming fusion," Fenollosa writes, "there must be no attempt to ignore the first theoretical groundwork. . . . I must go back to my work on Hegel. I must inform myself on present psychologic progress,[55] and I must bring them together on the basis of Buddhist mysticism. Here, having established intellectual foundations, I may afterward pass beyond this beginning, and fearlessly construct on the basis of the mystical view."[56] This formulation of a Hegelian Buddhism is not something we can wholly attribute to Fenollosa, however; the nature of this syncretism as well as many of its specific cultural and historical elements can be traced to the *Shin Bukkyô* movement within which he was actively engaged.

Shin Bukkyô, Tendai Philosophy, and Fenollosa's "Poetics of Emptiness"

While it is obvious that Fenollosa's own geopolitics reflect a shared conflation of ideology and philosophy/religion with the New Buddhist movement, this does not mean that his Buddhism can be reduced to its political dimensions. After all, Fenollosa received a more orthodox Tendai training before (and after) his reception into the Sangha on September 21, 1885.[57] Central to his training would have been a familiarization with Tendai's central teaching of the "middle way," or "threefold truths": (1) all things are empty (of inherent existence); (2) all things have a provisional/interrelated reality; and (3) all things are both empty of ultimate reality and provisionally real at the same time. Expounding a verse from Nāgārjuna's *Madhyamaka-kārikās*, Zhiyi (智顗, b. 538–d. 597) held that an object (e.g., a chair) does not exist autonomously without causes and conditions and is therefore said to be empty of absolute existence (first proposition); but it is not therefore true that there are no such things as chairs. Such things are perceptible and can be designated in language, so they have a provisional existence (second proposition). But neither the empty nor the provisional truth about the chair fully captures its reality: it is both provisional/conventional and empty, and neither (merely) provisional nor (merely) empty (third proposition). The reality of the mean is neither 有 (*you*, substance or existent) nor 空 (*kong*, empty or nonexistent), but a reconciliation of the two extremes of nihilism and materialism in 圓道 ("the perfect way").[58]

In Inoue's New Buddhist manifesto, *Bukkyo katsuron: Joron*, he organizes Western philosophy by means of a simplified version of the Hegelian dialectic, grouping the entire body of work of individual philosophers or entire schools into threes, with each philosopher (or school) occupying the position of thesis, antithesis, or synthesis.[59] Inoue argues:

> The so-called Middle Way is not being nor is it emptiness; it is both being and emptiness, and materialism and idealism are reconciled within it. It is a Middle Way that simultaneously embraces subjectivity and objectivity. It is a Middle Way that integrates experience and nature. . . . Within the Middle Way, all the ancient theories meet. . . . As a theory it lacks nothing. . . . It is the great ocean of thought and the fountainhead of philosophy.[60]

Given the convenient tripartite structure of both Hegelian and Tendai philosophy, it is not surprising that Fenollosa would also subscribe to a vision of a Hegelian (Tendai) Buddhism. In an essay entitled "Remarks on Japanese Art in General," Fenollosa writes, "[Supplemented] by Western Science, and the theory of Western Synthetic Logic [Hegel], it [Buddhism] can be made adequate to express the highest needs of intellectual life and to satisfy the highest claims of Pure Reason, and that, without ceasing to remain essentially Buddhism."[61] Fenollosa's biographer, Lawrence Chisholm, citing personal notebooks dating to the year of Fenollosa's return to Japan (1896), writes, "More than ever Buddhism seemed a key to all speculations. Tendai Buddhism offered a truly 'synthetic' philosophy with all the color and texture which Hegel lacked."[62] While Fenollosa favored Hegel's notions of dialectical synthesis, he also worked hard to undermine Hegel's acidic anti-Chinese views. While Hegel saw Chinese characters as too "concrete" and therefore limiting for abstract thought, Fenollosa sought to show that it is alphabetic writing which is too limiting, due to the inability to see the aggregative nature of both signification and the things signified. Nevertheless, Fenollosa, like other New Buddhists, saw the combination of Mahayana Buddhism and dialectical logic as the telos of the current age of history. This philosophical line of thinking also supported the New Buddhist assertion that Japanese Buddhism was the final realization of Chinese Buddhism (if not civilization more generally). In *Epochs*, Fenollosa writes that the founders of Japanese Tendai, enriched by the height of Chinese civilized thought, established a "mystical theocracy such as never existed in China or any other Buddhist Kingdom."[63]

Tendai's emptying of conventional reality of unified, autonomous meaning (especially as embodied in words), among other investments, led Fenollosa to disagree with the mavericks of Western Buddhology, Rhys Davids and Max Müller, concerning their positivist claims to textual authority.[64] Both Davids and Müller argued that the only authentic Buddhism existed in the Pali texts, since these texts could be traced back to the historical Buddha. Believing, then, that the Western scholarly exegesis of the original texts provided the only authentic knowledge of Buddhism, they argued that all subsequent Mahayana Buddhism merely amounted to degenerate cultural accretions and local superstitions. While this argument gave Orientalists greater authority over Buddhism than its (then) present practitioners held, Fenollosa chose to anchor his claims to those made by the New Buddhists' delegates at the parliament rather than to the Pali texts.

Relying on the same Social Darwinist supports deployed by Japanese Buddhists at the parliament, Fenollosa contested both Christian and Western Buddhological claims to textual authority by labeling the older Theravada tradition (the branch of Buddhism associated with the Pali) a "static" tradition lacking the growth and vitality of Mahayana practice. In effect, Fenollosa deployed Social Darwinist claims as a means of reclaiming Buddhism as a progressive and dynamic form of Asian Modernity rather than a set of ancient texts.[65] In his massive study *Ep-*

ochs of Chinese & Japanese Art, Fenollosa writes, "The great truth that they [Western Buddhologists] forget is that Buddhism, like Christianity . . . has been an evolutionary religion, never content with old formalisms, but, filled with spiritual ardour, continually re-adapting itself to the needs of the human nature with which it finds itself in contact."[66] So while the New Buddhists could not escape Western knowledge claims by allowing Eurocentric discourses to frame the very terms of their dissent, this hybrid idiom would likely not have disturbed Fenollosa, whose appropriation of New Buddhist rhetoric granted him an unusual sense of authority, and thus enabled him to contest established Western Orientalist claims without having to question his overarching Eurocentric investments.

While it is important to explore the imperialist and essentializing elements of Fenollosa's Buddhist positioning, which helps one understand the imperialist tone of the opening paragraphs of the CWC, one must return to the core Tendai tripartite formulation of the "Middle Way" espoused by Inoue to address the Buddhist thought in the CWC itself. Read in the context of Fenollosa's Tendai epistemology, the central argument is not the perfect isomorphism of signifier and signified—which is one of the most important elements of Pound's reading of the essay—but that Western languages and logic have mistaken accuracy for truth, taxonomy for knowledge, and abstraction for reality.

The Buddhist "Chinese Written Character as a Medium for Poetry"

The notion that philosophers and poets might turn to the openness of language infused by interrelation and conditionality rather than hypotactic strings of autonomous "things" would have pleased Fenollosa. His essay offers an example of a language and poetic tradition that, from his perspective, avoids the positivist pitfalls of Western logic by foregrounding its ultimate emptiness, while at the same time offering conventional truths (and beauty). For Fenollosa, many characters appear as "snapshots" of their interdependent origination, a "bundle" not only arising from these aggregates, but also prone to undetermined meanings when syntactically set adrift with other such "aggregated bundles." Using these "snap-shots" of "dependently originating bundles," a poet, for Fenollosa, can actually "mimic" nature's own "infinitely interpenetrating flux," while at the same time establish conventional truths in "beautiful" harmonies within the patterns of language and nature itself.

Fenollosa begins his assault on the logical categorization of language and thought with a challenge to traditional Western notions of syntactic completeness. He gives two definitions of syntactic completion: "a sentence [that] expresses a 'complete thought'"; or one that achieves its completion through a simple "union of subject and predicate." So, therefore, the kind of completeness demonstrated by the "practical completeness" of, say, simple interjections like "Hi there" or "Scat!" is "only conventionally complete," since "no full sentence really completes a thought."[67] It is important to draw attention to Fenollosa's distinction between "conventional" completeness, represented in what he defines as "natural syntax," and any notion of "ultimate completion" (which he argues is not possible in language of any kind), for it is this very distinction between "conventional" and "ultimate" truth that lies at the center of Tendai's "Middle Path." One might say, from this perspective, that language (and syntax specifically) is "conventionally real," because it is useful, it is used; but it is not "ultimately real," because it does not positively exist as something (holding presences as complete things within it) beyond its usefulness.

Fenollosa gives an example of a "natural sentence," "Man sees horse 人見馬," as a model of "conventional completeness," yet he shows how it falls short of any ultimate completion because it is not an isolated event: "The man who sees and the horse which is seen will not stand still. The man was planning a ride before he looked. The horse kicked when the man tried to catch him." He continues, "The truth is that acts are successive, even continuous; one causes or passes into another. And though we may string ever so many clauses into a single, compound sentence, motion leaks everywhere, like electricity from an exposed wire." He concludes that "all processes in nature are inter-related; and thus there could be no complete sentence (according to this definition) save one which it would take all time to pronounce."[68] Throughout Fenollosa's analysis one can detect both the spatially oriented Kegon definition of emptiness as a "web" (all things are empty of autonomous "completeness" because all things are "interrelated") and the more temporally oriented Madhyamika definition of emptiness ("one cause passing into another," or *pratītya-samutpāda* [dependent arising]) to communicate the merely conventional completeness of syntax.[69]

The influence of Kegon along with that of Tendai Buddhism on Fenollosa's thinking is present from early on. In an earlier lecture, Fenollosa deploys an even more powerful Buddhist articulation of his argument by comparing static *things* to temporary waves on the surface of a deep, still sea:

If we take an instantaneous photograph of the sea in motion, we may fix the momentary form of a wave, and call it a thing; yet it was only an incessant vibration of water. So other things, more things, apparently more stable, are only large vibrations of living substance; and when we trace them to their origin and decay, they are seen to be only parts of something else. And these essential processes of nature are not simple; there are waves upon waves, process below processes, systems within systems;—and apparently so on forever.[70]

In this passage Fenollosa is invoking a common Buddhist metaphor by comparing transience (conventional or empty phenomena) to waves, and absolute emptiness to the sea. The metaphor's origin likely stems from the Sanskrit word *paramita*, which means "having arrived at the other shore" and is often explained as "being apart from coming into being and ceasing to be." For before one is released from attachment, coming into being and ceasing to be "arise like waves on water."[71] To transcend the states of existence, which would release one from coming into being or ceasing to be, entails a shift in perception likened to the freely flowing water rather than its surface waves.[72] But Fenollosa's discussion of "waves upon waves, processes below processes, and systems within systems" specifically invokes Kegon epistemology (and, by extension, aesthetics), mentioned earlier, in which a vast web of interpenetration (referred to by the metaphor of "Indra's net") is envisaged as a vast net of interconnections where at every intersection of every causal connection (figured here as horizontal and vertical threads) one finds a jewel reflecting every other jewel in the net. Unlike Tendai's "Middle Path," Kegon's "net" granted Fenollosa a more aesthetic theory of emptiness, capable of embodying both his epistemological concerns and what we will come to see, in Chapter 2, as his aesthetic, and even cosmological, concerns.

Fenollosa follows his critique of syntactic completeness by challenging what he sees as the next linguistic obstacle to the "Middle Path": semantic completeness. Nouns are problematic in this regard because to Fenollosa they represent the abstracted principle of stasis, isolation, and individual semantic autonomy. He writes, "A true noun, an isolated thing, does not exist in nature. Things are only the terminal points, or rather the meeting points of actions, cross-sections cut through actions, snap-shots."[73] Later he continues, "To get a tolerably concrete noun, we have to leave behind the verb and adjective roots, and light upon a thing arbitrarily cut off from its power of action, say 'the sun' or 'the moon.'" Yet, he argues that "there is nothing in nature so cut off, and therefore this nounizing is itself an abstraction."[74] Finally, he mocks: "Fancy picking up a man and telling him that he is a noun, a dead thing rather than a bundle of functions!"[75] He offers the example of the word for man (男), explaining that rather than slipping into a hypostatized noun, Chinese characters reveal an aggregate concept drawn from a relationship of causes and conditions: 力 labor in the context of a 田 field combine to signify the "bundle of functions" we come to think of as man 男. In this sense, we might say that characters are dependently arisen, or 汉字是因緣生的, caused by prior causes and conditions. For Fenollosa, therefore, English words, especially nouns, delude their users into believing they are semantically stable and complete unto themselves (事 things—what in Buddhist terminology one might call 自生, or self-born). By following the same method of destabilization used to undermine syntactic completeness (interdependent and causal origination), Fenollosa argues that nouns are just as empty of autonomous completeness as are sentences.

Fenollosa moves on to discuss the shortcomings of adjectival categories, in a manner highly reminiscent of his Buddhist "wave" metaphor. He argues that adjectives are merely derivations of processes: "Green is only a certain rapidity of vibration, hardness a degree of tenseness in cohering."[76] In this manner, Fenollosa continues to show how each grammatical convention cannot prevent motion from leaking "everywhere, like electricity from an exposed wire." Since he asserts that "isolated thing[s] do not exist in nature," his essay argues that "the verb must be the primary fact of nature, since motion and change are all that we can recognize in her,"[77] and, concordantly, any poetics based upon the operations of nature will necessarily be one that privileges transitive verbs over nouns and "relations over things," or the interrelatedness of the "ocean" over individual "waves" (*shi*). After nouns, therefore, Fenollosa finds value in the various parts of speech to the extent to which they foreground the interrelated (and thus ultimately incomplete/empty) nature of signification—their transience—or as Fenollosa would have it, transitive-ness. Should it be surprising that Fenollosa values transitive verbs above all other parts of speech? After all, the Buddhist valuation of the "transient" and Fenollosa's "transitive" are but present and past participles of the same Latin word *transire*, "to go over/pass through."[78]

After moving through the parts of speech, Fenollosa embarks on his most critical and lengthy attack on logical categories and their linguistic conventions. He writes:

> European logic . . . is a kind of brickyard. It is baked into little hard units or concepts. These are piled in rows according to size and then labeled with words for future use. This use consists in picking out a few bricks, each by its convenient label, and sticking them together into a sort of wall called a sentence by the use either of white mortar for the positive copula "is," or of black mortar for the negative copula "is not."[79]

By moving from grammar proper to the logic behind English grammar's "movement toward" taxonomical knowledge as its ultimate function, Fenollosa hopes to reveal the link between language and the limitation of thought and knowledge itself.

In an earlier draft of the CWC, Fenollosa explains why logic fails as a foundation for ultimate knowledge, since it "purchases its sharpness by its thinness. Its accuracy by its isolation." He continues, "Now things, a notion, are *not* isolated. Their processes are *not* simple. Their Meanings are *not* shredded . . . life is infinite and all at once. The truth of things, lies not in their abstraction, but in some organic law which governs their complex interrelations." Fenollosa thus concludes that "the sheer loss and weakness of this [logical] method" is "apparent and flagrant," since "such logic cannot deal with any kind of interaction or with any multiplicity of function."[80] As I mentioned in the opening section of this chapter, Fenollosa sees these weaknesses as the root of cultural "degeneracy," to which, precisely, the integration of Eastern philosophy with the Western mind was to provide the cure. For Fenollosa, then, the kinds of "truths" offered by taxonomical and positivist structures of knowledge can only address conventional needs but are not suited for serious philosophical study, let alone poetry and art. Yet he, like others on Tendai's Middle Path, sees value in language's practical applications. For Fenollosa, Chinese offers its users a perfect middle path by negating the idea of autonomous things/words (all can be shown to be composites and not "real" unities), while offering its users a practical language capable of communicating conventional truths at the same time. At the same time, the ideogram's aggregative nature offers, for Fenollosa, a model language incapable of hypostatization, and, therefore, a means to deal with the positivism of Western logic and contemporary Confucianism, which he saw as the principal catalyst for "cultural degeneration" and tyranny in the modern world.[81]

Ezra Pound and Ernest Fenollosa

For Ezra Pound to take Fenollosa's essay as a modernist "ars poetica," he had to assume that Fenollosa's stance against logical abstractions was arguing for a "direct treatment of the thing." In other words, Pound heard in Fenollosa the argument that Western logic prevents one from seeing "real things," like "cherry trees," "directly." Pound writes, "Get your 'red' down to rose, rust, cherry if you want to know what you are talking about. We have too much talk about vibrations and infinities."[82] In a letter to Harriet Monroe, Pound writes, "Language is made out of concrete things";[83] and later, in his *ABC of Reading*, he writes:

> In Europe, if you ask a man to define anything, his definitions always move away from the simple things that he knows perfectly well, it recedes into an unknown region, that is a region of remoter and progressively remoter abstraction. . . . By contrast to the method of abstraction, or of defining things in more and still more general terms, Fenollosa emphasizes the method of science, "which is the method of poetry," as distinct from "philosophic discussion," and is the way the Chinese go about it in their ideograph or abbreviated picture writing.[84]

Pound was conditioned to read Fenollosa in this manner due to his own imagist aesthetics, which sought the "direct treatment of the thing,"[85] but he later found this desire for linguistic mimesis consummated by his unique reading of Confucian terms like 正名 (*zheng ming,* often translated as "the rectification of names"). The term *zheng ming* originates in the *Lun yu* 13:3, which records a conversation between Confucius and his disciple Zi Lu, who asks his master what his priorities would be if he were made the Lord of Wei. Confucius answered that he would first *zheng ming,* or "rectify" or "correct," names. Confucius argues that if the *ming* were not *zheng* then language would cease to function properly, which would lead to a collapse of functioning laws, properly performed rites, and, finally, society itself. Pound's translation of the passage reads:

The men of old wanting to clarify and diffuse throughout the empire that light which comes from looking straight into the heart and then acting, first set up good government in their own states; wanting order in the home, they first discipline themselves; desiring self-discipline, they rectified their hearts, and wanting to rectify their hearts, they sought precise verbal definitions of their inarticulate thoughts, the tones given off by the mind; wanting to attain precise verbal definitions, they set to extend their knowledge to the upmost.[86]

In his book, *Ezra Pound and Confucianism: Remaking Humanism in the Face of Modernity*, Feng Lan argues that Pound first began taking the notion of *zheng ming* seriously in the mid-1920s. But it was not until Pound's *Confucius: Digest of the Analects*, published in 1937, that he translated the *zheng ming* passage. The most famous translation of *Lun Yu* appeared in 1950:

> 5. If words (terminology) are not (is not) precise, they cannot be followed out, or completed in action according to specifications . . .
> 7. Therefore the proper man must have terms that can be spoken, and when uttered be carried into effect; the proper man's words must cohere to things, correspond to them (exactly) and no more fuss about it.[87]

Lan points out that Pound's reading of *zheng ming* differs from the "feudalistic specificity" regarding the proper execution of the Confucian rites by abstracting it to a point whereby it applies to "all language." The father of Chinese history, Sima Qian, (b. 145–d. 86?) argued that *zheng ming* refers to rectifying feudal social relations between father and son by appealing to Confucius's historical context. For Sima, Confucius worried that Zhe (the Lord of Wei during Confucius's time) should respect his obligation to hand the lordship back over to Zhe's exiled father, Kuai Kui. Lan points out that there exist less historically contingent/contextual interpretations of *zheng ming*, however. These interpretations, like Pound's, tended to abstract *ming* into "written words/language." Yet most of these have been considered heterodox, and none share Pound's sense of absolute linguistic transparency/accuracy.[88]

In Mary Paterson Cheadle's *Ezra Pound's Confucian Translations*, she explains that Pound's unorthodox definition of another key Confucian term, 誠 (*cheng*), which Pound translates as "precise verbal meaning," is "not the result of his own inventive imagination but what seems to have been some fairly extensive research in Morrison's dictionary." She continues, "Bringing together the composite of definitions that Pound saw operating in *cheng*—meanings such as spear, lance, guarding the frontiers, guarding the boundaries—and combining this, in turn, with the sign for 'word' on the left side of the compound, he arrived, in paragraph 4 of *The Great Digest* at 'precise verbal definitions,' or as he gives it in the 'Terminology section preceding the translation,' 'the sun's lance coming to rest on the precise spot verbally.'"[89] While it is clear from both Lan and Cheadle that Pound's positivist/neoplatonic interpretation of Confucian terms cannot be attributed to Confucianist discourses themselves, many (Western) literary critics still see Confucianism as one of the points of origin for Pound's fascist beliefs.[90]

While Pound values Chinese characters for their "verbal precision" as "short hand pictures of things," it is important to remember that Fenollosa seems to take the opposite view of characters—for example, when he contrasts them with the "the untruth of a painting or a photograph" that, "in spite of its concreteness and vividness," "drops the element of natural succession."[91] So while both would argue that "brightness" is too abstract a concept in English and would prefer the aggregate of sun 日 and moon 月 to produce the idea of brightness 明, Fenollosa does not place value on the concreteness of "pictures of things" to build higher-order images, as Pound sees it, but values their clearly aggregative character in order to dismantle "thingness" itself by showing the dependency on contextual causes and conditions. In his most recent book, *Transpacific Imaginations,* Yunte Huang sheds some new light upon Ezra Pound's quintessentially imagistic poem, "In a Station of the Metro," that may help further differentiate Pound and Fenollosa's poetics:

The apparition   of these faces   in the crowd
      Petals   on a wet, black   bough[92]

Huang writes that "the apparition is not just that of the faces, but what hovers between the two lines that resist a metaphoric collapse: faces (as) petals. By calling it an image rather than a simile, Pound tries to make the gap disappear, if not in space, then at least in time."[93] Huang points to Pound's definition of the poetic image as "that which presents an intellectual and emotional complex *in an instant of time.*"[94] As I have already discussed, Fenollosa also uses the "snapshot" to describe the ideogrammic composite, but he clearly uses the elision of time to discredit what he argues is the falseness of the photographic image, which purchases its realism by dropping the truth of temporal flux (hence, impermanence). Instead, he points to the way aggregative characters reveal the metaphorical (linguistic) stratigraphy of concepts in causal time as a way of recalling the untruth of hypostatization itself. Pound, on the other hand, points to the *instant of time* as something that erases the contextual flux of signification, locking down positivist correlations between concrete images and their unchanging, clarified domains of signification. Quite simply, Pound either did not see, or had no need for, Fenollosa's dehypostatizing reading of characters and developed a constructive reading of "ideograms" largely discordant with Fenollosa's.

As a method, the ideogram represented for Pound far more than a poetic form like a sonnet or a haiku; it was a far-reaching concept of artful representation (or configuration) linked to other global movements from Cubism and the collage artists like Max Ernst and Kurt Schwitters, where image and meaning find forms outside normative conventions and syntaxes. As wonderfully fruitful as Pound's interpretation has been, later readers of the CWC, following Pound's "direct treatment of the thing" approach, succeeded in overshadowing Fenollosa's explicitly Buddhist poetics. Nevertheless, the theoretical and aesthetic "gist" of these heterocultural elements remains a vital part of the published version. So while the dominating call for a "unified," "harmonious" "interpenetration of overtones" cannot claim a significant impact on the modernist, disjunctive poetic forms inspired by Pound's ideogrammic method, the Buddhist epistemological arguments that underlie Fenollosa's theory of aggregative bundles and non-syntactic completeness certainly can.

While Fenollosa's Buddhists' investments have shaped the text we have come to know as "The Chinese Written Character as a Medium for Poetry," this is only half of the story, since Ezra Pound did not include the second half of Fenollosa's original text when he published the work, and never mentioned this second half throughout the decades that followed. While the Buddhism that informs the first half persists throughout the whole work, the second half of the text deals principally with issues of prosody and sound, and draws upon Chinese classical poetics and a rich assortment of concepts culled from notions of correlative cosmology (albeit always through the prism of Fenollosa's Japanese instructors) and existing trends in Western philosophical and aesthetic traditions. In the following chapter, I will show how this admixture both complicates and complements Fenollosa's poetics, as it draws upon different notions of emptiness from these heterogeneous discourses.

Patterned Harmony: Buddhism, Sound, and Ernest Fenollosa's Poetics of Correlative Cosmology

The whole delicate substance of speech is built upon substrata metaphor. Abstract terms, pressed by etymology, reveal their ancient roots still embedded in direct action. But the primitive metaphors do not spring from arbitrary subjective processes. They are possible only because they follow objective lines of relation in nature herself.
—ERNEST FENOLLOSA, "THE CHINESE WRITTEN CHARACTER AS A MEDIUM FOR POETRY: AN ARS POETICA" (1918, 1936)

Poetry surpasses prose in this fact especially, that the poet carefully selects those words for juxtaposition in a sentence whose overtones of meaning blend into a delicate and transparent harmony.
—ERNEST FENOLLOSA, "THE CHINESE WRITTEN LANGUAGE AS THE MEDIUM FOR POETRY" (FINAL DRAFT, CA. 1906)

In the late summer of 2004, I was leafing through the Fenollosa papers held in the Ezra Pound archive at Yale University's Beinecke Library when I happened upon a startling find: its second half. While many scholars have mentioned the earlier drafts of "The Chinese Written Character as a Medium for Poetry," no one had ever mentioned the important fact that the essay published by Pound represents only one half of Fenollosa's lectures on Chinese as a medium for poetry.[1] This "second half" is entitled "Chinese and Japanese. Draft of Lecture I. Vol. II." I am calling it the "second half" because Fenollosa clearly sees the CWC as "Lecture I. Vol. I," to be followed by "Vol. II." This view is validated further by a text that combines the two lectures, entitled "Synopsis of Lectures on Chinese and Japanese Poetry."[2] This scholarly oversight is particularly important to take note of since one of the most persistent criticisms of Fenollosa's work is the near total absence of sound from his discussion of Chinese, and the second half of the CWC is largely devoted to this very subject. Pound only mentions the second half of the lecture one time, when he states, "From his lecture on the Chinese Character I took what seemed to me most needed, omitting the passages re/ sound."[3] After reading through the missing lecture, it becomes perfectly clear why

Ezra Pound would not find what he "most needed" in the omitted passages: most of that lecture argues for metered and rhymed translations of classical Chinese poetry, which contradicts both Pound's imagist program and the break from English formalism represented so powerfully by his book of free-verse Chinese translations, *Cathay*. Yet this second lecture, when read in the context of still other writings only now being published,[4] offers more than a translation theory: it reveals a complex set of Buddhist reasons why Fenollosa chose to transliterate Chinese into Japanese (which Pound continued to do for many decades), reveals a greater philosophical context to understand his non-Buddhist predilection for "harmony" and belief in "concrete relations within nature," and, perhaps most importantly, reveals that Fenollosa possessed a far more richly textured knowledge of classical Chinese (cosmological) poetics from which he created a notion of poetic agency grounded in largely Daoist notions of emptiness. Not only did Fenollosa apparently know a great deal about Chinese prosody and poetic theory, but by following the synthesizing impulse that lies at the core of his New Buddhist agenda, he hoped to import key concepts of Chinese cosmology into both Western poetry and society more generally.

In a few words, Fenollosa believed that English verse, unlike the classical Chinese poetry and poetics (by which he meant traditional Chinese prosody and genres) had little to no relationship to philosophical, social, political, or spiritual discourses and therefore had become increasingly irrelevant and metaphysically bankrupt. Following arguments that paralleled his critique of "medieval logic" outlined in Chapter 1, Fenollosa believed that traditional English formalism could be saved from its own irrelevancy and decay by appropriating Chinese poetic theories of "correlative harmony" (which Fenollosa took to be "universal"). In this chapter, I will offer a detailed sketch of what Fenollosa knew about classical Chinese cosmology and poetics, how he hoped to import these ideas and forms into English, and why. As a point of contrast, I bring Ezra Pound back into the discussion to compare his early and later ideas on "Chinese sonority" as they drew upon his own desire to import Confucian concepts into Western poetic, philosophical, and political discourses. Finally, I present an analysis of the political ideologies that connect (or could have connected) their projects together. The following chapter, therefore, not only illuminates Fenollosa's understanding of the relationship of sound and East Asian philosophy, but explores how these ideas relate to the interface of sound and East Asian philosophy in the work of the man who, by dismissing Fenollosa's thoughts on the subject, succeeded in keeping them from entering the history of twentieth-century American poetry and poetics.

Emptiness vs. Harmony

In the previous chapter, I attempted to show how Ernest Fenollosa's heterocultural reading of classical Chinese poetry and poetics came about through a complex weave of Buddhist notions of śūnatā, 空 (kong, emptiness) and Western intellectual trends of the period. For Fenollosa, so-called Chinese ideograms resist positivist dreams for a one-to-one correspondence between signifier and signified by constantly reminding their users of the contextual, dynamic, aggregate nature of signification, as well as the "things" signified. In contrast to both popular Western thinking and sophisticated Western philosophy, in which individual things tend to be hypostatized—that is, regarded as concrete or fixed realities—Fenollosa's Buddhism emphasizes the aggregative, dependent nature of all "things." For instance, a chair, from a commonsensical Western standpoint, will be viewed as an autonomous "thing" or object, whereas, from Fenollosa's Buddhist standpoint, a chair might be understood to be an aggregate of its many parts (legs, seat, back), each of which can be broken into its own parts, causes, and conditions, and its color, which is merely a phenomenon that arises at the meeting place of vibrations of light and sight organs, which are themselves a complex nexus of processes hypostasized as an "eye" or a "person." Neither the chair nor its color is simply "there." Fenollosa could, for instance, point to the character for chair 椅 and comment upon its aggregate of "wood" 木 that pleases 可 people 大 who sit upon it. While such "visual etymologies" are not correct, from a linguistic point of view, they offered Fenollosa a linguistic analogue for his Tendai Buddhist beliefs. In contrast to the image of a world of objects defined by their ideal, or essential, forms—the kind of world that lends itself to maps, taxonomies, hierarchies, and the formulation of scientific laws—we have an image of a world that never comes to rest in any given form, but can be conventionally designated in language for practical reasons or orchestrated for aesthetic reasons.

Fenollosa, a student of American and British transcendentalism, was prepared to find harmony, unity, and synthesis in this world of flux (after all, these are important terms in both Romanticism and transcendentalism),[5] yet a closer analysis of his wider writings will demonstrate that his poetic and aesthetic theories cannot be reduced to derivative Romantic transcendentalism. While we will encounter terms popularized by Coleridge, Schelling, Hegel, and Emerson, we will find that over his two decades studying East Asian philosophy, aesthetics, and poetics, Fenollosa's terms took on distinctly new, heterocultural values. Regardless of where concepts of "harmony" enter Fenollosa's poetics, they are difficult to reconcile with the dehypostatizing theory of the ideogram, parts of speech, and syntax discussed in the previous chapter (but here we will explore how other elements of his Buddhist investments impact his aural theories of poetry).

This idea of "harmonizing" is not, in Indian Buddhist terms, particularly compatible with notions of "dependent origination." All things are dependent upon prior causes and conditions, but there is no discussion of "harmony" within these aggregates, since harmony is not the point, dehypostatization is. According to Whalen Lai, the movement from concepts of emptiness grounded upon notions of "dependent origination" to Chinese Buddhist forms of emptiness which introduced notions of "harmony," resulted from a reinterpretation of emptiness along the "organisimic"[6] principles of 本 (ben, root or origin) and 末 (mo, end or dust),[7] a construction grounded in the notion of a Dao as "mother to all things." This organic reinterpretation of dependent origination, Lai claims, laid stress on native Chinese notions of organic, harmonious becoming already present in a cosmological system dominated by the correlative cosmology illustrated in the yin/yang–wu-xing cosmogony of the Yijing. We can gain a better understanding of the differences between the Indian- and Chinese-influenced models of emptiness by returning to the wave-water metaphor used by Fenollosa (discussed in the previous chapter). In the waves-to-water metaphor, water (tathatā) generates waves in saṃsāra through the causal conditions of ignorance. Yet the waves are still water, and water still waves. They are One, yet the Kegon notion of "Indra's net"[8] goes even further by stating that "every particular wave interpenetrates all other particular waves both individually and as a whole, and every drop of water interpenetrates every other drop and the Whole." Lai continues:

> There is, I think, an important difference between interdependence and harmonism. Things can be mutually dependent without necessarily adding up to a whole, to a unity. Yin/yang harmonism, however, implies this oneness through complementation. It can be seen that this sense of oneness or harmony . . . was derived

unconsciously more from the native Chinese cosmic monism than from Nāgārjuna who might not agree with such a theory of mutual penetration.[9]

While Fenollosa's assimilation of Kegon ideas moves him closer to an integration of dehypostatizing emptiness and an aesthetic of harmony, it still cannot account for Fenollosa's notion of artistic agency in creating such "harmonies." To explore these elements of Fenollosa's poetics, we must reach beyond his late Meiji Shin Bukkyô (New Buddhist) world-view and focus on his understanding of classical Chinese poetics derived in large measure from Chinese correlative cosmology.

In the epigrams that begin this chapter, one can see two distinct notions of poetic agency: the first is perceptive/receptive in nature, as Fenollosa charges poets with the task of not so much inventing meta-phors but of uncovering preexisting correlations in nature from which to derive "objective metaphors." The second quote, however, reveals a more creative role for the poet who must juxtapose words so that they "blend into a delicate and transparent harmony." In this later quote from the CWC (which was altered by Pound in the published edition[10]), Fenollosa emphasizes the poet's role as harmonizer, rather than etymologist (or phenomenologist). Yet I would argue that these are not, in fact, contra-dictory notions when understood within Fenollosa's "universal theory of literature": 文 (Ja: *bun*, Ch: *wen*, pattern).

In contrast to Fenollosa's understanding of "emptiness," discussed in Chapter 1 of this study as essentially the law of dependent origination, he invokes a wholly distinct understanding of emptiness drawn largely from Daoist notions (filtered through Western Romanticism) to describe poetic/creative genius, which he views as the result of an author's abil-ity to "empty" the self of personality, or interfering ego.[11] He compares composition to a "priestly trance," whereby "he" does not "act himself," but lets the "affinities do their own work" "through fluidity of conscious-ness."[12] This notion of creative emptying resembles Zhuang Zi's notion of 心齋坐忘 (*xinzhai zuowang*, "to fast the heart and sit in forgetfulness") in order to perceive the Dao.[13] One might ascribe such statements to Em-erson's "invisible eyeball" and Keats's "negative capability" if it were not for other passages that reveal a closer affinity to clear classical Chinese poetics. Fenollosa refines this idea of an ego-less creativity by redefining the term "individuality" as "spontaneous origination." He uses the term "individuality," reinscribed with non-Western references:

> . . . not that sickly cast of thought, that morbid self-consciousness, which is sometimes spoken of as the feeling of personality. This has been necessarily absent from creative periods, whether in the East or in the West. I mean by individuality, not the self we think, but the self by which we do. It is the power to produce freshly from within, to react and adapt under rapid change of environment, transcend institution, custom, love of approbation, fear of disapproval, all slowly acting forces of sheer mass. It is spontaneous origination.[14]

Fenollosa's notion of "spontaneous origination" is a fairly straightforward translation of the Chinese concept of 自然 (*ziran*, self-so(ing)/self-generating nature). His adoption of this concept situates his description of an "emptied priestly trance" to existing artistic theories tied to Daoist metaphysics/ethics insofar as he argues that the self's imposition of personality, or even analytic categories, on the *ziran* of 物 (*wu*, things) violates their individualistic "self-generating nature."[15]

Fenollosa warns his readers that the differences between his principle of "individuality" and "the modern romantic theory of subjectivity" used in Western philosophy and art/literary criticism are irreconcilably different. "Such a phrase as Flaubert's, 'the style is the man,' or 'that it is the very oddity of personalities that constitutes genius,'" are for Fenollosa "distorted shadows of the truth." Instead, he posits that art "creates itself, through the hidden affinities of things, and thoughts, and forms."[16] He continues by arguing that the literary genius "must not let his personality intrude," since "self-interest or prejudice" would "disturb the free re-distribution of the affinities."[17] Lastly, Fenollosa argues that "abstract objectivity is too crude for art," but that "abstract subjectivity is too small and mean"; and therefore, we "must penetrate deeper to that state where objectivity and subjectivity become one." For Fenollosa this unity (or *wen*) can be found in the "true synthetic logic" of *ziran*: "Logic of art is its self-hood of harmonious combination."[18]

Implied in Fenollosa's emptying notion of creativity lies a particular form of poetic agency, namely, that the poet is needed to fully manifest, or channel, the "self-hood of harmonious combination." He writes, "Its qualities, its affinities, its harmonies, its individuality are inherent. . . . A literary genius is a soul that has the capacity of giving birth to such roots."[19] Fenollosa argues that literary genius is, therefore, predicated on an "infinite sensitivity to affinities," or a "kind of instinct."[20] Yet, "without his mediumship, his human individuality," "the affinities will not combine."[21] Here, Fenollosa's notion of *wen* is nearly identical with the term as defined by the sinologist Stephan Owen, who writes: "*Wen*, aesthetic pattern, is the outward manifestation of some latent order"; and "In the human, wen's outwardness does not appear on the physical body; wen is here manifest through the essential human characteristic mind (*xin*). The outward manifest form of the activities of 'mind' is 'writing,' *wen*—or in its essential form, 'literature.'"[22] Owen concludes: "Literature thus stands as the entelechy, the fully realized form, of a universal process of manifestation."[23]

Zong-qi Cai uses the term *wen*-Dao to denote the notion of authorial mediumship whereby literature, *wen,* is understood to be a manifestation of the Dao. Cai cites passages from Liu Zongyuan (柳宗元, b. 773–d. 819), who argues that his writing (文)者以明道 ("is for illuminating the Dao"), as well as passages by Han Yu (韓愈, b. 768–d. 824) and Bai Juyi (白居易, b. 772–d. 846), who likewise argue that *wen* can reveal "or even embody the cosmological Dao." But for Cai, and others, it is Liu Xie's 文心雕龍 (*Wenxin diaolong* [*The Literary Mind and the Carving of Dragons*]) that forms the foundation of this view. In his prologue to *Chinese Aesthetics,* Cai traces this view to the first line of Liu Xie's work, which begins: "文之為德也大矣，天地並生者何哉？"[24] Zong-qi Cai translates this line as: "The Pattern (*wen*) as a power is great. It is both together with heaven and earth, and why is it so?"[25] In an alternate and more liberal translation by Siu-kit Wong, Allan Chung-hang Lo, and Kwong-tai Lam, we get a translation closer to Fenollosa's interpretation of *wen*: "Harmony, harmony such as you see in poetry, is universal; with the beginnings of earth and sky it was born."[26] In both translations we see the link between *wen* as pattern and *wen* as harmony.

Liu Xie ends this passage with a discussion of *wen* in relation to human language: "新生而言立，言立而文明，自然之道也。"[27] From Cai we get: "When language was formed, the pattern became manifest. This is the Dao, the natural course of things."[28] And from Siu-kit Wong et al. we have: "When sentience quickens, language takes form; and when language has taken form, harmony, the harmony of poetry, the harmony of the refined, the cultured, becomes clear. This is the Way of Being."[29] In both translations one can see Liu Xie's attempt to link *wen* as cosmological pattern to *wen* as human language, and, in particular, literature/poetry. While one can criticize both Cai and Fenollosa for being too transhistorical in their selection of *wen* as the central theory of Chinese poetics, they are by no means alone. Even James Liu, one of the most well-known scholars of Chinese poetics during the 1970s and 1980s, advocates a similar idea when he argues that the "metaphysical schools," with *wen*-Dao poetics at their center, "are the theories from which distinctively Chinese contributions to an eventual universal theory of literature are most likely to be derived."[30]

Like other important cosmological terms (Dao or *yinyang*, etc.), *wen* (pattern/literature) is a multilayered term with many meanings, ranging from marks on stones to literature and culture. For Fenollosa, *wen* "is not merely social" (or an epistemological imposition) but "a universal state" (or an ontological fact).[31] He continues to argue that *wen* is not derived from "attempts to show how animals united to become men, and so evolved in time, perhaps, a higher nature, *spirit* (as with Spencer)," but is instead manifested "from the nature of heaven," which, he argues, "realizes its very law of harmony in human institutions."[32] Fenollosa finds *wen*'s most important expression in "human products like Music, Painting, and Literature," but also sees it underlying all classical Chinese sociological and transcendental categories.[33] He cites the term's application in "not only literary accomplishments (Writing, Prose, Poetry) but also Music, Morals, Ceremony, Politics, etc., in short all human product which exhibits rational harmony."[34]

To more fully articulate the ontological ground of *wen*, Fenollosa favorably compares it to both 乱 (Ja: *ran*, Ch: *luan*), which he defines as "disorder" or "a mere heap of bricks, or broken confused sounds, discordant colors" and as "the opposite of harmony, the absence of affinity," and to 理 (Ja: *ri*, Ch: *li*), which he calls "the lower or Analytical Reason" or "an externally arranged series, in short analysis."[35] As already seen in his CWC, analysis, for Fenollosa, is the lowest form of human intellectual endeavor, capable only of dealing with the mundane world, while "harmonious synthesis" or *wen*, is the highest form of intellectual realization.[36] Armed with these terms, Fenollosa argues that the "Aristotelian logic" he so scorns in the CWC and elsewhere is roughly analogous to "Ri,"[37] and the West's "egocentric" notions of society can be likened to *ran*, since law in the West "is a negative concept," or "a selfish restraint" used to "curb our Egotism to the end that we may the better enjoy it."[38] He writes, "This in contrast to the East where the principle of struggle would be regarded as immoral, the separate person is *ran*. *Therefore Law is positive, namely, the natural conditions of harmony*."[39] Using both *ri/li* and *ran/luan* as points of comparison to Western equivalents, he is able to situate *wen* as a superior, and even universal, concept (again foreshadowing both James Liu and Zong-qi Cai in recent decades).[40] I will explore the implicit political and sociological dimensions of Fenollosa's appropriation of *wen* at the end of the chapter, as it relates to Ezra Pound's own ideological cooptation of Confucian terms and concepts. For the moment, however, it is important to note the subtle shift away from the poet as "medium" attuned to affinities, to the fact of these "affinities" themselves. *Wen,* for Fenollosa, is the result of bringing one's writing into harmony with the correlative structure of nature itself (through channeling them), but this implies a world in which these harmonies and affinities exist in an objective reality. In the final draft of the CWC, Fenollosa writes:

> The whole delicate substance of speech is built upon substrata of metaphor. Abstract terms, pressed by etymology, reveal their ancient roots still embedded in direct action. . . . Similar lines of resistance, half curbing outward-pressing vitalities, govern the branching of rivers, and the branching of nations. Thus a nerve, a wire, a roadway and a clearing house are only varying channels which communication forces for itself. This is more than analogy; it is identity of structure.[41]

Pound excised the next, and most important, line of Fenollosa's argument: "Laws of structure are the same in the spiritual and the material world. Human character grows with the same stresses and knots as mountain pines."[42] In Fenollosa's "universal theory of literature," *wen* is shown to be a part of correlative nature and should therefore try to harmonize with it by adopting (if not manifesting/channeling) its correlative structure.

In the second half of Fenollosa's lecture on Chinese language and poetry, he argues that humankind should not be seen as separate from nature, which in the West (apparently exempting his transcendentalist—Emerson and Thoreau—and Romantic—Wordsworth—forebearers), he asserts, has traditionally been characterized "as something awful and devilish," but as a part of nature's correlative structure, as reflected in Chinese poetic formalism (parallelism, rhyme, and tonal prosody, which will be discussed in a moment). He writes:

> In China, this idea is present almost from the beginning. The very philosophy of the Book of Changes, reinforced by Confucius, re-

gards all nature as a harmony, nature and man, harmonious with each other because heaven works through both. In later days, as the wonderful mountain and river beauties of central and southern China became explored, while scholarly poets & painters, enforced its doctrines of harmony, by presenting these natural excellences as types of simple human beauty and spontaneity. Still later this language of nature became spiritual down to its minutest shades of expression. No form of shrub, or rock, or land, or motion of water could arise, which did not seem alive with individuality of character, and as such a clear key to the study of man. That[s] why so much in Chinese poetry is figurative and allusive, why this is the very solid depth of its coloring. With us poetry tends to be dramatic, to exhibit directly struggle & sadness—with them it tends to be lyric, to show all that is sad and sweet with human individuality, by merging it into the form of natural harmonies.[43]

Another example of Fenollosa's belief in the correspondence between humans and nature appears in his description of Zen training in his art history book, *Epochs*: "The wise teacher set him [the Chan/Zen adept] down before rocks and clouds, and asked him what he saw. . . . It was his [the priest's] very purpose to let the mind build up its own view of the subtle affinities between things; to construct an organic web of new categories."[44] From passages like these scattered through Fenollosa's work we see his strong belief in the "concrete analogies" between not only various elements and phases, but between human psychology and nature as well. Such passages help one understand the culturally specific desire for poets to harmonize their work by finding and utilizing metaphors derived from "concrete" relations in nature.[45]

Implicit in Fenollosa's CWC (yet far more explicitly present in his wider writings) is the desire to show how Western poets can, as an alternative to reaching back to pre-Aristotelian Western thinking, embrace the still existent cultural discourses that led to the heights of East Asian civilization (which, as we will recall from Chapter 1, remain available through Japan's interpretation and preservation of China's cultural treasures). In other words, the ability to find true analogies and trace out the correlations or patterns (*wen*) between elements in nature as a way of realizing its fundamental unity (as a net) is, for Fenollosa, still available through a study and emulation of Chinese poetics. By employing these correlative structures, Fenollosa implies that all poets, East and West, can create poetry of the highest order by cultivating what he describes as the highest order of artistic beauty: "synthetic harmony" (*wen*).[46]

Cosmological Formalism

It should not be surprising that correlative cosmology assumes a central position in Fenollosa's poetics; after all, one can see it running through almost every aspect of classical Chinese religious, political, and aesthetic theory. Many of these elements are widely seen in Chinese traditional medicine, for instance, where the body is treated through an understanding of its correlative relations: points in the feet or ears correspond to certain internal organs, herbs with particular properties correspond to *yin* or *yang*, and the five elements (discussed below) are ingested to bring harmony to excessive or deficient amounts of their correlative elements in the body. Everything from Chinese cooking to martial arts and geomancy (*fengshui*) operates within this paradigm.

Both Confucians and Daoists use correlative cosmology to reach their different goals. Confucians focused on perfecting mankind's moral character as a means of bringing order to the world, whereas Daoists used correlative cosmology in private and public rituals, meditative practices, and alchemy to achieve regeneration within the Dao. Yet there would also be ample evidence that the correlative worldview is not, and never has been, a disinterested philosophy but an extension of consecutive dynastic ideologies, all of which required adherence to the belief in an ordered universe with the state at its center (I will return to this sociopolitical reading of correlative cosmology at the end of the chapter). Regardless of the reasons we attribute to correlative cosmology, it is important to note here that this paradigm of resonant interrelations is a general system within which other systems of thought exist.

Table 2.1 shows some common examples of correlative cosmology. At first glance, these webs of correspondences may not look so dissimilar to Western taxonomical and classificatory schemes, but, unlike the static categories of Western taxonomy, implied in every classification within this correlative cosmology is the idea of transformation, birth, and decay generated within and between these elemental correspondences. The transformative nature is often described as a movement between *yin* and *yang* within various elements, which interact to create and de-create one another.

In Figure 2.1, we see that fire creates earth, which creates metal, which creates water (condensation), which creates wood, which creates fire,

Element	Heavenly Stems	Planets	Color	Taste	Animal
Wood	Chia and Yi	Jupiter	Green	Sour	Tiger and Rabbit
Fire	Ping and Ting	Mars	Red	Bitter	Horse and Snake
Earth	Wu and Chi	Saturn	Yellow	Sweet	Dog and Snake
Metal	Keng and Hsin	Venus	White	Acrid	Cock and Monkey
Water	Jen and Kuei	Mercury	Black	Salt	Pig and Rat

TABLE 2.1. Correlative cosmology. Based on a diagram in *T'ung Shu: The Ancient Chinese Almanac*. Ed. Martin Palmer (Boston: 1986), 34.

which melts metal, which splits wood, which covers earth, which holds/contains water, which extinguishes fire. Implicit in this correlative cosmological paradigm is a worldview based on the principle of harmonious (ordered) change/flux. Everything that exists comes into existence through a unique "self-origination," but the nature of this "becoming" follows more-or-less prescribed patterns of harmonic interaction and transformation. For poets to manifest/channel *wen* in their writing, they would need to know how correlative harmony unfolds in nature and attempt to bring their own creative efforts (metaphors) into harmony with these "objective relations in nature" (and notions like "fasting the mind" would allow a poet to attune him- or herself to these relations without imposing what Wai-lim Yip calls "epistemological elaborations"[47]).

To understand how Fenollosa came to integrate correlative cosmology into his poetics, we must return to his second sojourn in Japan, from 1896 to 1900, when he began his studies of Chinese cosmological thought under Michiaki Nemoto, Japan's leading 易経 (Ja: *Eki*, Ch: *Yijing*, commonly spelled *I Ching*) scholar. Since Fenollosa did not leave behind notes from his meetings with Nemoto, we cannot know exactly what he might have taken from these lessons. It is probably safe to assume, however, that Nemoto introduced Fenollosa to the conceptual and symbolic devices deployed in the *Yijing*, including the 八卦 (*bagua*, eight trigrams) and their sixty-four combinations, as well as the *yin/yang* dynamics that underlie the *Yijing*'s cosmology. Akiko Murakata notes that Fenollosa also possessed Legge's translation of the *Yijing*.[48] In that translation, Fenollosa would have encountered an orderly world captured by the text's correlative cosmology.

Legge describes the correlative structure of the *bagua* (eight trigrams, the foundational symbols of the *Yijing*):

[The symbols of] heaven and earth received their determinate posi-

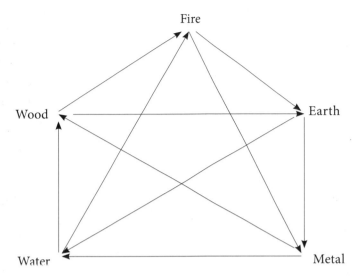

FIGURE 2.1. This standard five-element diagram shows both the creative and de-creative relationships.

tions; (those for) mountains and collections of water interchanged their influences; (those for) thunder and wind excited each other the more; and (those for) water and fire did each other no harm.[49]

To explain the relationship between the trigrams and the maps from which they are derived, Legge writes:

The difference [of] Yin and Yang, the dark and the bright, the moon-like and the sun-like; for the sun is called the Great Brightness (Thâi Yang, [taiyang] 太陽), and the moon the Great Obscurity (Thâi Yin, [taiyin] 太陰). Fû-hsî in making the trigrams, and king Wăn, if it was he who first multiplied them to the 64 hexagrams, found it convenient to use lines instead of the circles—the whole line (——) for the bright circle (O), and the divided line (— —) for the dark ●. The first, the third, and the fifth lines in a hexagram, if they are "correct" as it is called, should all be whole, and the second, fourth, and sixth lines should all be divided. Yang lines are strong (or hard), and Yin lines are weak (or soft). The former indicate vigor and authority; the latter, feebleness and submission. It is the part of the former to command; of the latter to obey.[50]

Legge continues:

The lines, moreover, in the two trigrams that make up the hexagrams, and characterize the subjects that they represent, are related to one another by their position, and have their significance modified accordingly. The first line and the fourth, the second and the fifth, the third and the sixth are all correlates; and to make the correlation perfect the two members of it should be lines of different qualities, one whole and the other divided. And, finally, the middle lines of the trigrams, the second and fifth, that is, of the hexagrams, have a peculiar value and force. If we have a whole line (——) in the fifth place, and a divided line (— —) in the second, or vice versa, the correlation is complete.[51]

I will need to return to Legge's description of the *Yijing*'s symbolic language when we discuss the aesthetic principles Fenollosa derives from this text. Until then, it is sufficient to point out that the *Yijing* symbolic language would be proof of a philosophical system not only freed from the "positivistic thinness of logic" critiqued by his Buddhist epistemology (as the *Yijing* takes change/flux as the ground of being), but also able to grant humans a window into the exact correlations, or "objective relations," within nature itself. We can safely assume that Fenollosa's aesthetic privileging of specific interrelations within his Buddhist "net" of totality can be located, at least in part, in his study of the *Yijing*.

We can also find references to the *Yijing* in his translation notes (which Pound used to produce *Cathay*). In his translation of the following line from "Song of the Bowman Shu," Fenollosa's writes:

日	歸	日	歸	歲	亦	陽*	止
etsu	ki	etsu	ki	sai	eki	yō	shi
[rì	guī	rì	guī	suì	yì	yáng	zhǐ]

We say to each other "when will we return to our Country?"
   —It will be October.

Fenollosa then adds the note:

In Eki [yi 易 "the Changes"] the Symbol of October is

i.e. all lines are "In" [*yin*, 陰].

He continues:

There is not "yo" [yang, 陽] at all, but "yo" comes under the earth, therefore October is called contrarily "the month of Yo."[52]

In his parenthetical note, Fenollosa not only recognizes the level to which the *Yijing* symbols have penetrated classical Chinese poetic diction, but also a good deal about what is the correlative nature of *yin* and *yang* dynamics within the hexagrams as well. Here, even in the most "*yin*" hexagram, Fenollosa knows there is incipient *yang*; the *yin,* having reached its full expression, will begin its transformation back into *yang,* giving the month its "contrary" name.

While it is unclear whether Fenollosa's Tendai or poetry teachers introduced him to Kukai's (空海) *Bunkyû hifuron* ("文鏡秘府論"), which includes the most extensive (and cosmologically oriented) collection of texts on Chinese classical prosody in existence, the fact that Fenollosa uses this term 文章 (Ja: *bunsho,* Ch: *wenzhang*),[53] not simply as the word for "literature" but as a metacritical term "synthetic harmony," as the central term of his "universal theory of literature" makes me believe that he may have been familiar with Kukai's description of the *yin/yang* cosmological roots of Chinese poetic form. Kukai writes:

> "one" (yi—) was the beginning of names, and patterns (*bun/wen*) was the well-spring of teaching. When you consider names and teachings as its ancestor, then literature (*bunsho* [文章]) is the key element in institutions and laws. Of those who are in the world or out of it (i.e., laymen and monks) who can ignore this: Therefore, someone who is well versed in the sutras and who bravely advances on the path to becoming a Bodhisattva must first of all understand literature.[54]

Even if Fenollosa did not have access to Kukai's collection on prosody, his notes include diagrams of Chinese rules for tonal prosody coded in *Yijing* symbols for *yin* and *yang.* Figures 2.2 and 2.3 show that they are arranged in the traditional manner: top to bottom, right to left. Each figures is followed by an English transcription. Fenollosa not only knew a great deal about meter, rhyme, and tonal prosody, but he has correctly grasped the way the four basic tones of Chinese (Ping Sheng, 平聲; Shang Sheng, 上聲; Qu Sheng, 去聲; and Ru Sheng, 入聲[55]) are "for poetry" bifurcated into "only two classes of tones, the modified and unmodified"[56] (also called *level* and *oblique*), which corresponds to the *yin/yang* cosmology he would have encountered in Nemoto's lectures and Legge's *Yijing.*

To reveal the relationship between cosmological textuality (with *Yijing* symbols) and classical Chinese poetic form, I have mapped tonal parallelism

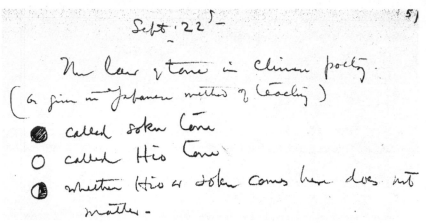

FIGURE 2.2. Fenollosa's notes on classical Chinese tonal prosody reveal a clear awareness of the relationship between correlative (*yin/yang*) cosmology and tonal prosody. "Chinese Poetry, Hirai and Shida: autograph ms.," Ezra Pound Papers YCAL MSS 43, box 99, folder 4220, p. 57. Beinecke Library, Yale University. Used with permission of New Directions Press.

in the following poems by Han Yu and Li Bai by assigning level tones a *yang* marker [——], and the oblique tones a *yin* marker [— —]. Also note that the first poem corresponds almost exactly to the first of Fenollosa's templates in the seven-character short form, *jueju*, but the second is a full *lushi*, composed in a five-character line (*wushi*) like Fenollosa's second example. I am displaying these poems in the modern horizontal style left to right and using the modern *pinyin* tonal markers as well, for the convenience of the reader. Following the transliteration, I provide my own translations that mimic the *prosodic* textures of the original (meter, rhyme, and tonal prosody) in the hope that the formal qualities of these genres can be better understood by non-Chinese readers. I am using the term "mimic" here self-consciously, however, since "translate" implies a transference of meaning and I believe that one cannot transfer the meanings available through sound since different audiences bring different expectations to the event and will inevitably respond differently to the same or similar aural textures. So while both Fenollosa and Pound (toward the end of his career) hoped to transfer the sound of Chinese into English, their acts of mimicry (like mine below), or even straight recitation (of the originals in both Chinese and Sino-Japanese) cannot overcome the hermeneutic horizons of the audience itself, who upon hearing either the affected English idioms or the original languages would not hear what native speakers would hear, since meaning arrives by way of interpretive contexts, not abstractly within language itself. Yet, if one never

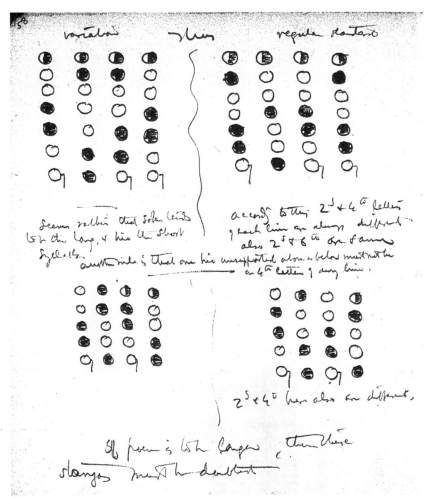

FIGURE 2.3. Section of Fenollosa's notes on classical Chinese tonal prosody. "Chinese Poetry, Hirai and Shida: autograph ms.," Ezra Pound Papers YCAL MSS 43, box 99, folder 4220, p. 58. Beinecke Library, Yale University. By Ezra Pound, from previously unpublished material, © 2009 by Mary de Rachewiltz and Omar S. Pound. Reprinted by permission of New Directions Publishing Corp.

places a metaphysical belief in transcendent translation, then all translation ever can be is mimicry, and therefore there is an equally good reason to mimic sound as there is in mimicking semantic content.[57]

I want to turn to the poetry of the consummate Confucian poet, Han Yu (韓愈), since his work is seen as a nearly perfect example of regulated tonal prosody (which would have signaled to his readers the degree to which he had internalized the Confucian interpretation of correlative cosmology as the foundation of state authority). Here is his poem "Spring Snow" (a tonal prosody chart for the poem appears in Figure 2.4):

春雪
新　年　都　未　有　芳　花
二　月　初　驚　見　草　芽
白　雪　卻　嫌　春　色　晚
故　穿　庭　樹　作　飛　花

chūn xuě

——　　　　——　　——　——　　　　——
xīn　nián /　dōu　wèi /　yǒu　fāng　huā

—— ——　——　　　　——　——　——
èr　yuè /　chū　jīng /　jiān　cǎo　yá

——　——　——　——　　　　——
bái　xuě /　què　xián /　chūn　sè　wǎn

—— ——　——　　——　——　　　　——
gù　chuān / tíng　shù /　zuò　fēi　huā

To give one a feeling for the form's formal qualities, here is a translation of my own that retains the formal elements of the original (the tonal marks are here to redirect one's natural English pronunciation—which tends to affect monosyllabic lines like these with nursery-rhyme cadences—toward uniquely Chinese prosodic textures).

sprīng snǒw

——　　　　——　　—— ——　—— ——　　　　——　　　　——
nēw　yéars /　comēs　bùt /　bloǒms　dōn't　grōw

—— ——　——　　　　——　　——　——　——
whèn　Màrch / neārs　nēw /　grāss　sproǔts　gróv

——　——　——　　　　——　　　　—— ——　——
yét　white /　snòw　thínks /　sprīng's　comè　lǎte

—— ——　——　　——　——　　　　——　　　　——
ànd　fàlls /　throúgh trèes /　like　bloōms　blōw

As one can see in Figure 2.4, the tonal chart, Han Yu's "level start" *qi-jue* only differs from the prescribed tonal template by a single character, which actually falls after the caesural pause that separates two of the level tones from the third. While a violation of the template, Han Yu's transgression takes place without violating the prosodic laws laid down by Shen Yu (discussed in the last section of this chapter).

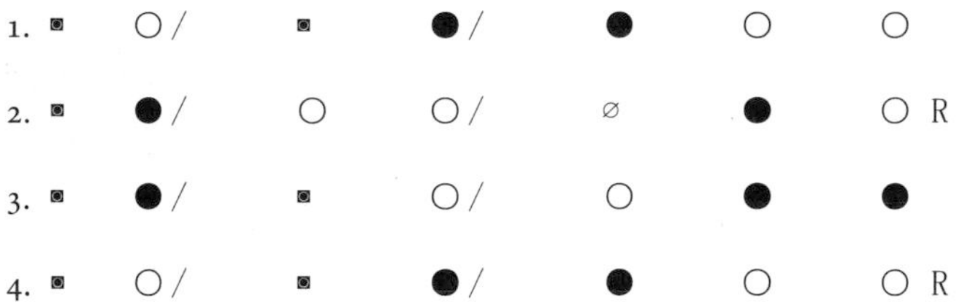

1. ▣ ○/ ▣ ●/ ● ○ ○

2. ▣ ●/ ○ ○/ ø ● ○ R

3. ▣ ●/ ▣ ○/ ○ ● ●

4. ▣ ○/ ▣ ●/ ● ○ ○ R

FIGURE 2.4. This tonal prosody chart reveals how incredibly filial the poet is to tonal prosody.

The second, longer poem is a *wushi*, or "five character poem," by Li Bai 李百, and is entitled "Seeing Off a Friend" (送有人):

清	山	橫遠	北東	郭城
白	水	一	為	別
此	地	萬	里	征
孤	蓬	遊	子	意
浮	雲	故	人	情
落	日	自	茲	去
揮	手	班	馬	鳴
蕭	蕭			

qīng	shān /	héng	běi	guō	Notice that the caesura operates as a crucial dividing line in the regulation of the tones. According to the rules of classical Chinese formalism we will discuss at the end of the chapter, one should not encounter three of the same tones in a row, unless they straddle the caesura. Fenollosa also discusses this point in some detail in the second half of the CWC (a point discussed in a moment). I have bolded the end-rhymed words in this poem to emphasize this element of the poem's aural parallelism.
bái	shuǐ /	rào	dōng	**chéng**	
cǐ	dì /	yì	wéi	bié	
gū	péng /	wàn	lǐ	**zhēng**	
fú	yún /	yóu	zǐ	yì	
lòu	rì /	gù	rén	**qíng**	
huī	shǒu /	zì	zī	qù	
xiāo	xiāo /	bān	mǎ	**míng**	

"Seeing Off a Friend"

| greēn | peāks | cróss | nŏrth | wāll |

—	— —	— —	—	—
whíte	streăms/	wìnd	eāst	**tówn**
— —	— —	— —	—	—
ŏnce	wè/	pàrt	thís	placé
—	—	— —	— —	—
mīles	páss/	weèds	rŏll	**roūnd**
—	—	— —	— —	— —
cloúds	floát/	nó-	măds	moòd
— —	—	— —	—	—
òld ·	friènds/	feèl	sún	**dówn**
—	— —	— —	—	— —
frōm	hĕre/	wàve	hānds	pàrt
—	—	—	— —	—
neīgh	neīgh/	strōng	hŏrse	**sóund**

In addition to the unifying nature of the tonal harmonies, Fenollosa points out that regulated verse (as with earlier verse forms) utilizes end rhymes on the even numbered lines. Regulated verse must also end even lines with a level tone (here indicated as *yang* by a yang line). One can rhyme the first line as well, as Li Bai does here, but the poem's tonal pattern must compensate for this addition by altering the whole pattern.

The tonal charts in Fenollosa's own handwriting reveal a considerable understanding of the link between correlative cosmology and poetic prosody, which he elaborates upon in his discussion of tonal prosody: "It is like pure & impure, or liquid and solid. It is manifest, that the order of these tones in the syllables of a line will have much to do with their musical value. If many successive syllables were unmodified, it would be too weak—If many modified, it would be too rough. The Right mixture gives strength and beauty together." Importantly, Fenollosa does not stop at a description of classical Chinese formalism: he offers a way to import the metaphysics that undergirds it through various translation methodologies.

Translating Correlative Prosody: The Lost Half of "The Chinese Written Character as a Medium for Poetry"

The last paragraph of the first half of the CWC introduces the themes and issues of the second half, and we can see Pound's editorial hand slashing through the paragraph. In another document, which details the full synopsis of the essay, we again see Pound's conscious decision to omit the second half as he brackets the sections that refer to visual elements from those that discuss sound.[58] Prior to Pound's editing, Fenollosa's essay ends with the following paragraph:

I had intended in this lecture to speak of the subject of visible Chinese metres and stanzas; but this will be better postponed to the second lecture, where we shall discuss as well the sounds of Chinese verse, and in which we shall exhibit an outline of its evolution. I have now justified, I think, my initial title, by showing that the Chinese written character constitutes indeed a wonderful natural medium for Poetry.[59]

He continues in the second half to write:

> Up to this time, it will be noticed, I have spoken of Chinese poetry, as if it were entirely addressed to the eye; as if it had no phonetic element at all. This is, of course, not true. Not only must a Chinese spoken language have preceded the written; but the early poetry itself was written to be pronounced and sung to music.[60]

As briefly mentioned earlier, in the second half of the CWC Fenollosa strongly advocates both traditional Chinese and English metrical poetic forms, so when it comes to explaining Chinese forms, he quite naturally looks for equivalents in English rhyme and meter. The Imagist criteria for what made poetry were not yet in view. Fenollosa attempts to map the formal qualities of Chinese poetic aurality (rhyme, meter, parallelism, and even tones, but in nonconventional ways discussed in a moment), criticizes earlier translators' inadequate attempts to convert these features into English poetry, and suggests ways in which elements of English metrical verse could be deployed toward these ends. For Fenollosa, the similarities between Western and Eastern poetic conventions reveal a common poetic ideal of patterned harmony. Like Pound, Fenollosa sees Chinese poetry and poetics as an important resource for improving the Western tradition. Unlike Pound, however, Fenollosa hopes to enrich traditional English verse forms with the metaphysical depth he finds in classical Chinese poetics.[61]

This second lecture is primarily concerned to prepare for Fenollosa's assertion of the universal aesthetic condition of 文 (wen, pattern, or sometimes in conjunction with the character for "order") 章 (Ja: Bunsho, what Fenollosa translates as "synthetic harmony"). He attempts to show how classical Chinese poetry, from the Shi Jing to the Li Sao and beyond, weaves its "heterogeneous materials" into a "fabric as pure as crystal" by blending all its elements into mellifluous semantic, visual, and sonic patterns.[62] Fenollosa discusses the historical development of Chinese verse as a series of metrical harmonies or patterns. Beginning with trimeters, Fenollosa progresses through tetrameters, pentameters, and hexameters (before Chinese verse forms "leaped over to the 7 character lines or the union of 4 and 3").[63] In each case, Fenollosa gives both Chinese and English examples to bolster his argument that each character constitutes a metrical (as well as visual) foot, and that the strict regulation of poetic feet contributes to the aural and temporal harmonization of a poem. He gives us the following example from Stephen Phillips's *Marpessa*:

Thŏu mēan/ĕst whāt/ thĕ sēa/ hăs striv'n/ tŏ sāy/
Thŏu ārt/whăt āll/ thĕ wīnds/ hăve ūt/terĕd nōt/[64]

Then comments:

Here it is only unimportant words, particles, and inflection-syllables of verbs which fall on the short beat. Every important word and root has the long stress. This is seen if we pronounce only the long syllables, leaving a "rest" in the place of the others. It is quite understandable. Now the Chinese, being an uninflected speech, and every word standing for an independent root, is quite in this position. There are practically no particles; all are verbs. And so it turns out that the character itself, even to the eye, constitutes a single foot; that is, all the characters make an even stress on the attention, one after the other. Thus a Chinese line of 3 characters corresponds to the stresses of our trimeter; of 4 characters to our tetrameter; of five characters to our pentameter; of 6 to our hexameter etc. The proof of this is that we can often make a literal translation into English, giving a measure of English sound to every character, in which measures the long stress is given to the root word that translates the characters, the small stress to particles, inflections, and unimportant parts of polysyllables.[65]

He then concludes: "There are no small words or particles to be slurred, as in English. Each is like the stroke of a bell. Thus, in translating, we can often follow measure for measure, and take our choice of translating a single word with a foot that shall be an iambic, an anapest, or dactyl."[66]

Fenollosa's translation theory highlights what he sees as an essential similarity between English and Chinese poetic form: namely, that the basic compositional unit is the foot, that the most important words fall on the stress, and that the subordinate particles and the like fall on the unstressed syllables. By creating verse forms that pair stresses with semantic weight, translators can use the full arsenal of English feet, from trochees and spondees to dactyls and anapests, to build metrical lines that match foot-for-foot the Chinese originals.

Fenollosa gives an example of his method by translating the hexameter of Wang Wei (王維, Ja: Omakitsu). Here is the poem and modern Mandarin transliteration:

桃	紅	復	含	宿	雨
táo	hóng	fù	hán	sù	yǔ
柳	綠	更	帶	春	煙
liǔ	lü	gèng	dài	chūn	yān
花	落	家	僮	未	掃
huā	luò	jiā	tóng	wèi	sǎo
鶯	啼	山	客	猶	眠
yīng	tí	shān	kè	yóu	mián[67]

Fenollosa gives a fairly literal translation, followed by his metrical translations:

Peach crimson, also holds lodged rain
Willow green, also belts spring smoke.
Flowers fall, house servant/maid not-yet sweep
~~Nightingales~~ larks cry, mountain guest ~~yet~~ still ~~sleep~~ slumber.

    -_ | -_ | -_ | -_ | -_ |-_ |
The blooms of peach have lodged the dews in ruby urns.
The willows silhouette belts in the April mists.
To sweep the fallen flowers no house maid yet appears.
No voice of larks avails to raise the mountain goat<guest>.

/   - -| /   - -|/   - -| /   -   - | /   -   - | |
Crimson the snare of the peaches that catch[es] the dews on the wing.
Verdant the face of the willows that bathe in winds of the spring.
Petals have fallen all night, but no dutiful maid is yet sweeping.
Larks have been up with the dawn, but the guest of the mtn. is sleeping.[68]

The first metrical version translates the poem into an alexandrine line of six feet or twelve syllables (here, iambs). But Fenollosa argues that this is not the best fit in English and instead offers the second, which is an alexandrine (hexametrical) dactyl, or a series of six feet, each of which is composed of one stressed and two unstressed syllables (as with the word "strawberry"). Given Fenollosa's theory of "foot-to-foot" translation, the dactyl would offer the translator the most space to match the content, meter, and rhyme. Here, he chooses to change the ABCB rhyme scheme to an AABB rhyme scheme, which was popularized by Giles and other Vicotrian translators of Chinese verse, but Fenollosa also applies Chinese-inspired rhyme schemes to different translations of his.[69] Clearly, his translation theory is, in part, inspired by popular nineteenth-century experimentation with metrical schemes imported by poets like Henry Longfellow (who famously uses a trochee inspired by the Finnish folkepic *The Kalavala* in his "Hiawatha"). Edward Fitzgerald's translation of *Ruba'iyat*[70] as the *Rubaiyat of Omar Khayyam* in 1859, which, like most classical Chinese quatrains, has an AABA rhyme scheme, stands as an obvious precursor to Fenollosa's ideas. Yet it is important to remember that Fenollosa is not interested in formalism for aesthetics per se, but for the correlative cosmology that he argues undergirds it and that makes poetic form matter as the foundation for poetic agency (the channel through which humans manifest their ultimate correlative *wen* in a world of correlative flux). Therefore, one can reflect on Fenollosa's desire to import philosophical and aesthetic notions as conceptually radical,[71] while remaining aesthetically conservative (traditional).

In addition to his translation theory, Fenollosa offers a sophisticated if very idiosyncratic transliteration theory as well. If translators are to translate Chinese poetry in such a way as to produce similar sonority and prosody, they will need to know what the sounds being translated are. Fenollosa, for a variety of (often prejudiced) reasons, rejects Mandarin transliteration as an insufficient orthographic, phonetic representation of original poetry's aurality. He asks, "If Chinese poetry is also made up of sounds, What sounds are they? The sounds of Confucius' day? the sound of the Yangtse valley? of 1000 years ago? or of Peking today?"[72] He argues that the original sounds of the Chinese are lost to us, and, with a grating air of both Western and Japanese bias, claims that Mandarin is ill suited for poetry, and that while many of the original rhyme schemes are still recognizable, "students of poetry" should look elsewhere to reproduce the original sounds of Chinese verse. Personal prejudices aside, Fenollosa, aware of the phonological differences between Middle and Modern dialects of spoken Chinese, in many ways foreshadowed the later interests of sinologists like Hugh Stimson, who apply reconstructed Chinese phonology to the reading and "total appreciation" of classical Chinese poetry.[73] But unlike Stimson, whose reconstructive efforts followed the pioneering phonological research of Bernhard Karlgren,[74] Fenollosa had to invent a method of his own.

While Fenollosa's and later Pound's insistence on using Japanese "spellings," or "rōmaji," of Chinese words has been the source of confusion and frustration for American readers (who have to jostle back and forth between proper names like Li Bai and Rihaku), it is important to note the complex heterocultural (here a mixture of classical Chinese poetics and esoteric Buddhism) conditions that inform this decision. "To get something like the real sounds," Fenollosa argues, "we must go to their partial preservation in the Southern dialects, of Amoy and Canton, or better still to Corean, which for many hundred years has fixed the sounds by an alphabet; or to Japanese, where the Chinese words have been preserved unchanged since the 5th century."[75] In *Epochs* he writes, "The Japanese still call their earliest ('Southern') pronunciation of Chinese Characters—preserved by their syllabary—'the Go sound.'"[76]

When Chinese characters were imported into Japanese, they came to be used in two distinct ways: "sound reading" (*yomi*, 音読み), which attempts to capture the Chinese sound, or "native reading" (*kun'yomi*, 訓読み), which uses Japanese words with similar meanings to the Chinese. For example: the Chinese character for man, 人 (*ren*), is read with its *kun*-reading as "hito," the pronunciation of the Japanese word for person, while the "sound reading" will read it as *jin*, as it is closer to the original Chinese. Fenollosa speculated that this pronunciation captured by the Japanese syllabic script—kana—served as a linguistic time capsule. The problem is that the "sound reading" of Chinese characters corresponded to different dialects, depending on when they were imported. It is clear that Fenollosa knew this, however, which is why he specifically speaks of the "Go sound" (呉音), which refers to the first "wave" of such "sound readings" that carried ancient Buddhist texts and concepts to Japan via the ancient Korean kingdom of *Baekje* in the middle of the fourth century (the dialect would be that spoken in the Yangzi Valley during this time).[77] And he speaks of the "second wave," which imported the dialect of the capital Xian, known as *kan-on* (漢音), which transcribed the influx of Tang poetry and literature at that time.[78] The idea of using these pronunciations to re-create classical pronunciations of characters did not end with Fenollosa either, as it can still be found in the massive Morohashi dictionary (the *Dai Kan-Wa jiten*, 大漢和辭典 [Great Chinese-Japanese dictionary]) used by sinologists from the middle of the twentieth century to the present day, and which offers both the Kan'on 漢音 and Go-on 呉音 pronunciations along with other reconstructive methods.

For Fenollosa, there was another compelling reason to transliterate Japanese pronunciations of classical Chinese verse: tones. This may seem strange at first, as "rōmaji," unlike Romanized Chinese (like that which I used in the earlier section discussing the tonal arrangements of classical Chinese prosody) does not include diacritical marks indicating one of the four tones. Yet Fenollosa, taking into consideration the *yin/yang* underpinnings of Chinese tonal prosody, emphasizes the importance of the missing tonal category of Ru Sheng (ending in the consonants p, t, or k), which is necessary to uphold cosmological harmony. Fenollosa writes:

> Now with the 4th tone, the Japanese have far better preserved this poetic value than the modern Mandarin pronunciation. It has lost the final consonant, and only retained the shortened vowel. But in the old pronunciation the final consonant strengthened and lengthened the syllables, as it does with us. Thus our word "stand" to be used on the unaccented beat of a measure because it could not pronounce all of the components in a short time. The vowel, however, is short, and if the final consonant was dropped, it would suddenly change technically from a long to short syllable. That is the kind of change which Mandarin has produced in the 4th tone; and we could hardly understand the aesthetic value of the poetical laws of tone were it not for the example of the Japanese preservation of the 4th tone consonant, to show that the value of the modified syllable is a strong or rough value.[79]

For Fenollosa the very cosmological backbone of Chinese prosody is at stake in the orthography one chooses to transcribe the poems themselves. Yet it is important to note that Fenollosa would have had another set of concerns, informed by his Buddhist practice, that would likely have fed his desire for "true sounds." He not only champions Japanese "sound readings" of Middle Chinese, but also points to its relationship to Buddhist textuality: "we have a still finer test of the relative accuracy of the oldest Japanese pronunciation of Chinese words, in its power, far greater than Mandarin, to transliterate the Indian and Sanskrit names that came into China, and chiefly Southern China in the 4th & 5th centuries. Pronounced in Japan today from Chinese characters, they are quite intelligible: pronounced in Mandarin, they are barbarous travesties. I will give several examples (also Shingon)."[80] Confirming the Buddhist context of this assertion, his argument ends with the otherwise nonsequitur, parenthetical "also Shingon." There are many reasons to bring up the Shingon sect of Tendai Buddhism (the sect to which Fenollosa belonged) in this context. The sect's name means "true word" (真言), and it was founded by Kūkai, who was thought of (during Fenollosa's time) as the father of the kana syllabic script.[81] For Fenollosa, the kana did more than accurately capture and preserve the various waves of "sound readings" of ancient Chinese: the kana was partly conceived on the model of the Sanskrit script Siddham, *bonji* (梵字). Siddham was one of the principal scripts used in the Buddhist texts that arrived in China via the Silk Road and has been historically closely tied to Tantric texts and mantras, which value the non-semantic sounds of Siddham as seed syllables with intrinsic power as sound vibrations.[82] Kūkai introduced the Siddham script to Japan when he returned from China in 806. And while it is clear that kana was influenced by the principles of Siddham's systematically ordered, syllable-based script, it is unclear if it phonetically "captures" these sounds as well as Fenollosa argues.[83] Nevertheless, it seems clear that Fenollosa's belief in the phonetic power of the kana to preserve Chinese sonority arises from this dense aggregate of historical forces. Far from an obsession with scholarly accuracy, I would argue that Fenollosa's close attention to the aural conditions of classical Chinese poetry follows Kūkai's efforts to do the same. After all, it is likely Kūkai's belief in the importance of sound to Buddhist practice is what led him to create the most elaborate and sophisticated study of Chinese poetic prosody still in existence (the *Bunkyû hifuron*).[84]

While Shingon notions of sound may have influenced Fenollosa's basic understanding of the problems, his solution was his own. He declares that his presentation of classical Chinese verse in transliterated kana represents the first time anyone had endeavored to do this:

I say, "for the first time," for though the Japanese have preserved in Buddhist and other learned diction, the actual sound of the Yangtse valley; they have never used those metrically in reading Chinese poetry. They have always had the habit of translating the thoughts of Chinese poetry into certain of their native polysyllabic words, and therefore it is literally true that no modern human ear for hundreds of years have heard Chinese poetry read even approximately as it sounded. The Chinese have not, because they have been using their barbarous Mandarin sounds. The Japanese have not, because they have read Japanese root words into them. Only now for the first time, when I have insisted on writing out under the characters, the monosyllabic words as preserved in Japanese Kana, and in reading them in the slow measured manner which takes one word for a foot, has a

We do not have any recordings of Fenollosa reciting these works, but one can still go to his extensive transliterations, "rōmaji," of classical Chinese poetry to "hear" them. For instance, in his essay *Chinese Poetry and Landscape Painting* Fenollosa offers an example of his Romanized Japanese transliteration of the Chinese on another hexametrical verse:

San ban cho -*Kei*- itsu wun
Ken ten chi -*Kei*- fu fun
Ju an ai   -*Kei*- fun wun
En fu Ken   -*Kei*- ku ban[85]

This particular stanza also includes voiced caesurae, "*kei*" (兮, *xi*), which appear as a breathed pause (like a sigh) in the Qu Yuan's epic poem *Li Sao*.[86] In Fenollosa's translation he uses the rhyme scheme from the original as he understands it from his Japanese transliteration:

The mountains myriad fold, starve, capped
    With a single veil
Heaven and earth are astray, free, free
    Like deer from a pale.
Forests somber and weird, ah me the breath they exhale!
Monkeys and bodiless voice, God, God!
    The mood of their wail![87]

Fenollosa concludes the second half of the CWC by lamenting previous attempts at "analytical translations" (as he calls them, following Max Müller) of Chinese poetry without regard for its poetics of harmonic, synthetic patterning, to reinforce his belief that translators must replicate the *wen*, "synthetic harmony," of Chinese poetry in their English translations. In other words, one must attempt to replicate the harmony of Chinese poetic conventions by synthesizing English metrical techniques with the overtones of a poem's meanings, sounds, and images so that Westerners may learn how to recognize the "universal" quality of harmony in their own canon and learn how to harmonize these planes within their own work.

Sounds of Modernism and Correlative Poetics

In 1913 a young Ezra Pound published "A Few Don'ts by an Imagiste" and altered the direction of American poetry through the present. Along with H.D. (Hilda Doolittle) and Richard Aldington, Pound wrote three principles upon which the Imagist coterie agreed:

1. Direct treatment *of* the "thing" whether subjective or objective.
2. To use absolutely no word that does not contribute to the presentation.
3. As regarding rhythm: to compose in the sequence *of* the musical phrase, not in sequence *of* a metronome.[88]

This list is a more distilled version of a longer "List of a Few Don'ts" Pound offers slightly later in his work.[89] Nearly one and a half millennia earlier, another literary coterie offered its own list of "Don'ts," initiating a very different poetic revolution, one that would have a profound effect on Chinese poetry up to the beginning of the twentieth century. This group of poets is usually referred to as "the eight friends of Jingling" (*jing ling ba you*), since the poets gathered around the Prince of Jingling, Xiao Ziliang (b. 460–d. 494). The most prominent poet of this group, Shen Yue (沈約, b. 441–d. 513), wrote a manifesto that appeared in the afterword of his prose work 宋書 (*Songshu,* The History of the [Liu] Song Dynasty), which struck an iconoclastic and didactic tone not so unlike Pound's own. Shen Yue writes:

> The reason why the five colors illuminate each other and the eight musical instruments harmonize with each other is because dark and light colors and *yin* and *yang* notes are each appropriate to specific objects. If you wish the notes *kung* (gong) and *yu* to alternate and the low and high tones to balance each other, then wherever there is a "floating sound" in front, there must follow a "cut-off sound." Within a line, initials and finals must be different; within a couplet, light and heavy sounds must be distinct. Only those who attain this subtle meaning can begin to discuss literature.[90]

While Shen Yue still uses the native Chinese terms *kung* (gong) and *yu*, which refer to notes in the Chinese pentatonic scale, his adoptions of tonal prosody proposed a totally original notion independent from the pentatonic scale used up to that time in Chinese poetry recitation and composition. In a very real sense, Shen Yue's manifesto presents an opposite orientation toward prosody from that presented by the early Pound. Shen Yue wants to free Chinese poetry from "the musical phrase" by adopting meter, just as Pound wants to free poetry from meter by appealing to the musical phrase.

Here is Shen Yue's own list of "don'ts":

八不 "Eight Don'ts"

1. Level Head. In any couplet, the first syllable of the first line and the first syllable of the second line may not be in the same tone, nor may the second syllable of both lines take the same tone.
2. Raised Tail. In any couplet, the final syllable of the first and second lines may not be in the same one of the four tones (unless the first line contributes to the end rhyme scheme in which case this is permitted).
3. Wasp's Waist. In any five-syllable line, the second and fifth syllables should not be in the same tone. [This rule was not observed closely in later regulated verse.]
4. Crane's Knee. In a series of lines of five-syllable verse, the fifth and fifteenth syllables should not be in the same one of the four tones. In other words the final syllables of successive non-rhyming lines should not be in the same tone.
5. Major Rhyme. This is a case where, within a couplet, there is another syllable that rhymes with the rhyme word.
6. Minor Rhyme. This is a case where within a couplet there is a rhyme, but exclusive of the rhyme with each other. [Note: rhyming binomes or pairs of words are common and excused from these rules. But other words which rhyme with the end rhyme scheme seriously alter the rhyme harmonies of the poem and are forbidden.]
7. Side Knot. This defect occurs if, within a line, there are two separated syllables sharing the same initial consonant. [Again reduplicative binomes or other paired words often create an alliterative sound and are a key element in aural prosody, so this rule only applies to separated words.]
8. Direct Knot. This defect occurs if, within a line, there are two separated syllables sharing the same initial consonant and the same medial vowel.[91]

What is most striking about pairing these two poetry lists of "Don'ts" is that one can see two very distinct poetic idioms and, very importantly, two very different ideas about what "good" poetry should sound like. I am juxtaposing these two lists to emphasize an important point left out of the image-laden, emptiness-centered discussions of Chinese poetry in the West: Imagist aesthetics and classical Chinese poetic forms are anything but apposite.

According to Zhaoming Qian, "Pound derives his break from meter on the model of Qu Yuan as he found his poetry described in the pages of Giles translations of Qu Yuan's 九歌 (*Jiu ge, Nine Songs*) in his *History*, and states that, 'The poet never ends his line in deference to a pre-scribed number of feet, but lengthens or shortens to suit the exigency of his thought.'"[92] Qian continues, "Now from Gile's *History,* Pound learned, to his amazement, that the Chinese poet Qu Yuan" had developed a proto *verse libre* "over two thousand years earlier."[93] If we are to acknowledge this transpacific connection between classical Chinese verse and *verse libre,* then we must limit this claim to Qu Yuan, and perhaps some of the poetry in the *Shijing* that predates the period of regulated verse most Americans associate with classical Chinese verse. This is an important corrective, however, since the formal qualities of Chinese poetry initiated by Shen Yue's own "Don'ts" one-and-a-half millennia earlier bear so little resemblance to American Modernism.

Yet it is important to note that I have been speaking of the young Ezra Pound, not the Pound who later learned to chant classical Chinese poetry and who expressed to his students at St. Mary's the importance of melopoeia (musical character) in Chinese poetry. I have not spoken of the Pound who fought a long battle with Harvard University Press in the hope of fulfilling his dream for a scholarly edition of the *Shijing* complete with a pronunciation guide and a "singing key" for each poem. Harvard, and later T. S. Eliot's Faber and Faber (and still later, New Directions), published a shorter edition of his translations, but the only notes on the sounds of the originals can be found in the short essay that prefaces the volume written by Achilles Fang from Harvard University Press. Fang's scholarly introduction indicates just how seriously the late Pound took classical Chinese prosody by underscoring Pound's awareness of the importance accorded music by Confucius and Confucianism more generally. Fang observes:

> It is possible that Confucius did set some of the Odes to music; but his admission that "when Music Master Chy began the ensemble finale of the fish-hawk song [Ode 1], came wave over wave

an ear-full and how!" indicates that his actual role was to put an already existing body of musical notation into order, perhaps retouching it here and there. At any rate Sy-ma Ts'ien (Sima Qian, 145 BC–86 BC) writes that Confucius sang the 305 Odes to his lute and made them harmonize with the modes of *shao, wu, ya,* and *sung. . . .* The Master must have worked hard on the music of the Odes all his life. Whether at home or on the road, his lute was always with him; "barring cogent reasons, a scholar is never without his lute."[94]

Fang continues:

As to how the Odes were sung by Confucius and his contemporaries, only a wide solution, as Sir Thomas Browne would say, is possible. No music of the fifth century BC is preserved for us; we do not know even the kind of intervals used at that time. But, apparently believing that such puzzling questions are "not beyond all conjecture," a number of curious musicians have tried their hand in reconstructing the music of the Odes.[95]

Fang then gives an example of one such re-creation before offering, "for the reader who wishes to try the music," "a syllable-for-syllable transcription of the ode as pronounced in North China 'a maunderin tongue in a poundian jowl'—*Finnegans Wake.*"[96]

So while Fang (and by extension Pound) could not give an exact transcription of the Chinese original, they, like Fenollosa before, did their best to transmit the sound of the original inasmuch as this was possible at this late date. Finally, Fang explains that while "there is no guarantee that Confucius read the Odes in a pronunciation like this (we know that both consonants and vowels were much richer in his time) or that he sang them in melody reconstructed more than a millennium afterward," "it cannot be too strongly insisted that the Odes were actually sung in Confucius' day. Poetry to the ancient Chinese seems to have been an art in which the art of words and music formed a single unit. In fact the term 'odes' applied to the 305 poems in this volume is to be understood in its etymological sense of songs meant to be sung."[97] To translate these sounds, Fang assures us that "Pound, the Confucian, 'the old hand as stylist still holding its cunning,' is intent on fusing words and music. For this purpose the choice of the ballad meter is a happy one, as it not only makes the translation readable, but accurately brings out the original rhythm of the Odes. For the Odes are essentially ballads; they were all sung, and some of them were probably dance songs."[98] So filial was Pound to the source text's prosody that a young and clearly upset Charles Olson complained in a short verse:

> To clank like you do
> He brings coolie verse
> To teach you equity,
> Who layed down such rails!
>
> . . . . . .
> . . . that the Master
> should now be embraced by the demon
> he drove off!. . . .
>
> . . . . . .
> That the great 'ear
> Can no longer hear![99]

What Olson could not have known is that Pound's Imagist, even ideogrammic, poetics that helped break the hold of the rhyming iamb became increasingly complicated by Pound's continued study of Confucianism and its historical relationship to "Chinese sonority." While Fang is only lightly treating the significance of music to Confucian sociopolitical thought, its importance to the Spring and Autumn period (春秋時代, 722 BCE–481 BCE) can easily be seen in the two most important texts of the period: 左傳 (Zuo zhuan, Zuo Commentary) and 國語 (Guo yu, Speeches of the States).[100] And there is no doubt that Pound would have, by the mid-1950s, recognized the importance of music to the function of a harmonious state found in the 樂記 (Shi Ji, Record of Music).[101]

If Fenollosa valued Chinese melopoeia for its correlation with cosmological and Buddhist esoteric philosophies, then Pound returned to Chinese sounds to advance his notions of a Confucian poetics at the service of a higher state intelligence. In the end, Pound's later translations can be seen as an interesting cognate of Fenollosa's, since both sought to bring new poetic forms into English as a vehicle for introducing the particular transpacific imaginaries (or East Asian philosophies) they believed animated these forms. Yet Pound's view of poetry as an assemblage of "concrete things" lies in stark contrast to Fenollosa's attempt to supplant the dream of "thingness" made available in the

English language with a language he believed could reveal Nature's infinite flux. Yet when we turn our attention to Fenollosa's appropriation of classical Chinese notions of "patterned harmony," we may get closer to Pound's authoritarian poetics than one might expect.

While Fenollosa's valuation of correlative cosmology relied on a Romantic treatment of its theories of harmonic correspondences within flux abstracted from history and the cultural fabric from which it came, it is important to acknowledge the full ideological scope of the correlative worldview so that we may come to a more full appreciation and critique of Fenollosa's heterocultural project, especially as it relates to Pound's. One can begin to appreciate the political dimension of Chinese poetic form and prosody by exploring why the Confucian exams 科舉 (605–1905) required civil servants to compose poems as the primary diagnostic for service to the state. The composition of poetry seems like an odd way to measure an applicant's capacity to run state affairs. Often I hear off-handed remarks from friends and colleagues that such poetic requirements reveal China's enlightened sense of governance, at least in comparison to the anti-intellectual climate of contemporary American politics. But certainly there is something in the composition of poetry that signaled an applicant's value to the central state beyond one's "creativity" or "poetic sensibility." Stephan Owen convincingly reveals what some of these values might have been:

> Within the highly circumscribed rhetorical moves of examination verse are found the formal embodiments of the imperial ideology—the politically legitimate sentiments, the attention to only the authorized aspects of the outer world, the parallelism and rules of rhetorical amplification which teach that all objects and events belong in a system of received relations. In other poetry the rigid rules of examination verse seem to be relaxed, but this liberation is only illusory: beneath the surface all the properties are either observed or denied in acceptable ways.[102]

He concludes that it is "the poem," as opposed to a formal pledge of allegiance, that "demonstrates a thorough assimilation of the correlative cosmology on which the government's authority, even its justification to exist, is founded."[103] The wealthy clans that occupied positions of authority throughout dynastic China would naturally have supported their own self-interests, but for nearly 1,300 years China administered exams, which brought ambitious lower officials and members of the merchant class (who would not necessarily share the same interests as the ruling elite) into civil government. The exams, and the requirement that one compose poetry based upon correlative models, gave proof that the applicant had internalized the central government's authorized view of the cosmos and their supplicant position therein. In other words, classical Chinese poetic form, at least in part, accepted and projected received notions of proper class, gender, ethnic, political, and other cultural roles.

It is fair to say, however, that Fenollosa did not consider the ideological dimension of this cosmology when he sought to revitalize Western poetic forms by connecting their harmonic patterns to the universal truth of his correlative universe. When he contrasts the West's use of law, as a "curbing of the ego so as to better enjoy individuality," to the East's, "where the principle of struggle would be regarded as immoral" and where *"law is positive, namely, the natural conditions of harmony,"*[104] one can safely assume that this assertion relies on the billowy clouds of a blissfully ahistorical idealism. What Fenollosa saw as Eastern "harmony" (the natural correlations between natural and human patterns) was certainly not understood as the internalization of state-enforced political ideology, but a philosophical attitude attained by individuals within a distinct cultural orientation.

In fact, Fenollosa vehemently condemned Confucian governments for destroying what he termed Buddho-Daoist "individualism" (one of his code words for *ziran*, or naturally becoming one's self through and as a part of flux without interference from outside analysis) during and after the Song dynasty, leading to, in the Social Darwinist terms of the period, "the softening of the Chinese Brain."[105] Fenollosa rationalized his paradoxical acceptance of correlative cosmology and his vehement disdain for institutionalized Confucianism by emphasizing the difference between the philosophical ideals of Confucius (whose views of social harmony he found "sublime and fruitful as philosophy") and the state-enforced doctrines of the "Confucian educational system itself."[106] Fenollosa went on to argue that "all the great imaginative art work of the Chinese mind has sprung from those elements in Chinese genius, which if not anti, were at least non-Confucian." He then continues to compare the genius of later poetry, beginning with the Daoist-oriented epic *Li-Sao* to the institutionalized canonization of the "primitive, short-lined moralizing Chow [Zhou] balladry of

Confucius' compilation" central to Pound's Confucianism.[107] It is clear that Fenollosa wanted to separate state interests (which he understood as intrinsically linked to Confucian ruling parties) from the correlative worldview they sponsored. After all, is Fenollosa not correct to mark a distinction between a philosophy or a religion's theology, for example, and the institutionalized and political forms that may wish to capitalize on the discourse for political gain? I would argue that he is justified in doing so, yet I would also argue that the agency offered by the correlative worldview, based upon the belief that flux is not only harmonious but can be accurately mapped, will always offer a foothold to authoritarian claims to knowledge, and hence be easily coopted as an extension of state interests. Philosophy is, in the end, responsible, at least in part, for the ease by which it can be appropriated and deployed toward oppressive ends. Yet it is hard to say just how much Fenollosa's own correlative views would have been decentered by his simultaneous belief in the limitations of all knowledge claims as understood through his Buddhist investments.

There is, in the end, an irony at the heart of Ezra Pound and Ernest Fenollosa's strange dance. Pound's ideogrammic method, which produced the *Cantos*, undermined his own poetics of concision, by not only denying a single, concise reading, but anything like a unified meaning. All the while, as Owen points out, the correlative patterns Fenollosa adopted were already "an extension of the Confucian doctrine of *cheng-ming* [*zhengming*] calling things by their 'proper names.'"[108] In other words, the doctrine that lay at the foundation of Pound's Confucian poetics could have found a safer harbor in the correlative formalism advocated by Fenollosa's desire to shore up the poverty of traditional English verse than in the uncontrolled waters of his disjunctive *Cantos*. It is equally interesting to point out that Fenollosa's desire for an indeterminate language capable of recalling its own impermanence, or emptiness, would have found a safer passage through Pound's poetry than the correlative cosmology at the heart of classical Chinese poetics, which, after all, threatens to know too much about where things have been and where they might be going. Given the important legacy of Pound's paratactic techniques inspired in part by Fenollosa's Tendai and Kegon metaphysics (albeit through considerable layers of misunderstanding), it is difficult to be upset by the loss of Fenollosa's correlative poetics to history, which while rich in their heterocultural scope would likely have detracted from the primary vision of his poetics of emptiness. Yet it is also important to note that in the absence of an introduction to correlative poetics and prosody, American poets and readers have entertained principally visual notions of Chinese poetry devoid of sound, and therefore largely discordant with classical Chinese poetics and aesthetics.

3 / 法 Teaching the Law: Gary Snyder's Poetics of Emptiness

Teaching the Law

At the end of Gary Snyder's book *Mountains and Rivers without End*, he offers a glimpse into his understanding of poetry's role in transmitting Buddhist dharma (teachings):

> The T'ang poet Po Chü-i said, "I have long had the desire that my actions in this world and any problems caused by my crazy words and extravagant language [*kyōgen kīgo*] will in times to come be transformed into a clarification of the Dharma, and be but another way to spread the Buddha's teachings."

Snyder then writes, regarding his own work, "May it be so!"[1]

For Snyder, poetry (especially Chinese and Japanese poetry) is a vital resource for transmitting Buddhist dharma 法, *fa* (or 佛法, *fofa*). The term 法 (*fa*), like 空 (*kong*) and 文 (*wen*), is complicated and signifies different concepts within a wide range of cultural discourses. In Buddhist discourses the term generally denotes "the law," or "teachings," of Buddhism but can also denote, for much Buddhist phenomenology, "momentary elements of consciousness" (which, depending on the branch of Buddhist thought, may or may not have a separate existence of their own). For the sake of this discussion, I would like to use the term's first Buddhist denotation and explore the ways in which Snyder's poetics responds to the task of transmitting "Buddhist law/teaching." In this sense, I will be discussing the didactic aspects of Snyder's poetry and poetics and will pay especially close attention to how he uses specialized poetic language and devices to convey (or enact) the Zen stereological notion of *tathāgatagarbha*, or *Buddha-dhātu* (Buddha matrix or Buddha Nature). Snyder's desire to transmit this particular dharma is especially compelling, as it requires him to envision a poetics of emptiness that leaves language itself behind.

While Zen Buddhism is famous for its experiential methodologies and its "non-reliance on words and phrases," poetry, as opposed to discursive prose, has played a central role in this branch of Mahayana Buddhism from its inception. "Zen Poetry," for Snyder, walks the "edge between what can be said and that which cannot be said." He continues, "Mantras or koans, or spells are actually superelliptical poems that the reader cannot understand except that he has to put hundreds of more hours of mediation in toward getting it than he has to put in to get the message out of a normal poem."[2] For Snyder, therefore, the work of expressing the dharma entails reaching beyond the normative parameters of language to an extralinguistic experience of the world, which he believes can be accomplished through some forms of poetry. He writes: "There are poets who claim that their poems are made to show the world through the prism of language. Their project is worthy. There is also the work of seeing the world without any prism of language, and to bring that seeing into language. The latter has been the direction of most Chinese and Japanese poetry."[3]

Snyder's vision (by which I mean to underscore the ocularcentric quality of his assertions) of East Asian poetry lies in large measure within Japanese Zen readings of Chinese poetry, which often foreground (and perhaps exaggerate) the difference between discursive, explanatory language available in sutra texts, which *wenzi chan* (literary Chan) often refer to as "dead words," 死句, or *siju*, and the disjunctive, non-discursive language play (or disruption) of classical Chinese poetry, which is referred to as 活句 (*huoju*, "live words"). Above all, Zen poetics values Chinese poetry's use of "live words" for its ability to leave a poetic resonance (that does not function grammatically) conducive to inducing heightened states of awareness.[4]

One can think of the word play within koan questions as an example of this distinction. Take, for instance, the following well-known koan attributed to Zhaozhou (趙州, Ja: Jōshū, b. 778–d. 897), "Does a dog possess Buddha Nature?" The ritualized response is "Mu!" "Mu" is the Japanese pronunciation of the Chinese character for emptiness 無 (Ch: *wu*). At first the answer can mean "No," implying that the respondent does not think a dog has "Buddha Nature." But the term is also the Japanese onomatopoetic equivalent of a dog bark (Eng: ruff). Upon further introspection, we can see that the dog answers for itself, with a single word, "emptiness," alone, which implies that dogs possess Buddha Nature for the same reason all things do, by way of their shared unity in emptiness. The language play within the koan sets in motion several interconnected chains of signification, initiated by the word "mu," thought to disrupt the normal cognitive patterns through which adepts claim to experience states of consciousness beyond "thinking" in any normative sense. (I think of Philip Whalen's assertion that poetry should, like koans, "wreck the mind."[5])

As we saw in the previous chapter, if one pays attention to the correlative patterns of classical Chinese poetic form, one sees the primacy of poetic agency to harmonize with natural patterns of correlation, but read through a Zennist lens, which does not participate in this cosmological economy, the poetic line looks loose, often indeterminate, and open to interpretation. In other words, the classical Chinese poetic line represents "live words." The Song dynasty poet Wu Ke (d. ca. 1174) brought this Chan/Zen distinction between "live words" and "dead words" (originally linked to koan practice) into poetry when he stated: "Dead poetry is a poetry the language of which is still language; live poetry is a poetry the language of which is no longer language."[6] In his foreword to *A Zen Forest, Sayings of the Masters,* Soiku Shigematsu's translation of the *Zenrinkushu,* Gary Snyder offers a reading of a poem by Du Fu similar to that, which may help illustrate Snyder's Zennist reading of classical Chinese verse. Snyder cites Du Fu's famous poem "Spring Scene" as an exemplar of Zen poetics, even though Du Fu was not a Buddhist.

> The country is ruined: yet
>> Mountains and rivers remain.
> It's spring in the walled town,
>> The grass growing wild.[7]

Snyder cites Burton Watson's evaluation of Du Fu's verse to reveal its use value for Zen practice, which apparently comes from the poem's "acute sensitivity to the small motions and creatures of nature. . . . Somewhere in all the ceaseless and seemingly insignificant activities of the natural world, he keeps implying truth is to be found.'"[8] The poet's turn from the world of human history to the minutia of natural phenomena moves the poem and the reader from the rhythm of society to the ceaseless transience of natural cycles, which are so often neglected by historical grand narratives. We can see that this shift in focus may represent a "live word"[9] for Snyder or other Zennist readers, whereby the poem turns the speaker's or reader's mind from its normative patterns. Read in this way, Du Fu's move away from the important historical time of the fall of the Tang capital of Chang An 長安 (today known as Xi An, 西安) to the "other time" of the "grass growing wild" consists of "live words," which, according to the the Buddhologist Dale Wright, "bespeak the identity or congruence of self and situation,"[10] insofar as this focus reminds the reader of the interconnected nature of all phenomena. These lines, in other words, point to interdependence and the permanent presence of transience "directly," rather than discursively explaining how war, loss, the poet, the reader, and the grass are "one" in emptiness, interconnected. In this sense, Du Fu's poem was written from a nirvanic perspective, or the perspective of one who is always aware or this "other time" and the interconnected nature of all things in impermanence.

Yet Watson's and Snyder's similar readings of Du Fu's poem interestingly do not presence many of the reasons why this poem, and not another, attained its preeminent position in the Chinese canon. Here is the whole poem:

chūn 春	wàng 望				Spring Scene
guó 国	pò 破	shān 山	hé 河	zài 在	Country broken / mountain
chéng 城	chūn 春	cáo 曹	mù 木	shēn 深	river still here
gǎn 感	shí 时	huā 花	jiàn 溅	lèi 泪	City spring / grass trees deep
hèn 恨	bié 别	niǎo 鸟	jīng 惊	xīn 心	Feel moment / flower splash tears
fēng 烽	huǒ 火	lián 连	sān 三	yuè 月	Regret parting / bird startle heart
jiā 家	shū 书	dǐ 抵	wàn 万	jīn 金	Beacon fire / join three months
bái 白	tóu 头	sāo 搔	gèng 更	duǎn 短	Family letters / equal ten thousand tael
hún 浑	yù 欲	bù 不	shèng 胜	zān 簪	White head / scratch become thin
					Simply be about to / not bear hairpin

Since Du Fu's "Spring Scene" is written in the genre of regulated verse (*lushi*), it conforms to the same tonal patterns, rhyme schemes, and semantic parallelism as the regulated verse discussed in the previous chapter. The success of a poem in this style can be gauged, in part, by the way it naturalizes these formal qualities in a way that leads to an overall unity of content and form. The first couplet can be read as a textbook example of the four-part progression of regulated verse, *qi* (or to begin, arise), insofar as it sets the time, location, and theme for the rest of the poem. And already we see a correlative interplay of dynamic tension between opposing (but correlatively connected) forces: human culture (country) / nature (mountains and rivers), what is broken / what endures, etc. This poem is particularly well known for its brilliant naturalization of semantic parallelism. As noted earlier, the middle couplets must be parallel, which Du Fu accomplishes with grace and naturalness:

Feel	moment /	flower	cry	tears
Emotion	time/space	natural nouns	shock	visceral response to shock
Regret	parting /	birds	startle	heart

Beacon fire /		join	three		months
Distant communications		linkage	cosmological numbers		noun measurements
Family letters /		equal	ten thousand		tael

The four couplets move in an orderly progression from the nonparallel, into parallel, and back to the nonparallel, and Zong-Qi Cai writes, "In traditional Chinese poetry criticism, the four couplets are each assigned a specific function: *qi* (to begin, to arise); *cheng* (to continue, apt to carry on); *zhuan* (to make a turn), and *he* (to close, to enclose)."[11] Du Fu's poem not only perfectly fulfills these functions in each of the couplets, but also ends the poem by returning to temporal progression, which highlights the decay of the poet himself. We can see this last couplet "*he*" is a return to time and decay, away from the atemporal, parallel stasis of the inner couplets organized by way of vertical symmetry and harmony (as opposed to horizontal syntax, which is temporal, insofar as events take place in time).

Du Fu's ability not only to conform to the rigors of *lushi* but also to make these conventions meaningful by revealing the seamlessness of poetic form and content has contributed to the lasting popularity of "Spring View." Snyder's and Watson's readings of the poem, however, arise from a particular context, namely, the way these lines have been anthologized within the *Zenrinkushu* (*A Zen Forest, Sayings of the Masters*), a collection of quotes from Chinese and Japanese sources used by Zen practitioners to move beyond conventional thought. The poem's inclusion in the volume equally reveals a specific, doctrinal reading of Chinese poetry as an "instrument" for enlightenment, which cannot be taken as representative of all Chinese poetry or poetics (which is why I wanted to once again call to mind a correlative reading). This instrumentalist reading of Chinese poetry as a vehicle for teaching the dharma, *fa*, is further revealed when Snyder argues that "the poets and the Chan masters" of China are "in a sense just the tip of the wave of a deep Chinese sensibility, an attitude toward life and nature that rose and flowed from the seventh to the fourteenth centuries and then slowly waned."[12] Certainly, the "wave" Snyder sees conditioning the "poets and Chan masters" is real, insofar as the particular Chinese practices of Chan/Zen poetry and poetics rise from the greater context of Chinese poetry and sensibilities toward life and nature. Yet it becomes problematic when the base of the wave and its tip are inverted, and Chan/Zennist poetry and poetics are seen as the greater context for Chinese poetry as a whole.[13]

While Wu Ke's notion of "live and dead words" is a doctrinal device, the liminality of language suggested in phrases like his was purposefully connected to existing non-Buddhist theories of "poetic resonance" or Chinese poetry's attenuation of signification, its afterglow, afterimages, lingering tastes, smells, and perhaps most importantly, sounds; in short, a classical Chinese poem has been traditionally valued by some critics for its "resonance," which is seen to bring language out of its cognitive structures and topographical certainties into the intuitive, suprarational, or what Snyder might call language's "wilderness." By the sixth century, Chinese poetics had already formed a wide variety of terms that signal this importance of poetic "resonance." An inchoate theory of resonance is grounded early on in terms like *yiyin* (lingering sound), *yiwei* (lasting flavor), *congzhi* (double meaning or multivalence).[14] But these terms are given a strong sotereological utility in Zen poetics, which one will not find in prior Chinese poetics.

In his poem "The Taste," Gary Snyder foregrounds the gustatory theory (taste beyond taste) that undergirds ideas of poetic resonance so central to his Zennist notion of Chinese poetry.

> I don't know where it went
> Or recall how it worked

What one did
What the steps were was it hands?
Or the words and the tune?
All that's left
is the flavor
that stays.[15]

Snyder's poem explores the limits of cognition: when the words have fallen away, when the body has forgotten the proper steps, something intuitive, ready to be, remains; something lingers. Working squarely within the modernist idiom of William Carlos Williams, the pacing and meter of Snyder's poem is marked by line breaks and grammar rather than by formal prosodic structures. Reminiscent of Williams's poems like "Nantucket," the appearance of disjunction within the poem is largely a result of line breaks, not syntax. Written in a more linear fashion replete with conventional punctuation, Snyder's poem would be only mildly disjunctive, as the poem generally unfolds in a syntactic, discursive way, ending with a marked redundancy that reinforces the poem's theme of lingering resonances. The poem's explanatory tone attempts to convey through conventional language (or its "content") the difficulty of bringing something from the outside (in this case, memory or thought) back inside. Yet, like Pound and other modernists, Snyder is very aware of the resonant quality that English is capable of producing from the grammatical interruption of line breaks. When the syntax is broken by line breaks, we find new potential meanings through enjambment or attenuated moments of indeterminacy. Meanings normally derived from a linear sentence's momentum can, thus, be redistributed or redirected throughout the poem's lines or semi-discrete units. Donald Davie writes that "it was only when the line was considered the unit of composition [as opposed to the stanza or sentence as the unit of composition] that there emerged the possibility of 'breaking' the line, of disrupting it from within, by throwing weight upon smaller units within the line."[16]

The poetic resonance in Snyder's work is produced by more than his line breaks, however: the resonance arises from the complex relationships between different subunits within a poem. Often Snyder does this by intertextually weaving together different source materials or juxtaposing unadorned visual datum. By exploring Snyder's use of poetic resonance within poems like "We Wash Our Bowls in This Water," we can begin to see how such "resonance" or "live words" function as instruments for Snyder to teach a dharma (that proposes an exit from language itself).

Let me cite a substantial excerpt from the poem, for a sense of context, before looking at the opening stanza in detail.

We Wash Our Bowls in This Water
> *"The 1.5 Billion cubic kilometers of water on earth are split by photosynthesis and reconstituted by respiration once every two million years or so."* [Snyder's italics]

A day on the ragged North Pacific coast get soaked by whipping mist, rainsqualls tumbling, mountain mirror ponds, snowfield slush, rock-wash creeks, earfuls of falls, sworls of ridge-edge snowflakes, swift gravelly rivers, tidewaters crumbly glaciers, high hanging glaciers, shore-side mud pools, icebergs, streams looping through tideflats, spume of brine, distant soft rain drooping

from a cloud,

sea lions lazing under the surface of the sea—

We wash our bowls in this water
It has the flavor of ambrosial dew—
....

. . . "Well, lets get going, get back to the rafts"
Swing the big oars,
head into the storm.

We offer it to all daemons and spirits
May all be filled and satisfied.
Om makalu sai svaha!

•

Su Tung-p'o sat out one whole night by a creek on the slopes of Mt. Lu. Next morning he showed this poem to his teacher:

The stream with its sounds   is a long broad tongue
The looming mountain   is a wide-awake body
Throughout the night song after song
How can I   speak at dawn.

Old Master Chang-tsung approved him. Two centuries later Dōgen said,
"Sounds of streams and shapes of mountains.
The sounds never stop and the shapes never cease.

Was it Su who woke
or was it the mountains and streams?
Billions of beings see the morning star
and all become Buddhas!
If *you*, who are valley streams and looming
mountains,
can't throw some light on the nature of ridges and rivers,

who can?"[17]

In the first paragraph/stanza, we see a network, or what in Snyder's often Kegon Buddhist–inflected language might be called a "web," or "net," of interrelated phases of the water cycle. Kegon is not a form of Zen, but its central concept of a "net" has had a strong influence on Snyder's poetics and ecological prose writing. As mentioned in the first chapter, the central teaching of the school holds that all phenomena are interconnected in an infinite web and every point in the web reflects every other point. While Snyder points to this interconnectivity, or what he often refers to as "interbirth,"[18] as an ontological foundation for his anti-anthropocentric worldview, I would argue that this concept cannot be equally applied with much success to his notion of Chinese poetics and its role in teaching "the Dharma." Given the wide proliferation of Buddhist schools and teachings, it is important to locate what "Dharma" Snyder hopes to transmit/teach through his poetry. This stanza, and the poem that follows it, helps us do just this. The fact that each of the images in the opening stanza of the poem represents a different manifestation of the same substance, water, reveals a debt to Yogācāra, and especially the class of teachings associated with the notion of *tathāgatagarbha*. I would argue that this distinction is central to understanding Snyder's poetics of emptiness, and by extension a major element of transpacific philosophical, aesthetic, and religious migrations into American poetry more generally.

Like most Buddhist schools, Yogācāra argues that ordinary experience is impermanent in its nature since it depends upon the momentary phenomena of causes and conditions, but it also argues that even though these external objects of perception are empty and devoid of any intrinsic reality (dependently arisen), the states of consciousness that cognize them are real (not dependently arisen). This uncaused "house of consciousness" is called the *alaya-vijnana* (often translated as "storehouse consciousness"), and in the course of Yogācāran practice a practitioner must cleanse the *alaya-vijnana* of its contents in order to return to the undivided, uncaused matrix of emptiness, emptied of and, therefore, free from causation. You will notice here a shift in the meaning of "emptiness" itself. In the class of sutras known as Tathāgatagarbha, under which are both the *Laṅkāvatāra Sutra* (楞伽經) and the *Nirvana Sutra* (涅槃經), the truth of emptiness understood as *pratītyasamutpāda* (dependent origination) central to Fenollosa's Buddhism, shifts to a positive expression of an ontological "Mind" or *citta*, which is not "empty," in the sense that it is contingent on causes and conditions (*pratītyasamutpāda*), but is empty of duality, discrimination, and contingency/change. The *Laṅkāvatāra Sutra*[19] teaches that this pure "One Mind" can only be experienced after one discards discrimination based on the dualistic (linguistic) intellect. Furthermore, this "positive expression of emptiness" as "*Buddha-dhātu*" (Buddha Nature, 佛性) or *tathāgatagarbha* ("embryo/sprout of the Buddha-nature," 如来蔵) can thus be seen as a shift away from the negative epistemology of Fenollosa's Buddhism to a positive ontology and soteriology meant to impart a lasting, permanent "true self" in, or more accurately, as *tathāgatagarbha*.[20]

To illustrate how this metaphysical structure enters Snyder's work, let me refer to its most common metaphor once again: water. The Mind is a deep still sea, and thoughts are but waves on its surface. Emptiness, or Buddha Nature, is this same deep, still sea, and all phenomena are but waves on its surface. Phenomena are not real in an ultimate sense since they are not autonomously existent; they are real only insofar as they are generated from Mind/Buddha Nature.

1 "Mind" is the basis for "phenomena"
2 "Mind" gives rise to "phenomena"
3 "Mind" is one, "phenomena" are many
4 "Mind" is real, "phenomena" are not real
5 "Mind" is the essential nature of "phenomena"
6 "Phenomena" are not ultimately real, but have some reality in that they have arisen from the "Mind" and share its nature[21]

While there is not a consensus on this issue, *tathāgatagarbha* can be thought of as a "generative monism" or a "positive expression of emptiness"[22] and is extended by way of the metaphor of water through the first stanza of Snyder's poem, insofar as snowflakes, rivers, glaciers, mist, rains, ponds, slush, creeks, falls, pools, icebergs, and clouds are all apparently discrete phenomena but are ultimately manifestations of a single Oneness. Clearly, such a vision of emptiness would find a seat kept

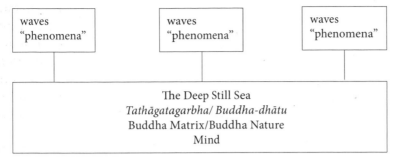

| waves
"phenomena" | waves
"phenomena" | waves
"phenomena" |

The Deep Still Sea
Tathāgatagarbha/ Buddha-dhātu
Buddha Matrix/Buddha Nature
Mind

FIGURE 3.1. *Tathāgatagarbha* diagram reveals the monistic dimensions of form. Based on diagrams presented in "Critical Buddhism," in *Pruning the Bodhi Tree*, 242.

warm by Romanticism's exaltation of idealism, mind, and nature, but it is important to not subsume Yogācāran monism under the umbrella of Romanticism, although one can see why this discourse might be more popular in the United States than non- or anti-monistic concepts of emptiness, such as the Madyamika-inspired notions of emptiness that undergird much of Fenollosa's poetics or, in a more radical sense, Leslie Scalapino's writing.[23]

Following the first stanza, we see the italicized lines, which represent quotes from a Zen prayer that would be intoned before mealtime in a Zen monastery:

We wash our bowls in this water
It has the flavor of ambrosial dew—

We find the whole prayer again in an essay by Snyder, entitled "Grace," in *The Practice of the Wild*. By inserting decontextualized lines of the prayer throughout the poem (Snyder does not indicate the origin of the lines in the poem), however, Snyder liberates the lines from their natural "communicative" context and sets them afloat within a sea of other semi-discrete units that constitute both the poem's form and content, further adding to their "resonant" quality. The reader, encountering the lines of the dinner prayer set adrift within the poem, immediately begins making connections between, say, the "this water" (which would ritually refer to an actual bowl of water) of the prayer's first line and the snowflakes and rivers of the opening stanza. In this way, the discursive prose, like the visual datum of the first stanza, can now be read as "live words," in the sense that its meanings are no longer predetermined by its original ritual or discursive contexts, but open to multiple levels of signification (which in the Zen poetics of Wu Ke is a feature of "live poetry," "the language of which is no longer language"). Yet Snyder's use of parataxis and juxtaposition does not ultimately seek to fragment reality, but aims instead at disrupting normative grammar in order to reveal the Dharma of "unity" in a broader metaphysical sense of an inclusive "Buddha Nature." Snyder's poem progresses by floating a discrete series of textual islands individually cut off from their broader discursive bodies and contexts. Here, set adrift within the poem, prayers invoke water, and prose islets written in the imperative tell us to integrate ourselves into this watery unity: "swing the big oars" and "head into the storm."

The second section of the poem provides us with a map of the intertextual and heterocultural tributaries through which this metaphysics of unity and resonance arise in Snyder's poetics more generally, for at the center of the Chan/Zen valuation of Chinese poetic resonance lies a single poem by the Song dynasty poet Su Shi (his Buddhist name is Su Dongbo, which I will use here, given the Buddhist context), which we actually encounter in its entirety in the second section of Snyder's poem.

While not explicitly "about" poetic resonance by itself, Su Dongbo's poem "贈东林总长老 ("Presented to Master Lin Zongchang") is rarely "by itself," but almost always encountered within *chan wenzixue,* or Zennist, readings of the poem.[24] Snyder's poem mentions the most famous commentary, made by Dogen (Dōgen Zenji, 道元禅師, b. 1200–d. 1253), the founder of the Soto school of Zen, in his essay *Keisei Sanshoku* 谿聲山色 ("Valley Sounds, Mountain Form").[25] In this essay, Dogen writes about how Su Dongpo traveled to Mount Lu to learn about the Buddhist doctrine known as the "inanimate thing teaching" from Master Lin Zongchang.[26] Afterward, he traveled back down the mountain and spent the night near a river. It was at this point that the lingering presence of the words of his master mixed with ambient sounds of the water flowing and Su Dongpo received the teaching. Dogen points out that, according to the "inanimate thing teaching," all things possess Buddha Nature, or are "One" within Buddha Nature, and therefore the teacher's words are one with the sound of the stream. This realization, enacted in Su Dongpo's poem, is experiential in a way that the discursive sutra read by the master could not communicate. Su's poem reads:

溪声便是广长舌，
The stream with its sounds   is a long broad tongue

Snyder translates the Zen term "universal tongue" as a "long broad tongue," but in both cases the Chinese term refers to the Buddhist notion of *upaya* (方便), which itself denotes the infinitely varied ways in which the dharma can be taught so that the hearer can understand.

山色岂非清净身。
The looming mountain　is a wide-awake body

This term "wide-awake body" is Snyder's translation of the Chinese term 净身 (*jingshen*), which is more literally translated as "purified body," but in either case refers to the monistic Buddhist concept of an all-encompassing Buddha Nature (especially when paired with the idea of *upaya*, for which the concept of *tathāgatagarbha* is a prominent example). After experiencing his "awakening" during the night, Su experiences a prolific flowing of poetry and song.

夜来八万四千偈，
Throughout the night　song after song

But in the light of the following day, or in the "clarity" of dead-explanatory language, he cannot express the true nature of his enlightenment.

他日如何举似人。
How can I　speak at dawn.

In relation to the doctrinal debate surrounding the question of Buddha Nature and sentience, Su Dongpo's poem takes a partisan stance, but unlike a sutra that "states" or "explains" using "dead words," Su's poem purportedly gives the reader a more direct experience of the universality of Buddha Nature by "showing" that the "valley sounds" *are* the words/teaching of the dharma, and that the mountain's form *is* the pure Buddha Body/Buddha Nature.

Snyder's poem ends with a quote from Dogen's essay:

Old Master Chang-tsung approved him. Two centuries later

"Sounds of streams and shapes of mountains.
The sounds never stop and the shapes never cease.
Was it Su who woke
or was it the mountains and streams?
Billions of beings see the morning star
and all become Buddhas!
If *you,* who are valley streams and looming

mountains,
can't throw some light on the nature of ridges and rivers,

who can?"²⁷

Dogen's commentary, like Snyder's opening stanza, is drawing upon a monistic metaphor of water as a generative Oneness: mountains are like waves on the surface of the water figured as ceaseless impermanence (their sounds, i.e., movement, never cease). The poet, too, is but a manifestation of this water and so should know something of the condition of being mountains as well as water. In this non-differentiated unity, the poet's enlightenment is not separate from the enlightenment of all other phenomena, since separateness is an illusion. Dogen's teaching here draws heavily upon a network of water-based Buddhist ideas and terminology that rely on a binary with mountains. Mountains, or 重山 (*zhongshan,* heavy mountains), offer the illusion of permanence and are often invoked as a metonym for delusion, while water is 流注 (*liuzhu,* constantly flowing) but in this sense also "ceaseless" 不斷 (*buduan,* unceasing).

Within this dichotomy, water, often figured as an ocean 海 (*hai*) (海 印, *haiyin:* the ocean as symbol), takes on a series of positive significations in a wide array of terms. This ocean often signifies an onto-theological monism: 眞如海 (*zhiruhai,* "the ocean of the *bhūtatathatā,* limitlessness"), 清淨覺海 (*qingjiu xueha,* "the pure ocean of enlightenment, which underlies the disturbed life of all"), 圓海 (*yuanhai,* "the all-embracing ocean of Buddhahood"), and 法性海 (*faxinghai,* "the ocean of the dharma-nature, vast, unfathomable"). Water is also used to signify enlightened epistemological states, 意水 (*yishui,* "the mind or will to become calm as still water, on entering *samādh*"); 清涼池 (*qingliangchi,* "the pure lake, or pool, i.e., nirvana"). In Snyder's poem (and, by extension, Su Dongpo's poem and Dogen's essay), water also operates as a soteriological agent which purifies, cleanses, and teaches the dharma directly (as in the vehicle of the "inanimate thing teaching received in/through Su's poem). Such a function is captured in the phrase 海潮音 (*haichaoyin,* "the ocean-tide [Buddha] voice"), and in terms like 法水 (*fashui,* "dharma likened to water able to wash away the stains of illusion"), or dharma likened to a 法河 (*fahe,* "deep river"), or, finally, 法性水 (*faxingshui,* "the water of the dharma-nature, i.e., pure").²⁸

On multiple occasions Snyder conjures this monistic 法海 (*fahai,* dharma ocean). In *Earth House Hold,* for instance, Snyder writes, "That level of mind—the cool water—not intellect and not—(as Romantics and after have confusingly thought) fantasy—dream world or unconscious. This is just the clear spring—it reflects all things and feeds all things but is of itself transparent."[29] This transparent "dharma ocean" "taught" by Su, Dogen, and Snyder in this poem rushes out to engulf the totality of the poem and all of its differentia, including the reader in what I would like to call Snyder's retroactive grammar of unifying emptiness. Snyder often chooses to end poems on figures of generative, all-encompassing emptiness that activate a grammar of relationships (that works backward) between the various elements of the poem. The poem "Wave," for instance, ends a poem filled with differentia that can be recalled into a monistic origin as merely phenomenal "waves" and that lands in the monistic emptiness "of my mind." The poem "Prayer for the Great Family" ends almost every stanza (filled with differentia) in the refrain, "in our minds so be it." The poem "Song of the Slip" ends in the expression "make home in the whole," and in "Kai, Today" Snyder ends with the single word "sea," and so on.[30] These poems might be read as a loose aggregate of indeterminate subunits, if it were not for this retroactive grammar of unifying emptiness.

This is an important distinguishing characteristic of Snyder's unique use of imagistic parataxis, for as Charles Altieri, following Thomas Parkinson,[31] has noted, "this lack of tension is important because it distinguishes Snyder's lyrics from the expectations created by Modernism. Insofar as his poems are based on dialectic and juxtaposition, Snyder remains traditional, but the lack of tension leads to radically different emotional and philosophical implications."[32] Altieri contrasts Snyder's "lack of tension" with the unresolvable conflict between particulars in Yeats's "gyres" or with Eliot's reliance on a "transcendent still point" to unify particulars,[33] and he argues that Snyder "does not require heroic enterprise; reconciliation need not be imposed; it exists in fact."[34] Altieri's positive reading of Snyder's poetics arrives in the context of an earlier modernist poetics that is widely condemned for its varied attempts at reconciling difference and determining reading outcomes. Understood through Snyder's ontology, however, there is no need to unify the world; there is only the soteriological need to help others see that it is always already unified in "Buddha Nature."

Snyder's poetics of emptiness, following as it does the Yogācāran monism described earlier, reveals that the differentia of the poem cannot be juxtaposed per se, as they are (from the Yogācāran perspective, or from the perspective of an inclusive "Buddha Nature") revealed to be of one single emptiness. I am tempted to rewrite Snyder's or Su Dongpo's poem to illustrate this point by substituting the character for emptiness for each of the poem's characters:

空空 空空空
空空 空空空
空空 空空空
空空 空空空[35]

Taken as a visual field, this conceptual poem might serve to illustrate the absence of juxtaposition (insofar as any differentia in the poem appear as merely other instances of the same thing). However, the poem above cannot escape its own contextual/linguistic nature and would end up undermining the monistic 空 (emptiness) that subsumes Snyder's and Su's poems, since the first instance of emptiness that appears in the poem is contextually emptied by every following reiteration. The first emptiness becomes empty of its emptiness, which is further emptied, and the emptiness of this emptiness of emptiness is emptied, etc. Therefore, 空 空 would not adequately express Snyder's poetics of emptiness, since his must transcend language altogether. While "We Wash Our Bowls in This Water" is a compelling poem for its careful blending of imagistic parataxis and intertextual weave, the "emptiness" that governs its articulation would be more adequately signaled by a singular character 空 (like the answer to the koan, we began by asking if dogs have Buddha Nature). It is important to pause and think for a moment about the difference between the emptiness that takes place in language 空 空 (or what we might call the emptiness of language) and that which seeks to transcend it through monism, 空.

Snyder's poetics of emptiness, like that of the Yogācāran notion of a non-dual Mind more generally, succeeds by way of overcoming distinctions and even the ontological category of "difference" itself.[36] And if we follow the structuralist and poststructuralist view of language, it is even more clear that Snyder would have to transcend or discard language, which is, after all, only a vast system of contingent differences. For Snyder's poetry to manifest or signal monistic emptiness, it must do away with the contingent relational nature of language, because all linguistic meanings are "caused" or "dependent" upon this contextual condition (part of language's causal matrix is not, other than the fact that its distinctions and discriminations arise out of (and return to) the monistic emptiness that undergirds all things (Buddha Nature). Unlike language, however, *tathāgatagarbha*, "Buddha Nature," is "uncaused" (not subject to the law of *pratītyasamutpāda)* and therefore cannot be captured in language. This extralinguistic reality, or *rigpa,* is, therefore, the impossible telos of Snyder's poetics of emptiness. Yet, in the end, is this not one of the elements of Snyder's poetics that makes his poetry so compelling? His poetry is offered to us as a "skillful means" (as instruments carefully crafted from highly selective diction and an array of formal devices borrowed from Zennist readings of Chinese poetry and American modernist aesthetics) to help us escape the dualistic confines of language itself.[37]

It is important to make a clear demarcation between Snyder's extralinguistic "vision" of emptiness and Fenollosa's poetics, which locates emptiness within the causal nexus of language itself (as dependent origination), for Snyder's poetics of emptiness may have been far more influential than Fenollosa's (which, again, has not been read in its Buddhist sense). Yet, important Buddhist writing at the end of the twentieth century, like that of Leslie Scalapino, begins where Fenollosa leaves off. In her nonreferential, highly disjunctive poetry, she brings attention to the contingent nature of meaning-making by foregrounding its materiality (the emptiness of signification) and denies the existence of an ontologically stable emptiness "outside" its own, relational "emptiness." In a lecture entitled "Practitioners of Reality," given at Stanford University in 2003, she writes:

> Words do have referents, but these referents have no substance to them, being themselves merely label entities that depend on other label entities in a giant web where the only reality is the interrelatedness of the entities. There's no real substratum to this, and the only existence that things can be said to have is a very weak conventional one that is reflected in the pattern of interconnection—that is in the usage of language.[38]

Again, with strong echoes of Fenollosa's distinction between conventional completeness and ultimate incompleteness in language (discussed in Chapter 1), Scalapino also combines Hua Yan's notion of "Indra's net" with Nāgārjuna's two truths to articulate a concept of emptiness as contingency: nothing can exist independent of causes and conditions or have nonrelational (and thus autonomous) meaning. In this view, even emptiness is empty of "emptiness" (positive, autonomous presence), as it relies on other, different signifiers, like "fullness" or "completeness," to derive its meaning (and is thus "caused"). So the word "emptiness" 空 by itself cannot represent ultimate reality, from this view, as it proposes a false sense of ontological stability by hiding its supplements, its relational, contingent nature, 他然. The seemingly insignificant introduction of even one more character, 空空, reveals the dependent nature of meaning-making and subjects "emptiness" to the contingent emptiness of language itself.

At one level the difference between "emptiness" and "empty emptiness" may be thought of as a doctrinal argument (between say Madyamika and Yogācāra[39]), but it is clear to me that, of the two primary expressions of emptiness (negative and positive), the road Snyder chose to travel would offer less resistance to Romantic and transcendental forms of monistic ontology.[40] But this might also be one of the reasons for Snyder's significant success in integrating Buddhist ideas of emptiness and American Modernism more generally. Nevertheless, the paratactic, largely imagistic form of poems like "We Wash Our Bowls in This Water" draws upon (Zennist readings of) classical Chinese and Japanese poetry, not Romanticism and transcendentalism, to transmit its vision of a monistic "Buddha Nature." And I believe the interlinguistic foundation of his poetics of emptiness should raise additional questions regarding the status of translation in Snyder's work.

As we have already discussed, the "compromised" linguistic nature of Su Dongpo's "enlightenment verse" speaks from an (assumed) enlightened point of view outside the contingency of language through apophatic gestures alone. In a similar apophatic gesture, Han Shan writes:

> The pine sings, but there's no wind.
> Who can leap the world's ties
> And sit with me among the white clouds?[41]

Like Su Dongpo, the enlightened Han Shan is able to hear the non-linguistic teaching of nature: "pine singing without wind." Yet he is alone in his enlightenment, and he cannot communicate (through the relational nature of language) that which he has experienced beyond it.

> They don't get what I say
> & I don't talk their language.
> All I can say to those I meet:
> "Try and make it to Cold Mountain"[42]

For Snyder, and for Zen soteriological readings of Chinese poetry more generally, these poems are not simply apophatic expressions but are communicative insofar as they embody *upāya* (skillfulness-in-means) capable of helping us reach through language to pull us beyond it. Han Shan is already there. His is a poetry from the other side.

> My heart's not the same as yours.
> If your heart was like mine
> You'd get it and be right back here.[43]

Given the apophatic orientation of the nirvanic perspective, the Zen translator encounters not only the limits of language, but the limits of at least two languages.

Buddhist Romanticism and Transcendent Translation

Given the extralinguistic source of classical Chinese poetry attributed by Snyder's poetics, it is clear that he will run into a similar problem (or imagine a similar problem, depending on one's own interpretive frame) as faced by Wai-lim Yip in the next chapter—namely, how does one bring into English an "extralinguistic" experience of emptiness uniquely formulated in a cultural and poetic idiom as distant as classical Chinese poetry? Unlike Yip and Fenollosa, Snyder does not see the uniqueness of Chinese poetry in the Chinese language, or explicitly within a "Chinese worldview," but in the realized vision of the poets within a shared philosophical and aesthetic tradition. Therefore, Snyder does not foreground the structural disparities between English and Chinese, nor does he see a need to critique translation's systemic distortion and erasure of what Yip sees as a pre-predicative "Chinese way of seeing." After all, from the perspective of Tathāgatagarbha doctrine, all such East-West discriminations and dichotomies are less important than (one) Mind that gives rise to them. Instead, Snyder's discussion of translation tends to foreground the poet's enlightened vision and explores the ways in which he personally attempts to communicate that vision back into (another) language. In *The Real Work,* Snyder describes his process of translating Han Shan:

> I get the verbal meaning into mind as clearly as I can, but then make an enormous effort of visualization, to "see" what the poem says, non-linguistically, like a movie in your mind, and to feel it. If I can do this (and much of the time the poem eludes this effort) then I write the scene down in English. It is not a translation of the words, it is the same poem in a different language, allowing for the peculiar distortions of my own vision—but keeping it straight as possible.[44]

Snyder's translation theory reinforces the purely instrumental notion of language we have already seen (not so dissimilar from the aphoristic notion put forth in the *Zhuangzi,* of "getting the fish tossing the trap"), which allows him to "see" the signifieds independent of the systems of signification they rely on for their articulation. While Tathāgatagarbha doctrines may not rely as heavily upon vision-centered language as Snyder does,[45] it is easy to see how ocular-centric language offers Snyder an appealing set of concepts intuitively consistent with the desire to bypass or discard language.

In a more recent essay, published in the collection *The Poem Behind the Poem,* Snyder reveals a contemporary continuity with his earlier account of translation:

> The translator who wishes to enter the creative territory must make an intellectual and imaginative jump into the mind and world of the poet, and no dictionary will make this easier. In working with the poems of Han-shan, I have several times had a powerful sense of apprehending auras of nonverbal meaning and experiencing the poet's own mind-of-composition.[46]

Snyder attributes his ability to "jump into the mind and world of Han Shan" to the purely physical side of the Han Shan world: "the imagery of cold, height, isolation, mountains—is still available to our contemporary experience." And Snyder has experienced these things for himself, making him "at home in the archetypal land of Han-shan."[47] While it is tempting to attribute Snyder's visionary translation to his experience in the Sierra Nevadas, to do so would be to miss the metaphysical importance of his translation theory. In *The Real Work,* Snyder attributes his ability to recall visual details "as vividly as the primary experience" to his practice of Zazen, which reveals special qualifications for translating "extra-linguistic" poetry.[48]

In his essay "Amazing Grace," Snyder cites two basic modes of learning, roughly analogous to both Romanticism's and Zen's privileging of pre-predicative experience over linguistically (culturally) mediated experience: "direct experience" and "hearsay." Snyder goes on to say: "Nowadays most that we know comes through hearsay—through books, teachers, and television—keyed to only a minimal ground of direct contact with the world."[49] For Snyder, then, one can read about the Sierra Nevadas, see an episode of *Nature* devoted to it, or hear a lecture on its ecosystems, but these are all secondary to the "direct experience" of unmediated seeing. To "see the world without dualities" would be to behold it without language.

And while this idea of "immediate experience" may be, as Bob Perelman notes, a vestige of "anti-theoretical, counter cultural romanticism,"[50] it also reflects the broad "Zennist" discourses circulating during the mid-twentieth century. While perhaps tempting, I do not believe we can call this an "anti-theoretical" tendency, just a theoretical position that is heavily critiqued by current poststructuralist (and so-called "critical Buddhist") discourses. Snyder's particular application of Zen is in line with his period (and is similar to the positions held by D. T. Suzuki—as well as by innumerable Zen teachers who easily accommodated existing Western values).

Prior to acquiring the tools derived from the theoretical paradigm shifts (the so-called "linguistic turn") of the last several decades, Zennists commonly spoke of "going straight to things" in an "unmediated experience of the real."[51] Today, with scholars like David Loy, Bernard Faure, Dale Wright, and Donald Lopez, and Zen teachers like Newman Glass, Norman Fischer, as well as the more recent proliferation of Madyamika Buddhist discourses published by scholars like Jeffrey Hopkins and Jay Garfield, Snyder's poetics, founded during an earlier "wave" of transpacific migrations, may seem outdated but one must remember that Snyder, like everyone else, speaks from within a discrete cultural and historical nexus, and that his Zen studies, with its Yogācāran elements in tow, are not "anti-theoretical" but do offer a theoretical paradigm discordant with contemporary literary criticism (which privileges difference and sees language as a constituent element of all we perceive and know) and should not be exempt from criticism just because of its explicit heterocultural conditions.

Snyder as *Hagazussa*

> *It's a process of tearing yourself out of your personality and culture and putting yourself back in it again.* —SNYDER, *THE REAL WORK*

In Clayton Eshleman's essay "Imagination's Body and Comradely Display," he asserts that "Gary Snyder's assimilation of Far Eastern religion and culture is the most thorough of any post–World War II American Artist." Snyder is "a kind of *hagazussa* [a fence rider or boundary crosser]," Eshleman continues, "who took the Far East as the goal of his flight and, instead of remaining there or becoming an Eastern guru here, has brought his flight information to bear upon our culture and ecology via a resolutely American personality."[52] It would be difficult to argue against Eshleman's claim that Snyder's poetry reflects the most sustained and thorough "assimilation of Far Eastern religion and culture" after World War II, if we limit our discussion to Anglo-American poets. Snyder's study of East Asian languages at the University of California at Berkeley (1952–56); his long-term study of Zen in Japan (1956–68); his extensive travels and social relationships throughout Asia; and his life of "real work" in poetics, ecological activism, and teaching infused with these studies have granted Snyder's transpacific status a unique "authenticity." Figured as a *hagazussa,* Gary Snyder is read by Eshleman as American poetry's (if not America's) primary cultural intermediary to Asia. While Ernest Fenollosa spent more time in Japan and arguably had a greater impact on Japanese history, it is Snyder's, not Fenollosa's, Buddhism that came to impact American letters in the most direct way.

As I have already mentioned, Snyder's invocation of classical Chinese poetic form authenticates his own poetics of emptiness via Zennist hermeneutics. Snyder's life story itself is perhaps the most often cited source for the "authenticity" of his work. As is often noted, Snyder's poetry commonly invokes place, which in the case of his East Asian travels, tends to further Eshleman's claim for Snyder's role as "cultural emissary." For example, in Snyder's poem "At Maple Bridge," the intertextual relationship of Snyder's work to earlier Chinese poems is further "authenticated" because Snyder's poem is composed (or written as such) at the very spot in China where the Chinese poem Snyder is reworking is set. The original, Chinese poem reads:

"Night Docking Near Maple Bridge"

月	落	烏	啼	霜	滿	天
江	楓	漁	父	對	愁	眠
姑	蘇	城	外	寒	山	寺
夜	半	鐘	聲	到	客	船

My translation:

Moon sets crows caw frost filled sky.
River maples fishing lights can't find sleep
Outside Su Zhou, Cold Mountain Temple
Mid-night bells reach a visitor's boat

And here is Snyder's reworking of the poem:

"At Maple Bridge"
Men are mixing gravel and cement
At Maple bridge,

Down an alley by a tea-stall
From Cold Mountain temple;
Where Chang Chi heard the bell.
The stones step moorage
Empty, lapping water,
And the bell sound has traveled
Far across the sea.[53]

The "at" in Snyder's title immediately reveals Snyder's proximity to the "real" Maple Bridge where Zhang Ji wrote his famous quatrain. After establishing this proximity, Snyder's poem, like Zhang's before him, figures the transmission of emptiness as or through sound. The figuration recalls the story of the Sixth Chan patriarch Hui Ke, told in the *Platform Sutra*, where Hui Ke becomes enlightened upon hearing the sound of his knife knocking against a stalk of bamboo,[54] but this connection between sound and enlightenment can be found in numerous sutras and Chinese poems as well.[55]

Snyder's poem starts by situating the reader in modern China, where the sounds of its modernization fill the air around Maple Bridge. He then brings our attention to the "Empty, lapping water," presumably across which "the bell sound traveled," to reach Zhang Ji. But when Snyder redirects the bell's ring through an act of virtual enjambment with the last line, "Far across the sea," the bell's reverberation appears to be a thematization of the transpacific pathway whereby Buddhism has traveled to America. The past tense construction of the last line "and the bell sound has traveled," when combined with the new sounds of industrialization filling the air with its white noise, leads me to believe that rather than simply resonating across the ocean, the bell has, itself, immigrated to a land "far across the sea." This is a provocative reading that may not reflect the strange paradox of rising commercialism and growing religious activity in China today, but one that reflects instead Snyder's skepticism toward a rapidly industrializing and modernizing China increasingly known for its embrace of free-market capitalism, harsh treatment of Tibetan Buddhism, and eco-unfriendly policies. Yet it is important to note that China is not a monolith but a nation-state that holds within its boundaries wildly diverse cultural developments and inclinations as capable as the United States is of simultaneous religious fervor and consumerist materialism.

This is of course not the only time Snyder's poetry takes on a seemingly "righteous" position and may reveal a problem inherent in his poetics' attempt to overcome difference (through unifying emptiness), as it tends to position the poetic voice inside monistic *tathāgatagarbha* (Buddha Nature). Such a nirvanic position of enunciation can invest even the slightest innuendo with what I imagine is an unintended degree of authority. This authority is further codified by the inescapable web of reference to his life experiences in Asia and his Buddhist training in his own poetry and poetics, but especially in the hagiographic writing that surrounds him (and the Beat Generation more generally).[56] I want to stop short of assigning Snyder the title of cultural *hagazussa*, however, as such terms still traffic in the currency of what Rey Chow calls an "economy of idealized otherness."[57] Returning to the cross-cultural models discussed in the Prologue, I find the metaphorical language of "fences" to be ill suited for heterocultural literary criticism, given its blunt conceptual limitations. It is my belief that a myopic reading focused on questions of "authenticity or appropriation" "across fences," while perhaps more applicable to discussions of Snyder's relationship to Native American cultural texts and practices given its historically specific uniqueness,[58] would more likely obfuscate the dynamic, heterocultural nature of Snyder's transpacific poetics, by reducing important theoretical and aesthetic practices into inert cultural artifacts more suited for adorning the walls of classrooms than for the critical conversations held within or without them. But I hope this chapter has more than adequately demonstrated that Snyder's transpacific imaginary does constitute, as Eshleman clearly signals in his reading of Snyder, an important and influential example of heterocultural production. Problematic (from the perspective of other schools of Buddhism and contemporary postmodern poetics) yet not illegitimate, influential and generative yet often too narrowly doctrinal and too closely fitted to existing Romantic values (monism), the significance of Snyder's transformation of classical Chinese poetry into the principal catalyst for an American poetics of emptiness cannot be overstated, yet should not be read uncritically either. He offers his readers a poetry that enacts (as much as it is possible) notions of positive emptiness, which reflect the views of a vast population of Mahayana Buddhists alive today, but his is not the only poetics of emptiness to emerge from the rising and falling mirrors of the Pacific.

PART TWO

Daoist Imaginaries

4 / 無 Language of Emptiness: Wai-lim Yip's Daoist Project

Thirty years ago before I was initiated into Chan, I saw mountains as mountains, rivers as rivers. Later when I got an entrance into knowledge, I saw mountains not as mountains, rivers not as rivers. Now that I have achieved understanding of the substance, mountains are still mountains, rivers still rivers.

—WAI-LIM YIP, *DIFFUSION OF DISTANCES*

In China Wai-lim Yip (葉維廉, Ye Weilian) is recognized as a major contributor to modern East-West poetics, and he was the central focus of an academic conference held at the Center for New Poetry at Beijing University in March 2008. At the conference, more than forty scholars from throughout China and abroad gave over two dozen papers exploring Yip's fifty years of poetic and critical writing, and Yip's book *Zhongguo shi xue* (Chinese poetics) was honored as "one of the most important books of the last century."[1] And while Yip has not received this kind of attention in America, his close ties to American poetry communities, coupled with a nearly four-decade-long (English) career as a translator, poet, anthologist, and teacher of East-West poetry at the University of California at San Diego, make him an important figure in the popularization of Chinese poetry and an explicitly "Daoist" poetics of emptiness in America as well.[2] Since the mid-1970s, Yip has offered American (and Chinese) readers a description of classical Chinese poetry as an immanent vision of the "real-life world," unmediated by ego, or temporal, spatial, or logical frames. He gives us a vision of a poetics of emptiness (Yip uses the term 無言 *wuyan*, "empty language") whereby poets, and even poetry itself, step out of the way to let things present themselves "as they are."

In this chapter, I want to explore how Yip combines equal parts translation theory, ancient Chinese philosophy, and American modernist poetics—the tradition of Pound and Fenollosa, among others—to create a unique and very influential poetics of emptiness. Moreover, I also want to use the discussion of Yip's work to introduce a more inclusive model of Daoist poetry and poetics, which I believe complements his life work by decoupling it from the vestiges of cultural essentialism too easily co-opted by the very discourses he sets out to undermine.

Locating Yip's Emptiness

When first encountering the poetics of emptiness espoused by Wai-lim Yip, one will likely draw strong connections to Gary Snyder's poetics. After all, they both see classical Chinese poetry as an attempt to bring a non-linguistic "real" into language through a uniquely endowed poetic tradition, and they both describe non-linguistic—that is, pure apprehension of the "real"—as a "seeing" authenticated by East Asian philosophical (or religious) discourses. Given the often murky waters that both connect and separate Daoist and Buddhist discourses (and Snyder's and Yip's in particular), it might be helpful to begin this chapter with a look at their radically divergent interpretations of the koan cited as the chapter's epigram. Yip's "Daoist" reading of this well-known Chan/Zen koan reveals the metaphysical presumptions he brings not only to East Asian philosophy and poetry, but also, as we will see, to his popular heterocultural vision of the imagist-objectivist-projectivist desire for a poetics of unmediated immediacy.

Yip's "Daoist reading" of the koan follows.

> This can be taken as representing three stages of our perception of reality. The first stage, "seeing mountains as mountains, rivers as rivers," is comparable to the innocent or naïve mode of apprehending reality. This mode is naïve in the sense that it is not cluttered by intellectuality [. . .] before any epistemological activity enters into their consciousness.[3]

We can see that Yip privileges this first stage as a period in life where the mind "naturally" relates to nature 自然 (*ziran*, natural/self-so) by not intervening in it, or 無為 (*wuwei*, non-intervention).[4] By engaging in *wuwei*, one can, according to Yip, apprehend things in their *ziran* (natural self-generating/transformation), due to the absence of "conscious intellectual language." Yip then argues that "when a conscious attempt to express this response in language is made, we find ourselves moving into the second stage of perception, 'seeing mountains not as mountains, rivers not as rivers,' in which epistemological activity is at work." Yip clearly reads this second "stage of perception" as an obfuscation and distortion of the "real," which lacks the proper ethical relation to nature's otherness. Yip continues, "This activity leads us away from the fresh, direct appeal of landscape to seek in the world of ideas for relationships and meanings." And finally he reads the third stage—"seeing mountains still as mountains, rivers still rivers"—"as an achieved perception" rather than a naïve one, where the onlooker comes to again affirm landscape in its "original existence as independent and self-sufficient [*ziran*]."[5]

Yip's interpretation is strikingly different from the standard Buddhist interpretations of this text since he takes for granted the ontological category of "landscape," or "things," whereas a Buddhist interpretation would use the koan to illustrate Nāgārjuna's "two truths," discussed in the Introduction: that phenomena are both ultimately empty and yet conventionally real. The tripartite formulation of the koan reveals the influence of Tiantai (Ja: Tendai) Buddhism as it reflects Zhiyi's "Three Truths," also discussed in the Introduction and Chapter 1. This first "stage of perception" represents not Yip's idealized non-linguistic perception, but simply the conventional (and erroneous) view that mountains have a self-inherent existence ("nouness" or "thingness" for Fenollosa). The second truth points to the law of *pratītya-samutpāda* (dependent origination/emptiness), which reveals that all "things" are empty. This understanding then leads one to no longer view mountains as mountains, but as dependently arising aggregates of phenomena. Yet, after further study one finds out that phenomena are both "conventionally real" and "ultimately empty" at the same time, and so one does not return to seeing mountains as mountains in an ultimate sense but does accept this provisional reality as conventionally true.

A Buddhist reader influenced by Yogācāra idealism, like Gary Snyder, may read the first stage in a fashion similar to the Tendai Buddhist interpretation above, but the emptiness of the second stage would be described in terms of the Mind. The second stage would encourage one to view mountains as transient manifestations of the Mind, or Suchness, rather than as "mountains" per se. In the third stage, one's understanding that "All" is "Suchness," or "Mind," reveals no need to differentiate between the Mind and its manifestations, which allows one to return to the conventional designations of things while never losing sight of their "emptiness" in Oneness.[6]

Yip's Daoist (mis)reading of the Buddhist koan follows a tradition of many Buddhist or Daoist partisans who have cited texts of the other tradition to illustrate a point that may violate the conventional hermeneutics of the tradition from which it was taken. So, while Fenollosa, Snyder, and Yip may all believe that Chinese poetry allows for a more direct experience of reality, what that reality is (or, more specifically, what its emptiness is) remains radically distinct.

Before exploring his Daoist poetics in more detail, I should note that many of Yip's foundational arguments originated before his serious engagement with Daoism. The seeds of Yip's Daoist project lie within his continual engagement with problems of translation and his peculiar journey as both a Chinese and American modernist poet, and long after his movement toward Daoism we will find translation at the heart of his poetics. Born in Zhongshan, Guangdong Province, Yip's early years were punctuated by harrowing escapes from Communist and Japanese military campaigns, which forced him to move to Hong Kong as an adolescent, and again later to Taiwan as an undergraduate (he received a BA from National Taiwan University and an MA from Taiwan Normal University); finally, he moved to the United States as a graduate student. Yip began writing poetry early on; he was an active member of the Hong Kong poetry scene during the 1950s and later became a noted member of Taiwanese modernists associated with the Epoch Poetry Society. Yet Yip did not publish his first important volume, *The Fugue,* until 1963—the same year he received his MFA from the University of Iowa. His next volume, *Crossing* (1969), came two years after he received his PhD from Princeton and a year after he accepted a teaching position at the University of California at San Diego. All of his later work has been published during his tenure at UCSD.

Yip's poetry, like his critical writings, reveals a uniquely transpacific vision of American and Chinese Modernism. During his years in Taiwan Yip's work integrated elements derived from his reading and later translations of T. S. Eliot's *Wasteland* and the "Burnt Norton" section of the *Four Quartets,* as well as works by St. John Perse. According to Julia Lin, one can trace Yip's characteristic use of ellipses, extreme compression, and intense lyricism to Eliot and other American modernists.[7] In Yip's volume *The Fugue,* we see and hear a heterocultural poetry, which, like Pound's and Eliot's work, is both thoroughly modern and traditional at the same time, insofar as it is composed in a literary, formal language borrowed from antiquity yet revitalized within thoroughly modernist verse forms. What I find most interesting about the progression of Yip's poetics is that he consistently reaches across the Pacific for poetic sustenance. When in Taiwan he drew heavily upon Eliot and Perse, and later, in the United States, he turned to a vision of Daoist poetics drawn from classical Chinese poetry. In both cases, however, this reaching is never complete, insofar as his poetics is always already informed by both traditions and always grappling with the limitations of translation.[8]

While Yip translated Eliot and Perse early on, it was not until his careful study of Ezra Pound's *Cathay* that we see him become fully invested in the philosophical, political, and cultural problems of translation. This is also the time when Yip breaks with Eliot and Perse, with their elusive discursive ironies, and begins his career as an American modernist in the mode of Pound, Williams, and Olson, all of whom sought a more direct engagement with things, their direct, ontological "thereness." He begins his study of *Cathay* with a list of "steps" that he believes will "not defend or condemn," but widen "the scope of understanding Pound as poet by discussing his role as translator of Chinese."[9] The first of these steps will preoccupy Yip through to the present:

> 1. To look at the problems of translation from Chinese into English, and in particular, to discuss the difficulty of approximating in English the peculiar mode of representation constituted by Chinese syntax.[10]

Following this directive, Yip problematizes a number of English translations of classical Chinese poetry that destroy the "peculiar mode" of Chinese syntax in a manner we have already seen in his later work (but without the explicit Daoist metaphysics at work). For example, he, like Snyder in the previous chapter,[11] gives us the first two lines of Du Fu's "Spring Scene," followed by a literal translation:

[	A	]	[	B	]
noun	verb	noun	noun	verb/adj	
guó	pò		shān	hé	zài
國	破		山	河	在
chéng	chūn		cǒo	mù	shēn
城	春		草	木	深

Empire (is) broken (:) mountains and rivers remain
Spring (in) city (:) grass and trees (grow) thick.

Yip then gives several English translations of the lines:

> W. J. B. Fletcher (1933):
> A nation though fallen, the land yet remains.

When spring fills the city, its foliage is dense.

Edna W. Underwood (1929)
The country is broken—Nothing but mountains and hills
When spring comes back to the city, the trees and the grasses grow
   green.[12]

Yip then asks, "What is the relationship of Group A and Group B, syntactically speaking? Is it true that one clause is subordinate to another, as both Fletcher and Underwood have it?"[13] Yip shows how another translator (in this case, William Hung in 1952) avoids subordination:

The country is shattered. Only the landscape remains.
Spring in the city? Yes, unpruned trees and overgrown weeds.[14]

But Yip argues that Hung's translation also "finds it [the relation of A and B] too abrupt to leave the two groups standing all by themselves without some kind of connection . . . and so reintroduces the relation (syntactic commitment), changing the basic mode of the original presentation." Finally, Yip concludes that "in the original, the two phases of perception [A and B], like two cones of light, cut into one another simultaneously. Any attempt to connect them even syntactically will destroy the simultaneity and fall back on the logic of succession."[15] Like Pound, who first resorts to a convoluted metaphor of intersecting cones of energy to explain vorticism before adopting the Chinese "ideogram" as his model,[16] Yip looks to a scientific language before remapping his ideas onto a self-described Daoist poetics.

Yip's transition to his later explicitly Daoist language follows closely the pioneering heterocultural writings of Chang Chung-yuan, a professor of philosophy at the University of Hawaii and the author of perhaps the most important (other than Yip's work) seed text for later configurations of Daoist-oriented transpacific poetics of emptiness, *Creativity and Taoism.*[17] In Chang's work, we see in English for the first time a comprehensive Daoist reading of classical Chinese poetry cast in a language not only accessible to American readers but nearly apposite with certain strains of American modernist poetics, a connection Yip would bring to its full fruition. While Yip does not cite Chang's work as a precedent to his own,[18] it is instructive to read Chang's description of classical Chinese poetry, for it is the coupling of these philosophical claims with the structuralist translation criticism of Yip that facilitates the full articulation of his Daoist American Modernism.

Like Yip, Chang offers English translations of particularly imagistic classical Chinese poems by poets like Wang Wei and Ma Zhiyuan before making philosophical claims regarding the forms of consciousness they make available: "The reader is directly confronted with the objective reality which the [Chinese] poet originally faced. The subjectivity of the reader and the objective reality in the poem interfuse without obstruction and distortion from the interference of the poet."[19] Chang goes on to state that "Chinese poets penetrate into the source of things and reveal their true nature . . . no mere visual description." And, making the philosophical claims even more clear and dramatic, he asserts that "the reader is made to experience what the poet originally experienced from the actual situation. He faces directly the objective reality in the poem and shares in the ontological experience of the poet."[20]

For Yip, classical Chinese poetry will share in these exact attributes, but unlike Chang, Yip converts this "Daoist" description of ancient Chinese poetry into a vibrant living poetics and critical methodology. Abstracted from this concept of an "empty language," *wuyan*, which allows readers to see the world without the prism of linguistic (or, by extension, epistemological mediation), Yip argues that his Daoist poetics offers tools capable of resolving cross-cultural misunderstanding and distortion as well. Writing prior to Edward Said's *Orientalism*, Yip claimed to have found a way to both acknowledge and challenge universal claims made by Western structures of knowledge, and he applied these critiques to translation practices decades before Lawrence Venuti or Tejaswini Niranjana's postcolonial translation theories, which raise similar concerns regarding translation's imperialist distortions.[21] Yip situates his ideas within the broader context of what Robert Duncan called a "symposium of the whole": "a totality [in which] all the old excluded orders must be included. The female, the proletariat, the foreign, the animal and the vegetative; the unconscious and the unknown."[22] For Yip, a close friend and colleague of Jerome Rothenberg at UCSD, was the principal figure to bring East-West studies and poetics to bear upon the discipline of ethnopoetics, for which UCSD convened conferences and issued anthologies, responding to Duncan's call for a "symposium of the whole."[23] According to Yip, such a symposium can only truly take place if it integrates the two central Daoist concepts, *ziran* (natural/self-so) and *wuwei* (non-intervention). He asks "whether the indigenous aesthetic horizon is allowed to represent itself *as it is* (*ziran*) and *not as it is framed* [i.e., intervened upon, the opposite of *wuwei*] within the hermeneutical habits and the poetic economy of the West."[24]

It is hard to overestimate the role colonial and postcolonial experiences have played in Yip's turn toward these Daoist ideals. In his still unpublished autobiography, Yip describes his early experience of Japanese imperialist aggression and his schooling in British-controlled Hong Kong, where "the goal of colonial education is to produce humans as mere service instruments void of national or cultural identity whose sole life purpose, as it were, is to emulate the life style of their colonizer."[25] And for Yip, Daoism provides a powerful anticolonial discourse capable of challenging uneven power differentials, like those in play during his life spent under various forms of colonial oppression (and later as a member of the Chinese Diaspora abroad). According to Yip, Daoism, or more specifically, the Lao-Zhuang tradition (which refers to two texts: the *Daodejing* 道德經 and the *Zhuangzi* 莊子 produced between 6 BC and 3 BC), was a response to the Confucian naming system (名制) of the feudalistic Zhou dynasty (12 BC–6 BC), which sustained various hierarchies in Chinese society by codifying separate and unequal classes where *subjects* 臣, *sons* 子, and *wives* 婦 were subjugated to the uncontested power of *lords* 君, *fathers* 父, and *husbands* 夫. According to Yip, "The Daoist Project is a counter-discourse to the territorializations of power, an act to disarm and deframe the tyranny of language."[26] So for Yip, Duncan's "symposium of the whole" offers a cognate concept of an inclusive worldview that would, like Daoism, allow for a free expression of self-generating, self-transforming phenomena, or what Yip calls, in shorthand, 無言獨化, "empty language, self-transforming nature."

After Edward Said, most discussions of cultural appropriations and distortions take as their starting point the colonial, postcolonial, and neocolonial contexts of cultural exchanges. Distortions take place because Western representations of the other serve to reify cultural differences as a means of legitimating cultural hierarchies, or in Said's words, "dominating, restructuring, and having authority over the Orient."[27]

While Yip's work may be sympathetic to the last point, he would have to disagree with Said's assertion that Orientalism (in its most pernicious sense) is a "style of thought based upon an ontological and epistemological distinction made between 'the Orient' and (most of the time) the 'Occident.'"[28] He would have to disagree with Said because Yip's work presupposes that the primary obstacle to more effective cross-cultural interpretation is the *a priori* existence of radically different cultural paradigms à la Benjamin Whorf's famous hypothesis of structural linguistic/metaphysical incompatibility.[29]

To illustrate what he sees as the difficulty of his critical Daoist project,

Yip cites an imaginary dialogue penned by Martin Heidegger between Heidegger and a Japanese intellectual in order to present the long-held belief that there is an insurmountable wall separating Asian and Western philosophy and poetics. Heidegger writes:

> Inquirer: The danger of our dialogues was hidden in language itself, not in what we discussed, not in the way in which we tried to do so.
>
> Japanese: But Count Kuki[30] had uncommonly good command of German, and of French and English, did he not?
>
> I: Of course, he could say in European languages whatever was under discussion. But we were discussing *Iki*[31] and here it was I to whom the spirit of the Japanese language remained closed—as it is to this day.
>
> J: The languages of the dialogue shifted everything into European.
>
> I: Yet the dialogue tried to say the essential nature of Eastasian art and poetry.
>
> J: Now I am beginning to understand better where you smell the danger. The language of dialogue constantly destroyed the possibility of saying what the dialogue is about.
>
> I: Some time ago I called language, clumsily enough, the house of Being. If man by virtue of his language dwells within the claim and call of Being, then we Europeans presumably dwell in an entirely different house than Eastasian man.
>
> J: Assuming that the languages of the two are not merely different but are other in nature, and radically so.
>
> I: And so, a dialogue from house to house remains nearly impossible.[32]

Here it is clear that Yip more or less accepts Heidegger's notion of cultural incompatibility as *a priori*, but he argues that Daoism may, by virtue of its ability to dissolve the dualism of subject and object, hold the key to dissolving the wall between the East and West. Again, he argues that the concept of *ziran,* a category of unmolested alterity (a term I am using, not Yip), and *wuwei,* the principal method whereby one integrates the self's *ziran* with the *ziran* of otherness without adequation, appropriation, or distortions together can provide a metaphysical foundation for ethical, heterocultural dynamics heretofore unavailable within Western philosophy.

As Yip argues: "The Taoist worldview rejects the premise that the structure of phenomenon (Nature), changing and ongoing, is the same as we conceive it to be. All conscious efforts to generalize, formulate, classify and order it will necessarily result in some form of restriction, reduction or even distortion." He continues, "We impose these conceptions, which, by definition, must be partial and incomplete, upon phenomena at the peril of losing touch with the concrete, original appeal of the totality of things."[33] Of course, this "Taoist worldview," insofar as Yip is describing it here, does not differ entirely from that of Western philosophy, whether one is concerned with Platonic idealism, Christian metaphysics, or the Kantian distinction between noumena and phenomena (among many more examples). Western philosophy has taken "nature" to be something distinct from how we conceive it to be. The difference with which Yip's Daoism is concerned, however, is that the primary obstacle standing between nature and its perception is the language we use (or do not use) to describe it. Of course, this point can also be found throughout Western philosophy to the present (apophatic Christianity, which claims that the nature of God cannot be captured in language, comes to mind here). Yet both the *Daodejing* and *Zhuangzi* take the linguistic barrier to be central to its philosophical agenda, more intently than Western philosophy and theology more generally. For Yip (and many earlier Chinese poet/critics from Lu Ji 陸機, Si Kongtu 司空圖, and Su Dongpo 蘇東坡, to Yan Yu 嚴羽, etc.[34]), classical Chinese poetry has directly engaged Lao-Zhuang's critique of language by developing poetic forms that attempt to avoid cognitive reductions and what Yip calls "epistemological elaborations." "The main aim [of Chinese poetry]," Yip writes," "is to receive, perceive, and disclose nature the way nature comes or discloses itself to us, undistorted."[35] The natural, unmediated, aesthetic *ziran* is, for Yip, the by-product of linguistic *wuwei*. By following *wuwei* to behold *ziran*, poets can avoid "disfiguring things in their immanent presences by allowing them to disclose the dimension of their immediate thereness."[36] If translators could do the same, they, too, according to this logic, could avoid "disfiguring" the original's ability to "allow things to disclose themselves."

To ground this otherwise abstract theoretical notion of a *wuyan*, Yip returns to the rhetorical and methodological trope of translation. For example, Yip gives us an interlinear translation for the first two lines of Li Bai's poem 送有人 ("Seeing off a friend"):

清　山　横　北　　郭
green/mountain(s)/lie across/north/wall
白　水　遶　東　　城
white/water/wind around/east/city[37]

As we have already seen, throughout both his critical prose and his anthologies of Chinese poetry, Yip gives the reader literal, word-for-word translations of the poetic line so that they can try to *see* their meanings without significant alteration. He wants the reader to notice the absence of authorial presence, the bare, near paratactic quality of the lines whereby *things* are allowed to exist side-by-side, as they might in a painting, which is to say, without what he calls "epistemological elaborations." Yip then compares his literal translations to two canonical English translations:

> *Where* blue hills cross the northern sky,
> *Beyond* the moat which girds the town,
> Twas here . . . Giles, 1898

> *With* a blue line of mountains north of the wall,
> And east of the city a white curve of water,
> Here you must . . . Bynner, 1920[38]

Yip then writes: "Whereas in the original we see things working upon us, in the versions of Giles and Bynner we are *led* to these things by way of intellectual, directive devices ('where,' 'with,' etc.). Clearly, what has happened here is that a different sort of hermeneutical habit of perceiving and reading has intruded upon a rather clear-cut condition or state of being."[39] In this later example drawn from Yip's self-consciously "Daoist" poetics, we can see many similarities to his earlier discussions of incompatible worldviews/languages. The difference lies in Yip's new language to describe the Chinese worldview, language that comes with powerful metaphysical claims that the reason the English always fails to capture the original lies in the fact that classical Chinese poetry is a *wuyan*. For Yip, most Western translators cannot stay "out of the poem," nor can they "think with the things," and therefore they cannot transmit the original's *wuyan*.

It is at this point that some readers might suspect that Yip is moving further than simply defending the distinct "Chinese worldview" animating classical Chinese poetry, to asserting its superiority over other languages and philosophical traditions.[40] In light of this, readers today might move to dismiss Yip's argument for its apparent cultural essentialism, and I will discuss this important point at some length in a moment, but I would argue that dismissing Yip's transpacific imaginary in this way would be an all too convenient way to avoid the complex heterocultural conditions that undergird it. If we are to come to understand Yip's significant influence on East-West poetry and poetics over the past several decades, we must be willing to move beyond such rhetorical tropes of Western literary criticism to explore the heterocultural configuration of American modernist and Daoist concepts and aesthetic in his poetics of emptiness. However, one cannot ignore this creeping essentialism either. Therefore, I would like to explore some of the most problematic aspects of Yip's "Daoist" project before turning more fully to its American modernist and Daoist origins.

The Problem of Translation

As I have been stressing from the beginning, Yip's poetics has been continually formulated in relation to his practice as a translator, and I would go so far as to say that even his understanding of Chinese philosophy cannot be decoupled from translation. Yet it would be a mistake to subject his poetics to its theories of translation since the translative moment is but an aperture through which Yip enters his Daoist "vision" of the real. While Yip is certainly right when he points to the impossibility of fully translating classical Chinese poetry into English without transforming it into something else, I have never been totally comfortable with his description of this transformation as a "distortion." In most cases, I would argue that a word like "distortion" used across the board to describe a translation process from one language to another places too much emphasis on stable source texts with a limited number of set reading practices, as opposed to an open polysemy that translation merely contributes to but cannot replace (or erase). If we were only talking about translation, it would appear to me that his concerns could be overcome by simply viewing translation as a supplementation of the sociolinguistic nexus of the original text, as opposed to its interlinguistic equivalent. Such a move would immediately undermine any attempt made by Western translators to assert authority over the Chinese "originals." However, Yip's assertion that English translations of classical Chinese poetry violently erase the original Chinese worldview is primarily concerned with his reading of Chinese philosophy (through translation) than with literary translation per se.

By arguing that Chinese poetry can be used as a *wuyan* capable of "getting out of the way of 'things themselves,'" Yip perhaps inadvertently replaces transcendent signifieds with translative origins. That is to say, in the context of translation, his terms situate Chinese *as* the "real-life world," which is dislocated from its pre-predicative state when translated into "obfuscating language" that is coded as discursive English. Language is, therefore, broken into two kinds: *wuyan*, as embodied in the non-obfuscating forms of nouns and verbs common to Chinese ("a spotlight that brightens objects emerging from the real world"), and obfuscating, predicative particles common to English, which force "the world" into closed "epistemological elaborations" removed from the perceptual act itself.[41] The bifurcation of language into these two distinct *kinds* not only overdetermines the transparency of Chinese, however, but it also conversely concretizes English (written in a discursive fashion) into a rigid system incapable of interpretive slippages, a truly untenable claim.

By using translation to replace the golden thread between signifier and transcendental signified with a new thread between English signifiers and Chinese signifieds (which is both the sign and referent), Yip's ethnographic mediation allows him a unique, almost oracular proximity to the "real." I say "oracular" because Yip's translations work as an oracle through which, he believes, he can *see* the "real-life world" without linguistic mediation. The transparency of *wuyan*/non-language poetry allows for a direct *vision* whereby the Chinese reader (in this instance, Yip) can *see* unmediated "life world," while non-Chinese readers must make do with language (translations). While Chang Chung-yuan presented an apposite view of classical Chinese, Chang's confidence in the transparent condition of translation led him to believe that the translations he provided his readers would grant them access to pre-predicative experience. For Yip, you need more than a Daoist poem; you need a Daoist translative methodology to grant access to this unmediated, empty language.

The Dao of American Modernism

However, as I hope to show, Yip does not stop, as Benjamin Whorf would have, at this essentialist reading of static language systems incapable of change (locking worldviews in place for all time). Instead, in a later essay, "Syntax and Horizon of Representation," Yip changes gears by arguing that the Pound-Williams strain of Modernism, drawing upon Chinese poetry, has found a means of accommodating the Daoist worldview in English. Yip writes: "In 1911, before he came into contact with Chinese poetry, Pound argued, 'The artist seeks out the luminous detail and presents it. He does not comment.' After his contact with Chinese poetry, he [Pound] wrote, 'It is because certain Chinese poets have been content to set forth their matter without moralizing and without comment that one labors to make a translation.'"[42] Later, Yip quotes William

Carlos Williams's famous dictum "no ideas but in things," and argues that "Williams wanted to see 'the thing itself' without forethought or afterthought but with great intensity of perception."[43] Finally, to complete his identification with the Pound/Williams/Projectivist poetic lineage, he points to the fact that Charles Olson and Robert Creeley (as well as Gary Snyder), "in step with Pound and Williams, postulated that 'The objects which occur at any given moment of composition . . . are, can be, must be treated exactly as they do occur therein and not by any idea or preoccupations from outside the poem . . . , must be handled as a series of objects in field . . . a series of tensions . . . space-tensions of a poem . . . the acting-on-you of the poem."[44] Stephen Fredman correctly points to several elements within Olson's "Projective Verse" that reflect notions largely in line with Buddhist values, but many of these would have struck Yip as further grounds for a Daoist Modernism:

> The admonition that the poet move from one perception to the next without stopping to cogitate ("in any given poem always, always one perception must must must MOVE, INSTANTER, ON ANOTHER!"); and the proposal of a new aesthetic of "objectism," which is "the getting rid of the lyrical interference of the individual as ego, of the 'subject' and his soul, that peculiar presumption by which western man has interposed himself between what he is as a creature of nature . . . and those other creations of nature which we may, with no derogation, call 'objects.'[45]

One will notice throughout Yip's writing, however, that his identification with this strain of American Modernism holds only so far as it tends to ascribe to the "peculiar mode of representation constituted by Chinese syntax," as distinct from the more conventional English syntax in which one finds connectives directing discursive thought from point to point.

If we return to Yip's initial allusion to Duncan's "symposium of the whole," we can see that for Yip, the Pound/Williams/Projectivist lineage of American Modernism has already succeeded in widening the "Western aesthetic horizon" to accommodate the "Chinese mode of perception."[46] By attempting to recover "the original ground, where we find the given as given," American modernists, like the poets of classical Chinese verse, "liberate themselves from the accustomed house of thought so that language acts try not to disfigure things in their immanent presences but to make them disclose the dimension of their immediate thereness."[47]

For Yip, therefore, one can deploy modernist aesthetic conventions to translate classical Chinese poems while preserving what Yip sees as the Daoist *wuyan*, the "transparent language" of the originals.

Take, for instance, the following translation of "Stayover at Chien River" (宿建德江):

yí	zhōu	jì	yān	zhǔ				
移	舟	泊	煙	渚	move	boat	moor smoke shore	
rì	mù	kè	chóu	xīn				
日	暮	客	愁	新	sun	dusk traveler	grief	new
yě	kuàng	tiān	dī	shù				
野	曠	天	低	樹	wilds far-reaching sky low/er tree			
jiāng	qīng	yuè	jìn	rén				
江	清	月	近	人	river clear	moon	near/s man	

Yip translates this poem as:

A boat slows,
Moors by
Beach-run in smoke.
Sun fades:
a traveler's sorrow
freshens.
Open wilderness.
Wide Sky.
A stretch of low trees.
Limpid river:
clear moon
close to
man.[48]

Compare the presentation of this poem to Williams's poetry and to any number of modernist American poets who employ the left-aligned, short-lined, vertical form of free verse. The utilization of short line breaks distributes the weight of a/the poem away from syntax's linear grammar toward an archipelago of visual datum suspended paratactically. The effect in English is not so dissimilar to the "horizon of syntax" Yip attributes to Daoist-infused classical Chinese poetry insofar as the poet recedes into the background, and the differentia of what Yip calls the "real-life world" are presented without "epistemological elaborations."

Yip's argument is most poignantly illustrated by his continual references to the imagistic poems of Gary Snyder, and particularly by a series of modernist montage poems by Robert Duncan that appear in Yip's essay "Syntax and Horizon of Representation":

The Fire   Passages 13

jump	stone	hand	leaf	shadow	sun
day	splash	coin	light	downstream	fish
first	loosen	under	boat	harbor	circle
old	earth	bronze	dark	wall	waver
new	smell	purl	close	wet	green
now	rise	foot	warm	hold	cool[49]

The above examples reveal for Yip how modernist montage, like classical Chinese poetry, allows words to stretch out into a horizon that "radiates more connections than conventional syntactical structures can handle."[50] In light of the overlapping aesthetics of Anglo-Modernism and Yip's "Daoist worldview," one might argue that Yip's poetics of emptiness is simply a rearticulation of American Modernism (with its desire for greater immediacy with the world) in a language culled from Daoist discourses. But it would be important to note that the transpacific migrations moved both ways, as Yip infused his ideas directly into the American poetry communities that inspired him by publishing his heterocultural poetics in collections of work, like George Quasha and Jerome Rothenberg's anthology *America: A Prophecy* in 1973.[51] Since the intent of ethnopoetics was to redefine the past and present of American poetry through translation methods imbued with "New American Poetry's" experimental forms,[52] it became a natural fit for Yip's work.

Yet Yip's "Daoist Modernism" (which he believes can break through the limitations of Western discursive language) also becomes his model for contemporary Chinese poetry, which he believes is in danger of losing its Daoist worldview to Western linguistic and epistemic encroachments. In his book *Modern Chinese Poetry,* Yip discusses the danger of the Westernization of *baihua* (modern, colloquial Chinese) in contemporary Chinese (in this case, Taiwanese) poetry, and introduces his modernist/Daoist poetics as a possible model of resistance. In this work, Yip leaves (in part) his role as literary critic behind and speaks from the position of the Daoist modernist poet himself. He writes:

One passenger, who is not sleeping, unconsciously becomes silence itself. . . . Limits of space and limits of time do not exist in the consciousness of this passenger. He has *another hearing, another vi-*

sion. He hears voices we normally do not hear. He sees activities across a space not to be seen by the physical eye. Nor is the passenger conscious of any linear, causal developments between or among these things . . . and prose is a linear structure defined by limits of space and time, so this passenger writes a poem.[53]

The passenger in Yip's poetics statement is himself, but following Yip's poetics, we could just as easily say the passenger is any Chinese poet today who shares his Daoist/modernist poetics. As a poet, Yip chooses to include far more classical Chinese words than his contemporaries, but, as a modernist, he has never sought a return to classical regulated verse forms. Nevertheless, he admonishes his fellow poets to adopt the Daoist metaphysics that underlie *wenyan*, classical Chinese. For he argues that *wenyan*, as opposed to *baihua* (modern colloquial Chinese), is "conductive to this cinematic presentation which emphasizes phases of perception through spotlighting activities rather than through analysis."[54] Yip, following Fenollosa, scorns the "analytical" abstraction of discursive language and argues that relying on *baihua* in one's poetry will lead to an abandonment of Chinese poetry's Daoist roots unless one consciously disrupts its propensity for "epistemological elaborations." Yip explains that the discursive quality of *baihua* results from its origin in classical narrative prose, which relies on linear plot developments, explanation, and causal relationships. Yet he argues:

> The situation is worsened by the intrusion of Western sciences, systems of logic, and forms of poetry. The *baihua* is being Europeanized (as the Chinese called it) in the process of translation (both journalistic and literary) . . . , introduction of Occidental syntax, adoption of foreign grammatical frameworks as bases for the Chinese sentence, and application of punctuation to regulate and clarify Chinese linguistic structures. All of these were intended, no doubt, to tell the world that we have just as much logic and are just as scientific as the West, as if poetic ambiguity and richness were a shame![55]

Yip argues that contemporary Chinese poets have to contend not only with these linguistic changes but also with the shift in aesthetic perception formed by the changes within poetic language itself. Yet Yip holds out hope for *baihua* poetry, since contemporary Chinese poets can eliminate connectives and other discursive particles, merge with objects, and use "anti-linear structures," etc. When addressing contemporary Chinese poets (and readers), Yip tends to emphasize not only the negative transpacific influences upon Chinese poetry (imposition of discursive logic), but also the positive influence of paratactic, montage, or elliptic compositional modes in modernist poetry as well. While he does not go as far as Chen Xiaomei in tracing the reciprocal influence of American Modernism (inspired by classical Chinese poetry) upon contemporary Chinese poetry,[56] both Yip's verse and his prose point to this transpacific interfluence. Yet Yip argues that Chinese (even *baihua*), unlike English, can accomplish this break with discursive structures without "deliberate dislocation of language, as in Pound and others,"[57] due to the fact that the language retains abilities to hold ambiguities without rupturing its linguistic fabric. It is important to note, however, that poets writing in the Poundian tradition (from Objectivists to New American poets, to so-called LANGUAGE and Post-language poetry) often locate their politics in the disjunctive moment and would not want to lose the "rupturing" of language Yip seems to dismiss as a shortcoming of English. In fact, it is this "rupture" that presents the materiality of language and, by extension, exposes the constructedness of reality[58] so prized in later developments in American poetry, or even in the Zennist sotoreological poetics of Snyder (*huoju*, "live words," etc.), which stands in sharp counterdistinction with Yip's valuation of disjunction as a mode of presenting things unhinged from the determinate, artificial linearity of discursive English in order to perceive them unmolested by language. The metaphysics at play in these different values for disjunction is as distinct as the different readings of emptiness and the koan at the beginning of the chapter.

Is one, therefore, to surmise that something called "Daoism," or something we might want to call "Classical Chinese Poetry," defined as an extension of this worldview, is incompatible with the turn toward disjunction as rupture in American poetics? Would a "Daoist poetics of emptiness" be, far from a break with the English poetic tradition, actually a veiled attempt to return to modern (if not premodern—to the point of raising specters of the Adamic) notions of language? The answer is not, of course, straightforward. For from the very beginning of twentieth-century transpacific poetics there has been a gross overstatement of the similarities between classical Chinese and American modernist poetry. The commonly held view that both traditions of poetry can be described by their shared economic use of words, maximum imagistic appeal, and limited use of non-imagistic language (often creating asyntactic assemblages) is arrived at ahistorically and transculturally, decontextualized from the traditions within which they are situated.[59] So before we can look at the different possible trajectories of a Daoist poetics of emptiness in American poetry, we must turn our attention to Yip's source material, to the gaps, ruptures, and disjunction within/between classical Chinese poetry, poetics, the heterogeneous family of discourses we call "Daoism," and the collective vision of these in Yip's transpacific imaginary.

Daoism and Poetic Form

One of the key limitations of American understanding of classical Chinese poetry and poetics lies in the relatively small number of classical Chinese poems (Yip, Chang, not to mention others) used to produce the vision of a highly imagistic, syntactically ambiguous poetic tradition (poems like Wang Wei's "Deer Fence," Ma Zhiyuan's "Sky Pure Sand," and palindromic verse are often cited). This reduction of the tradition's great stylistic diversity to a single monolithic description has several drawbacks, but there are two specific problems most germane to our discussion of Yip's poetics of emptiness. First, at the level of poetic form, Yip must ignore the important role of correlative thought in not only his vision of "Daoism" but in classical Chinese poetics more generally. Second, Yip and other American poets, critics, and apologists have largely ignored the explicitly "Daoist" poetry, preferring the transcultural, transtemporal language of Lao-Zhuang thought to the explicitly religious language of the wider Daoist poetic imagination.[60] Far from being a critique of Yip's poetics, I want to offer the remainder of this chapter as a supplement to his poetic criticism, which I see as a historically important heterocultural project that cannot be dismissed but must be continued by way of challenges and supplementation.

Just as Ezra Pound's "Confucian" dream of a "rectification of names" through ideogrammic composition had to reject classical Chinese formalism (prosody, meter, rhyme—prior to Pound's late translation of *Confucian Odes* anyhow; and the poetics that undergird it—what Fenollosa called "synthetic harmony"[61]), Yip must also downplay these elements in order to make Chinese poetry appear as a model or foundation for his *wuyan,* poetics of emptiness. Of course, Yip's description of Chinese poetry as an asyntactic archipelago of juxtaposed images reminiscent of a Chinese landscape is shared by a host of American poet-translators/commentators, from Chang Chung-yuan to Sam Hamill and Tony Barnstone (and even, if in an altered form, Gary Snyder), among others.

Yip takes the Six Dynasties (六朝 , 220 CE–582 CE) genre known as "mountain and water," or "landscape," poetry (*shanshui shi*, 山水詩) as the origin of his *wuyan*. He argues that *shanshui* poetry "calls for the poet to release the objects of phenomenon from their seeming irrelevance and bring forth their original freshness and thingness—return to their first innocence, so to speak—thus, making them relevant as 'self-so-complete' [*ziran*] objects in their coextensive existence." He continues, "The poet's job is to approximate the cuts and turns of our immediate perceiving contact with the objects in their original condition."[62] Clearly, we have seen this argument before, but what makes this worthy of attention now is a peculiar omission that if it were included would, in fact, complicate Yip's *wuyan* before it had a chance to get off the ground. I am referring to his convenient omission of parallelism, which began in earnest at the same time as the new valuation of natural scenery so central to Yip's poetics.

To get a sense of the importance of parallelism to *shanshui* poetry, one need not look further than Yip's own excellent translations of the founder of *shanshui* poetry, Xie Lingyun (謝靈運, b. 385–d. 422). Xie, who belonged to one of the two most powerful families of the Jin dynasty, lived a peripatetic and perilous political life, held several offices, and was eventually sent to a rural post, where he became not only the most important *shanshui* poet but arguably one of the most important founders of cosmological formalism. In the following translation, Yip does an excellent job bringing the parallel structure of the original into English, which reveals that he not only knows about this innovation of Xie's, but that he has a deep appreciation of the aesthetic effect of parallelism as well. By paying close attention to the vertical relationship between like categories within the couplets, as well as the alternating motion between mountain and water scenery, one will get a sense of the highly structured nature of parallelism in Xie's poetry.

"Scene From South Hill to North Hill Passing the Lake . . . "

1. **Dawn:** *off from* the **south** *cliff.*   (mountain scene)
2. **Sundown**: *rest on* the **north** *peak.* (mountain scene)

3. **Boat** *left* **ashore**, so *to pour* into **distant** *islands.* (water scene)
4. **Staff** *laid* **aside**,   *to lean* on a **thick**   *pine.* (mountain scene)

5. **Sidepaths**   *lean and long* (mountain scene)
6. **Round islets** *bright and clear* (water scene)

7. **Looking**   *down*:   **tips**   of   *tall*   **trees**. (mountain scene)[63]

8. **Harkening** *above*: **water** rushes from *large* **valleys**. (water scene)

9. A **crisscross** rock *splits* the **stream**. (water scene)
10. A **dense**   forest *blocks* all **paths** (mountain scene)

11. **Sky** *thaws*: **thundering rains: how about them?**
12. **Vegetation** *rises* **up in profusion.**

13. First **bamboo-shoots** *wrapped* in **green** *sheaths*.
14. New **reeds**   *hold*   **purple** *fluffs*.

15. **Seagulls** *sport* on **spring** *shores*.
16. **Pheasants** *play* in **mild** *winds*.

17. **Cherish** *Transformation*: **mind** *will be unbound*.
18. **Embrace** *things*:   **love** *will deepen*.

19. One need not regret that men of past are distant.
20. Sad it is to find no one of like mind
21. To roam alone is not emotional relief:
22. Appreciation now abandoned—cosmic scheme: who knows?[64]

By alternating bold and italics and slightly altering Yip's spacing, one can see that he has gone to great lengths to foreground Xie's use of parallelism. Lines 11–18 alternate between land and water flora and birds instead of scenery. Foreshadowing later poetic formal rules, Xie ends the poem without parallelism. This will be discussed more momentarily.

So why does he not mention this element of Xie's work when discussing not only his poetry but also Chinese poetry/poetics more generally? The answer is fairly straightforward: just as the Zennist reading of classical Chinese poetry had to abandon correlative cosmology to emphasize the "live words" of the disjunctive moment, if Yip were to address parallelism he would have to abandon his model of a *wuyan* where poetry is but a transparent mirror of visual nature. Yip has no place in his poetics of *wuwei/ziran* to fit parallelism.[65] In fact, the idea that a poet must arrange the contents of the poem (including images) in highly structured, correlative patterns contradicts his description of Chinese landscape poetry's (*shanshui shi*) mandate: "The Central force in shaping this landscape awareness is the Taoist mental horizon which begins by rejecting the premise that the structure of Phenomenon is the same as we conceive it. All conscious efforts in ordering it will result in superficial structures imposed upon undifferentiated existence and hence distorting it."[66]

Yet Xie Lingyun's important position in Chinese poetics rests largely upon his innovation of such formal techniques. So well received were these formal innovations that almost all subsequent Chinese poems either conform to parallelism or consciously chose not to conform (which is to say, even not using parallelism becomes meaningful within the context of Xie's innovations, a point that will arise in the context of more explicitly Daoist poetry). So are we to assume that Xie deviates from Daoist poetics (even though Yip locates the beginning of his *ziran* poetics with Xie) because of non-Daoistic elements? Xie was after all an early adherent of proto-Chan Buddhism (though still very much engaged in neo-Daoist discourses) and a high-profile politician (which implies a deep familiarity with Confucianism). I would argue, however, that while it would be an overstatement to say that it was Daoism itself that influenced the rise of parallelism in Xie's work, Daoism as it is understood beyond the confines of Lao-Zhuang thought is inextricably linked to its cultural moment, infused by *yin/yang* correlative cosmology, Daoist cosmogony, and a sense of poetic agency derived from elements of Daoism rarely mentioned in Western poetics outside of a few lines of Fenollosa's lost work.

The webs of correspondences and resonances that form the bread and butter of classical Chinese cosmology describe, as we have seen in Chapter 2, a world of flux characterized by transformation, birth, and decay generated within and between these elemental correspondences, understood as a movement between *yin* and *yang*. The semantic (and already to a certain extent aural) patterning in Xie's work reveals a textual condition embedded within a historically and culturally distinct place and time. Yet there is more to Xie's parallelism than this simple "influence-model" I have sketched so far. Xie's work represents a unique philosophical and poetic breakthrough that had a tremendous impact on Chinese poetry and art for one and a half millennia to come. To cut to the chase, Xie brought attention to the materiality of language itself, to its elemental properties and possible cosmological values, in new ways. His poetry follows on the heels of a Daoist movement in poetry known as *xuanyan shi,* or "dark/mysterious language poetry," which is characterized by its discursive treatment of neo-Daoist philosophical themes developed in a form of public philosophical debate called 清談 (*qingtan,* "clear speech") popular during the period. These poems focused on themes of emptiness, articulated in the language of the *Daodejing, Zhuangzi,* and the *Yijing,* and were further enriched by early Buddhist ideas entering philosophical discourses at that time. The resultant poetry, while philosophically rich, did not apply the theories of language and emptiness discussed in the philosophy to the genre aesthetically. In fact, the poetry of this period was so widely denounced later for its bland, self-referential qualities that few examples exist today. What makes Xie's poetry so interesting is his ability to fuse poetic content with form, or more precisely in his work, to move from discursive theory to poetic praxis. Liu Xie 劉勰 (d. 522), the author of the 文心雕龍 *Wenxin Diaolong,* describes this general shift from Lao-Zhuang thought to landscape poetry as follows: "Discussion of the *Zhuangzi* and *Laozi* receded into the background and depiction of mountains and rivers began to flourish (壯老告退而山水方滋)."[67] But this shift does not represent a rupture with Lao-Zhuang thought, just an application of its sensibilities to aesthetics concerns. Rather than discursively discussing emptying the self or being with things, Xie Lingyun's poetry displaces the speaking subject by bringing phenomenon into the foreground and allowing the expressive voice to recede from view. Of course, this is precisely the point Yip gives as the birth of *wuyan.* But there is another important theoretical component being transformed from theory to poetic praxis, namely, the correlative cosmology of the *Yijing,* also central to Neo-Daoism[68] (and Daoism more generally).

Rather than discussing the relationship between the five elements or *yin* and *yang,* or relying only upon references to hexagrams and images from the *Yijing* (which Xie still invokes[69]), he takes language as a correlative element and seeks to harmonize grammatical and semantic elements as a doctor might seek to balance the elemental phases of a patient's body, diet, and medicinal treatments. For Xie, parallelism offers a very different interface between poet and nature than that pointed to by Yip. After all, parallelism has almost nothing to do with the so-called transparent "presentation" (as opposed to re-presentation) of a scene, "unmodified by the poet's mediation." In the purely metaphysical terms I want to pursue here, the function of parallelism signals either that one grasps the spiritual/cosmological reality underlying a scene's beauty by presencing its balance and harmony or, perhaps, that one thinks of parallelism as a function of poetic agency, an "ordering" or "harmonizing" of the natural world itself, as my comparison of parallelism and traditional Chinese medicine implies. After all, it is well known that Liu Xie elevates human writing, *wen,* to a new cosmological significance, implying a more important role for poets as not only seers but also as agents of harmonization themselves, and he implies that poetry naturally harmonizes the cosmos. And in the chapter "*Li Ci,*" of this work, Liu Xie points to the cosmological foundation of parallelism:

Nature, creating living beings, endows them always with limbs in pairs. The divine reason operates in such a way that nothing stands alone. The mind creates literary expressions, and organizes and shapes one hundred different thoughts, making what is high supplement what is low, and spontaneously producing parallelism.

造化賦形，支體必雙，神理為用，事不孤立。夫心生文辭，運裁百慮，高下相須，自然成對。[70]

Yip's Lao-Zhuang poetics would have to disavow such an idea as un-Daoist (after all, such a notion of poetic agency directly conflicts with his understanding of *wuwei*). Yet it needs to be stressed that the correlative underpinning of poetic agency as it appears in Liu Xie and elsewhere can be traced to not only Confucian, but also, importantly, to Daoist classics like the 內業 (*Nei Ye*) and 淮南子 (*Huainanzi*), not to mention the huge corpus of "self-cultivation texts" that discuss human agency in cosmological terms. After all, Daoism's primary pursuit of immortality through alchemy (both laboratory and meditative or hygienic forms, which will be discussed in the next chapter in more detail) entails careful manipulation and refinement of different elements so as to create in the microcosm of the body (or cauldron) the macrocosmic balance of becoming in and through the Dao. Unlike Fenollosa, who attempted to marry his Buddhist poetics of emptiness to classical Chinese correlative poetics, with mixed success, Yip offers a far less contradictory Daoist poetics of emptiness, but only by ignoring those elements that get in the way. Of course, there is not a problem with Yip choosing to leave something out of his personal transpacific poetics, but the absence of cosmology should let us see that his "Daoist Project" is not the only Daoist-related poetic paradigm out there.

What should we make of Wai-lim Yip's Daoist poetics, then? Is it "Daoist"? Is it a "romantic Western invention"? Or is it something else entirely, something I have already referred to as Daoist-Modernism? In Steve Bradbury's essay "The American Conquest of Philosophical Taoism," he locates one of the most egregious areas of American distortions and appropriations of Daoism as Yip's American poetry community itself. Critiquing Bynner's translation of the *Daodejing* as a "patchwork of Yankee transcendentalism," Bradbury continues:

Imperially confident American poets, like Kenneth Rexroth, Robert Lowell, Robert Bly and Steven Mitchell, have followed Pound's example, not just in the translation of Chinese lyric poetry, of course, but other genres from other cultures; everything from

Zen koans to Sanskrit love poems, from Noh plays to Amerindian prayers. . . . Electing themselves the mediators and interpreters of exotic literary traditions, they have taken possession of antiquity, not on the basis of a substantive knowledge of the language or culture, but . . . through a desire to translate antiquity into the American present. . . . Nowhere has the appetite of Americans to make for themselves what is old and to find themselves in it been more apparent than in the translation of philosophical Taoism.[71]

Finally, Bradbury concludes: "The legacy of American translations of philosophical Taoism is, at best, a tribute to an essentialistic faith in the autonomous American self's capacity to transcend cultural, linguistic and temporal boundaries."[72] Yip's transhistorical/transcultural Daoist poetics would likely lead Bradbury to lump him in with the poets mentioned above. And while it is important to acknowledge the appropriative element of American "poetics of emptiness," is it sufficient to reduce heterocultural literary production to historicized acts of appropriation without also exploring the heterocultural productions produced through such interactions? Bradbury's comments, while helpful on one level, reinforce the idea that cultures must remain pure (and immutable). According to Bradbury, therefore, translation must remain the purview of sinologists (itself an example of Orientalist rhetoric), and poets have no business messing around in cultural texts they do not have the training to comprehend.

In a short essay called "The Chinese Poem: The Visible and the Invisible in Chinese Poetry," Michelle Yeh argues that "implicit in the Anglo-American perception of the Chinese poem is a particular kind of correlation between stylistics and epistemology (namely Buddho-Daoist). It is this correlation that I find questionable."[73] While Yeh's critique of the Anglo-American perception of Chinese poetry is dead on, this description of the problem, like Bradbury's, may be as misleading as it is helpful, for a number of reasons: grounded in a Saidian paradigm, Yeh follows Robert Kern's thesis in his influential work *Orientalism and Modernism,* which reduces the transpacific qualities of American Modernism to an Orientalist projection on to the blank page of an exotic poetry, later re-presented as authentically "other."[74] Yeh is right to point out the error of this "Buddho-Daoist projection" (denaturalizing this projection is central to this work as a whole), but she, like Bradbury, cannot place this conflation upon "Yankee transcendentalism" or "Orientalist romanticism" alone, since this "conflation of epistemology and stylistics" is in part due to a historically limited access to Daoist texts and traditions and, perhaps equally important, to a long-established element in Chinese poetics itself that has been continued by scholars in the Chinese Diaspora, like Chang Chung-yuan and Yip himself.

The late Qing dynasty (1644–1912) syncretic critic Wang Guowei (王國維, 1877–1927), who gives us the phrase 無我之境 ("the territory of the—emptied—non-self"), in which 物 (wu, objects/things) and 我 (wo, subject) cannot be differentiated, could be claimed as Yip's next most recent Chinese literary influence.[75] Yet time and again, Yip correctly points to an even longer lineage of precedents for his poetics. Regarding the link between the "Daoist world view and Chinese poetry," he writes: "Perhaps it is because of this mystical tincture amidst a poetics of the real and the concrete that all later literary and art theorists, Daoist and Confucian alike, from Lu Ji 陸機, Liu Xie 劉勰, to Zhang Yanyuan 張彥遠, Si Kong-tu 司空圖, Su Dongbo 蘇東坡, Yan Yu 嚴羽, and post-Song critics, have made it into the pivot of their theoretical formulations."[76] Given the fact that Yip draws heavily upon a "conflation of stylistics and epistemology" found throughout what James Liu has called the "metaphysical" lineage of Chinese poetics,[77] we must hold in check the contemporary desire to see cultural impositions as originating strictly via an East/West binary à la Said. And as sympathetic as I may be to Bradbury's frustration with the myopic view of Daoism limited to Lao-Zhuang thought, the application of this limited spectrum of Daoism to poetry and poetics cannot be wholly attributed to an "aggressive market capitalism and humanitarian idealism," as he charges, but can be traced to earlier poet/critics throughout Chinese literary history. These earlier poetic precedents may exonerate Yip from charges of cultural fabrication, but it would be a mistake to ignore the transhistorical brush with which Yip creates his poetic vision today, and we must be careful not to adopt a too narrow idea of what "Daoist poetics" may actually demarcate. As Stephan Owen writes of Yip's poetics: "Every serious reader of Chinese poetry should understand these theories Yip presents. They need not, however, agree with them."[78]

Daoism in the Dark

The other curious absence in the transpacific Daoist imaginary presented by Yip (but again not limited to him) includes the explicitly Daoist poetry and poetics of what Rania Huntington calls the "maternal lineage" of the *Chu ci* 楚辭 (Songs of the South) and the *weishu* 緯書 (apocrypha), other *youxian shi* 游仙诗 (songs of celestial wandering), and extracanonical texts that stand on the outside of the "paternal lineage" of the *Shi Jing* 詩經 and the rest of the canon. Huntington draws attention to a poetry and poetics "inspired through possession," with a central focus on 仙 transcendents, or immortals, injecting a strong presence of shamans, mediums, and celestial travelers fulfilling the role of intermediaries between different realms or dimensions of reality. The imaginaries offered by this poetry bifurcated into two interpretive camps: the orthodox tradition reinscribed the "spirit journey" as a "vision of poetic imagination" or as allegory, while the other camp saw *xian*, or transcendents, as actual people who experience transformations and travel into alien realms.[79] In the context of the American Daoist imaginary, the difference between these interpretive camps is secondary to the simple absence of the poetry in the first place. While it is clear why Japanese Zennists would not draw upon works saturated with the Daoist/shamanistic imaginary, it is less clear at first glance why Yip and others interested in offering a "Daoist poetics" would not have included this tradition as well. After all, it would seem that in the spirit of ethnopoetics, following the lead of Jerome Rothenberg, there would be no reason to cut these poetic imaginaries off from the "symposium of the whole."

Just as Yip and others have neglected to address correlative formalism in their descriptions of classical Chinese poetry, because it interferes with the idea of a transparent, non-language *wuyan,* the explicitly Daoist poems of the "matrilineal tradition" also muddy the waters of Yip's configuration of a "Daoist poetics of emptiness." For instance, these works often use the personal lyric expressive "I," which undermines the claim that the absence of the subjective pronoun is a prerequisite for a "Daoist poetry." Furthermore, the culturally and historically specific religious, liturgical, alchemical, and shamanistic language appears to contemporary readers as irrevocably foreign and so exaggerated in its claims as to appear garish. Such verse presents a picture of Chinese poetry wholly discordant with the common perception of its natural, minimalist, imagistic, trans-temporal/trans-cultural aesthetics. Yet, most profoundly of all, and perhaps most importantly in the context of Yip's poetics of emptiness, this explicitly Daoist poetry of the matrilineal line offers a belief system—concepts of language, reality, and perception—that contradict the epistemological claims of Yip's modernist Lao-Zhuang thought.

Let us take a closer look at an example of a poem by Chen Zi'ang 陈子昂 in this tradition of 游仙诗 (songs of celestial wandering). Chen is the author of thirty-eight poems known collectively as 感遇 *Ganyu* (most often understood as "Moved by things encountered"). He is best known as a poet with a keen political mind, which he puts to use through thick allegorical language, but this interpretation, falling within Huntington's charge of patralinial containment, does not pay enough attention to the poem's Daoist language and themes. Living the life of a wandering knight-errant in the frontiers of the Chinese empire, Chen spent years as a Daoist adept in reclusion before he met his premature death, at forty-one, in prison for his political idealism. It is likely this end that has forced his work into the hermeneutics of political allegory:

吾观龙变化。
乃知至阳精。
石林何冥密。
幽洞无留行。
古之得仙道。
信与元化并。
玄感非象识。
谁能测沈冥。
世人拘目见。
酣酒笑丹经。
昆仑有瑶树。
安得采其英。

Moved by Events I Encounter, No. 6

I behold the transformations of the dragon—
Now, the Yang essence is at its fullest.
How dark and dense the stone forest—
Nothing in the shadowy caves can hinder its course.
The ancients who attained the way of the Transcendents—
Indeed were the equals of Primordial Transformation
Awareness of the Obscure is not the same as muddled knowledge—
Who can fathom the deepest dark?
Worldly people are bound by what eyes see,
Heady with drink they laugh at alchemy handbooks.
On Kunlun Mountain there is a jasper tree
How can they hope to pluck its blossoms?[80]

The poem is flooded with the explicitly Daoist language of religious treatises and scriptures and brings to the fore an important distinction first formulated in the discourse associated with 玄學, or obscure learning—namely, a distinction between two ways of "seeing":

Who can fathom the deepest dark?
Worldly people are bound by what eyes see.

In the second line, we find the verb 见 *jian* (Fenollosa found the traditional character 見 an inspiring aggregate of an eye moving out on legs), which is the common verb for "seeing," as in the casual phrase "See you later" (再见, *zaijian*). However, it is clear that the poet does not believe the "seeing" accomplished with the eyes can penetrate the obscurity of the "deepest dark," here named by the term 冥 *ming*. How, the poet asks, through what kind of seeing, can one behold/fathom the deepest dark? To borrow the language of a very different time and place from the French thinker Maurice Blanchot, we might ask: "How can we discover the obscure? How can it be brought into the open? What would this experience of the obscure be whereby the obscure would give itself in its obscurity?"[81] In the first line of the poem, Chen gives us an alternative verb, 观 *guan*, which in the context of this poem, Cai Zong-qi argues, indicates "in a general sense, he who *beholds* actively applies his attention to an object or sense, observing its appearance in order to understand, to 'fathom,' the essence beneath the surface," but which is here directed specifically into this darkness. Cai continues, "Clearly, vision to which it refers does not depend on the eyes alone."[82] I submit that Yip's poetics of emptiness is incompatible with Chen's (but does not have to remain so) because this distinct notion of vision offers an anti-ocularcentrism that stands in sharp contrast with Yip's and American Modernism's epistemologies and ontology (but which may offer ways to extend or broaden Yip's poetic project in the future).

While Yip supports his theories of Chinese poetry based largely upon references to Lao-Zhuang thought, to his credit, most of his own theories are more specifically grounded within language cited from the *Zhuangzi* commentator Guo Xiang's work. Guo Xiang (郭象, d. 312 CE) is known as one of the two founders (along with Wang Bi 王弼, b. 226 CE–d. 249 CE) of Neo-Daoism, or 玄學 (*xuanxue*, "dark/obscure learning"), and is responsible for assembling the present form of the *Zhuangzi* itself. Toward the end of his essay "Language and the Real-Life World," Yip addresses the ways in which Guo Xiang's commentaries on the *Zhuangzi* challenge and revise potential ontotheological readings of Lao-Zhuang thought: "Guo Xiang helped to clear away the possible mystical as well as metaphysical meanings unduly attributed to the word Dao. . . . He unequivocally said in his preface 'Above, there is no Creator, below, things create themselves'" (Yip, "Language and the Real-Life World," 96). The famous first lines of the *Daodejing* read:

道可道 非常道
名可名 非常名

The Dao that can be told of is not the eternal Dao
The name that can be named is not the eternal name.[83]

Note that the skepticism toward language as a medium for ultimate knowledge actually proposes the existence of an eternal, extralinguistic non-being, an *a priori* Dao. But Guo Xiang shifts attention to terminology less invested in monistic thought. Yip cites Guo Xiang: "All things are what they are without knowing why and how they are. . . . Although things are different, they are the same in that they exist spontaneously as they are."[84] Here Guo Xiang shifts the emphasis away from the monistic Dao toward his central concept of *ziran*, which as we have already seen becomes central to Yip's poetics. What Guo Xiang's notion of *ziran* does is to replace the "unknowability of the Eternal Dao" with the unknowabilty of all things, individually. Clearly, the category of "unknowability" refers to the way language (thought) cannot capture the spontaneous, shifting, and ultimately obscure nature of "becoming." So language is no longer simply insufficient to capture the nature a transtemporal Dao, but cannot capture the *ziran* of any thing (hence the ethical charge to not impose one's will on anything, or *wuwei*).

While I believe that the fact that Yip goes to Guo Xiang's commentaries as inspiration for his poetics shows a resourcefulness and a comfort with the more-nuanced aspects of Lao-Zhuang thought, his application of Guo's *ziran* as a linguistic/translative practice, whereby one is "to receive, perceive, and disclose nature the way nature comes or discloses itself to us, undistorted,"[85] gives me pause, for how could this be done in any language or poetic form? If Yip's description of classical Chinese poetry were limited to showing how Daoist concerns conditioned its aesthetics, this would be one thing. Yet clearly Yip's claims are not limited to aesthetics. He argues that Chinese is uniquely suited to actually "disclose" the world as it is received "undistorted." Yet Yip's project is far more important than its creeping essentialism; it is an attempt to engage contemporary philosophical, political, ethical, and poetic issues through a dynamic heterocultural Daoist poetics that I believe should not be abandoned, but generatively rethought through a different reading of Guo Xiang more in line with Chen Zi'ang's poem discussed above.

For Yip to make Guo Xiang the foundation of his theories, he has had to shift attention away from prominent elements of Guo Xiang's Neo-Daoism, which, if we recuperate now will move away from the ocularcentric essentialism that endagers it[86] toward the matrilineal line of thought embodied in Chen's poem discussed above. Guo Xiang seeks to reveal the violence of vision as a form of cognition by offering an alternative to 明白 (mingbai, which implies visual clarity and is privileged by Yip): he argues that the way to *ziran* lies in the dark *ming* (冥, dark or obscure). We see this character as the principal attribute of the mysterious obscure in both lines three and eight (石林何冥密, 谁能测沈冥。). But Guo Xiang uses *ming*, not in its normative adjectival or nominal sense, but as an action verb: "one *mings* with things, with transformations, with what one encounters . . . as a way of relating to them without the mediation of traces, and hence it's precisely the opposite of *ming*, brightness."[87] Brook Ziporyn defines this "dark" *ming* as a "vanishing into," which "implies a 'dimming' and 'darkening' of the perceived object, and a 'dimming' or 'darkening' of oneself *into* that thing."[88] Following this reverse heliotropism ("darken 冥 into things," not "bringing things into the 明 light"), Guo argues one can move beyond the cognitive consciousness delivered through the clarity of language framed as/by vision by leaving the self and others (things) in their uncognized solitude, "free of the reflections and comparisons to other things that they would have if made objects of relative knowledge."[89] In many ways, this is apposite to Yip's interdiffusion of subject and object, and to his phrase 無言獨化, which blends "empty language" with Guo Xiang's term "self-so transformation" (a cognate of *ziran*). And I believe that a shift in our reading of Yip's principal source of Daoist philosophical terms and concepts (Guo Xiang) can provide new and exciting ways to think of Yip's poetics of emptiness.

To be sure, adopting a "darker" reading of Guo Xiang's *ziran/wuwei* would do strange things to the question of linguistic mediation Yip attempts to resolve with his *wuyan*.[90] Yet I cannot stress enough the fundamental contradiction between the desire to behold "clarity" and "presence" that Yip finds in the imagist aesthetic of "no ideas but in things," and the supreme value accorded mystery and obscurity throughout much of Lao-Zhuang thought and the wider Daoist cannon. After all, not even "obscurity," we learn in the first chapter of the *Daodejing*, should be our goal, but the "obscurity within/of obscurity" (玄之又玄). Language may not be able to deliver the world unmediated, but it can generatively reflect back upon itself to uncover the grottos within.

Conclusion

Having reached new heights of popularity in Mainland China, Yip must now worry about how his work will be read as we enter a very different century for Sino-Western relations. In the late 1970s, Yip's "Daoist Project" challenged an uncontested Western literary hegemony through what we might call, following Gayatri Chakravorty Spivak, a "strategic essentialism." Unlike "negritude," however, which deployed similar tactics in the 1930s and 1940s to challenge the Western claim to universality, China is no longer in a radically disadvantaged position geopolitically vis-à-vis the West. Instead, Chinese state ideology, searching for a new rhetorical foundation after the decline of Marxism, is now in a position to exploit the essentialist tendencies in Yip's work to promote a Sinocentric paradigm not unlike the essentialist discourses that underwrote Japan's imperial aspirations discussed in Chapter 1.[91] If left unmodified, Yip's "Daoist Project" could follow in the footsteps of "New Buddhism"'s mixed legacy: on the one hand, Yip's "Daoist-Modernism" resembles New Buddhism's influential fusion of Western and Asian philosophy, but on the other hand, it could also be used to validate Sinocentric nativism not so dissimilar to New Buddhism's ultimately imperialist doctrine of *nihonjinron* (日本人論) theories of Japanese exceptionalism.[92] While Yip's poetics of emptiness, like Ernest Fenollosa's, can be appreciated for its important heterocultural scope, it is important to note how such work has been repurposed for purely ideological and political agendas in the past and can be again in the future. Clearly, it would be a shame to see Yip's "Daoist Project," which he sees as a "counter-discourse to the territorializations of power,"[93] become reterritorialized in a China-centered nationalist discourse similar to that which created the colonial conditions Yip had to flee from during his youth.

It is not Yip's reliance on classical Chinese philosophical terms like *ziran* and *wuwei* that lends itself to essentialist discourses. After all, these terms offer a powerful ethics that privileges otherness over the subject and is meant to help us avoid molesting the obscure self-becoming of alterity. Yet Yip reads these ideas through the Anglo-American modernist dictum "no ideas but in things" and envisions classical Chinese poetry as having already achieved this goal. And if classical Chinese poetry is the "poem behind the poem" of twentieth-century American poetry, as in Tony Barnstone's argument parsed at the beginning of this study, then Yip shows how English can mimic its "emptiness" but never be more than its linguistic shadow. Yet Zhuang Zi and Lao Zi were not thinking about English when they developed their distrust of language, and terms like *ziran* and *wuwei* offer a still more radical challenge to epistemological knowledge than that offered by Yip's vision-centered ontology. As I hope my "dark" re-reading of Guo Xiang shows, there are ways to read these terms not as epistemological, or ontological, but essentially sotoriological (kenotic) in orientation, where the viewer/subject vanishes into the act of perception itself. (When discussing the Daoist imaginary, it is important to remember its foundation in a diverse group of religious discourses.) Certainly, it is not easy to fathom how this "dark" reading of Guo Xiang might form the basis for a new poetics of emptiness, but this is the imaginative universe explored in the matrilineal Daoist tradition (with its shamanism and trance states in tow), which has waited for some time now to be welcomed into the "symposium of the whole."

5 / Pacing the Void: Theresa Hak Kyung Cha's *Dictée*

On the white surface of the virtual screen, an image as she partly describes it appears: in a dim performance space, separated from the viewer by a cheesecloth curtain whose effect is that of "an opaque transparency," the performer slowly moves about in a candlelit, oval-shaped area, wearing a white robe and unfurling "20 meters of black and red cloth from underneath."

—TRINH T. MINH-HA, DESCRIBING "A BLE W AIL"

Through an atmosphere generated by a loose gathering of visual and cultural textures and culturally specific cues, "A BLE W AIL" calls to mind a shamanic rite, or *kut*, and perhaps more specifically, the *Chinogwi kut*, where a shaman (which in the Korean context would almost always be a woman) channels the spirit of Princess Pari, the mother of Korean shamanism, to cross over the great divide between this world and the afterlife, bringing with her long strips of cotton with which she will find the recently deceased and pull them out from the lower hells to a permanent resting place in paradise. While not a reenactment of this rite, Cha's performance is striking for the prominence it accords to the white fabric worn by shamans (and during mourning), its ritualized movements (used in many shamanic rites), and the two lengths of fabric Princess Pari and those who channel her take with them to the afterlife. Cha's description of Princess Pari's journey, at the end of her novel/poem *Dictée*, is also remarkably close to Cha's own description of "A BLE W AIL."[1] As is the case with all of Cha's heavily heterocultural work, many cultural discourses simultaneously find their way into a state of *media res*, an in-betweenness. But it is important to note that the explicit and suggestive references to Asian religious, philosophical, and mythopoetic figures that permeate her work are not superficial exoticization, ornamental orientalism, or even instances of code switching—what Bill Ashcroft might call a metonymic gap, or places in a text that stand in for the unbridgeable distances between distinct cultural discourses.[2] Instead, I would argue that their forcefields of meanings are as (or arguably more) active as the historical, poststruc-

FIGURE 5.1. Image of Cha performing "A BLE W AIL," 1975. Photograph
by Trip Callaghan, image no. 1992.4.32. From, *The Dream of the Audience*,
93, © Regents of the University of California. Published by the University of
California Press.

turalist, feminist, postcolonial, Greek, French, and Catholic discourses
that have been commented on at great length. Yet works like "A BLE W
AIL," and *Dictée*, Cha's well-known novel/poem, make available distinct
cultural spaces conditioned by unique shamanic and Daoist cosmogonies
left unaddressed by the growing field of Cha scholarship. Clearly, Cha's
Daoist imaginary can be seen as an outgrowth of her years of studying the
Daoist art of *taiji chuan*[3] and exploration of Chang Chung-yuan's Daoist
poetics (among other figures in the transpacific imaginary),[4] but it can also
be traced back to the source of her poststructuralism—Roland Barthes.[5]
It is important to note from the outset, however, that while Cha's Dao-
ist imaginary is informed by Barthes's, it cannot be subsumed under his
imaginary or that of the broader "Chinese dreams" of the Tel Quel group
(Julia Kristeva, Philippe Sollers, Barthes, and others whose "dream" is the
subject of Eric Hayot's elegant book, *Chinese Dreams*). Cha does not turn
to Kristeva's "China," a figure of the "bizarre, aberrant, lunatic,"[6] or to Bre-
cht's "China" as a figure of alienating "strangeness"[7] (although she might
employ elements of her transpacific imaginary to these ends). Instead, her
use of key Daoist concepts reflects some of the same contours as the Daoist

(informed also by Buddhism, which I do not foreground in this chapter so that the more active Daoist elements can be more clearly seen) imaginary of late Barthes, who, years after having moved on from his early "utopian dreams" of Maoist China,[8] returns to Daoism (and rekindles his admiration of Zen) in a series of lectures (collectively known as "The Neutral" [Le neutre]) he gave during his first year at the Collège de France (the year after Cha studied at the Centre d'Etudes Américain du Cinéma in 1976[9]). I will return to Barthes's Daoism and how it may have conditioned Cha's work at a later time, but it should suffice to say that Cha's efforts to fuse Barthes's poststructuralism with Daoist concepts of self-emptying was likely influenced by his own attempts to do this.

It should be noted, however, that Cha draws upon Daoism and performs it in ways quite distinct from Barthes as well, for Cha articulates its "other logic"[10] through a distinct "Daoist imaginary" that was not on the horizon of the Paris avant-garde–Korean shamanism. As an indigenous, gendered (matrilineal) discourse threatened by both Japanese and Christian imperialism, which fuses Korean indigenous and Chinese folk Daoist elements into a unique episteme, Cha had recourse to a much richer, living tradition that her predecessors could not have imagined. I hope to show that her particular Daoist imaginary (especially as it is refigured in shamanic language and practice) is far more than simply another fractured surface set afloat in her work (like those discourses that belong to Greek mythology). Instead, Daoist notions of "self-emptying" supplement and in turn transform the poststructural theory that undergirds her work, and this heterocultural admixture, aimed at disrupting the dominant Western episteme, offers a poetics of emptiness unlike any other we have seen.

Over the past decade, many of the most influential books of literary criticism have examined Theresa Hak Kyung Cha's novel/poem *Dictée*: Lisa Lowe's *Immigrant Acts: On Asian American Cultural Politics,* Juliana Spahr's *Everybody's Autonomy,* Laura Hyun Yi Kang's *Compositional Subjects,* and Yunte Huang's *Transpacific Imaginations.* These works, along with numerous scholarly articles,[11] investigate Cha's work as an important critique of gendered postcolonial resistance, and the mid-1990s volume of critical essays devoted to *Dictée, Writing Self, Writing Nation,* along with the establishment of the Theresa Hak Kyung Cha archive by the UC Berkeley Art Museum and Pacific Film Archive, have all helped establish *Dictée* as arguably the most important postmodern transpacific text. This proliferation of Cha criticism is responding to the highly subjective, largely disjunctive, continually interrupted nature of a text that offers its readers images without captions, quotes and letters without citations, and an overall embarrassment of signs (or of riches) without clear referents. A cursory description of the text reveals several distinct narrative strains loosely organized around the Korean revolutionary Yu Guan Soon; Queen Min; Joan of Arc; Demeter and Persephone; Cha's mother, Hyung Soon Huo; and Cha herself. Cha's book uses intensely lyrical fragmentation to interrogate the dislocation of memory, language, and selfhood experienced by these distinct gendered spaces. She does not shore up this fragmentation, nor does she attempt to recuperate a more coherent expression of a stable identity, but offers fragmentation as a method of opening alternative modes of knowing.

While Cha's desire to open new epistemologies not subject to colonialization is correctly seen as an extension of her engagement with critical theorists like Roland Barthes, Cha's appropriation of Daoist and shamanic language and concepts (which, as I have already mentioned, is also conditioned by Barthes) also sheds light on the warp and weft of the epistemological insights offered by this text. Unlike Yip, who responds to what he sees as the loss of a "Chinese worldview" by producing a coherent Daoist aesthetic and hermeneutic; or Snyder, who offers a "Zennist" poetics authenticated by decades of "Zen practice"; or Fenollosa, who offers an unruly "synthesis" of East Asian heterocultural claims—Cha enfolds Daoist and shamanic language and concepts without recourse to any of the cultural supports we have seen previously. With a few notable exceptions, Cha, following the syncretic nature of Korean shamanism more generally, freely draws upon Daoist language and ideas (especially Daoist alchemical discourses), as well as distinctly matrilineal shamanic practice. Unlike the previous figures discussed in this work, she is not interested in defending East Asian philosophy as a distinct or superior mode of knowing the world, but as a potential site of rupture within the way we do. Here, in Cha's *Dictée,* Daoist discourses are released decontextualized into an already polyvalent assemblage of dislocated texts and images. The Daoist references, tropes, or even guiding metaphysical frames present in Cha's poetics are never presented at face value, but arrive in the dark, without proper citations or set definitions in tow.

Trinh T. Minh-ha arrives at a reading of "A BLE W AIL" in which she places Cha in the "ancient role of both a medium and a magnetizer," and the one to which "falls the magical task of resurrecting voices" and "letting shadows appear and speak in her folds."[12] Minh-ha's not too subtle reference to the shamanistic aura of Cha's performance opens an important and heretofore largely unexplored element of Cha's poetics, namely its connection to Korean shamanism, spirit possession, and celestial wondering intimately tied to the folk Daoism and the matrilineal line of Chinese poetry and poetics, which I have discussed briefly as the principal domains of Daoism excluded from Yip's work.[13] As a point of contrast, we might recall that in Yip's idea of *wuwo*, emptied self, one is primarily concerned with perceiving the world without language or "epistemological elaborations" (an attempt to restore the subject's ability to behold the life-world "as it is"), which tacitly retains a subject/object dichotomy insofar as the viewer enjoys direct access to the world of objects. On the other hand, I would argue that the shamanic medium of Cha's own *wuwo* empties the subject more radically by channeling other voices, by offering one's position of enunciation as the space and time for others (readers) to actively co-create meaning in the world. Her subject, in the end, finds liberation not in reconnecting to the presence of things, but in vanishing into the interdiffusion of reading and writing that takes place within the "plurality of entrances" Barthes describes as the "infinity of languages." In both cases we could argue that a "housed emptiness" is being proposed. Cha's "housed emptiness," however, following in the matrilineal folk Daoism tradition, is filled with *actual* possession, trances, and ecstatic flights, where one's "fasting the mind" leads to the displacement of the subject by foreign voices, multiple consciousnesses, and mixed languages, or a displaced consciousness that prepares the emptied self for more religious/mystical possibilities.

What in the classical Chinese context was a conflict between the poetic and hermeneutic orthodoxy of the patrilineal and matrilineal line of Chinese poetry and Chinese poetics, divided so strongly on the subject of shamanic possession and celestial flight, became in the Korean context an explicit conflict between orthodox Daoist cosmologists (men literate in classical Chinese philosophy and cosmology, largely concerned with the *Yijing*) and shamans (women initiated into an oral tradition, seeped in all "three teachings": Daoism, Confucianism, and Buddhism). While men historically patronized Daoist cosmologists as mediators between this world and the afterlife, Korean women have steadfastly supported shamanism to this day.[14] So while the patrilineal orthodoxy looked down on shamanic possession and ritual, the shamanic tradition drew liberally upon state religions, in much the same way as Chinese folk religions have in China. So while I will speak of "Daoist language" in this chapter, it is important to recognize the radically heterocultural nature of these discourses in Korea, and especially within Cha's work.

Void as Loss

One of the most important interpretive challenges offered by Cha's heterocultural Daoism lies within the key concept of 虛, "the void." It would be difficult to take in the full arc of Cha's work without noticing the centrality of the void. But East Asian philosophical discourses do not have a monopoly on concepts of emptiness or "voidness," so critics may not have felt the need to explore this recurring concept in relation to Daoist philosophy. The problem with discussing Cha's uses of emptiness without reference to the cultural discourses she is both drawing from and contributing to, however, is that critics too often promote readings of the void limited to a particular metaphysical orientation (in this case Eurocentric).

Often the figure of the void appears as a negative, even violent, result of colonialism, religious indoctrination, and marginalization in Cha criticism. While I do not want to supplant this important interpretation, the void, in the Daoist studies Cha encountered through Barthes's work and Chang Chung-yuan's *Creativity and Taoism*, is a generative, transformative term underlying Daoist cosmology and, by extension, its philosophical discourses and religious/ritual practices. If we turn to Elaine Kim's reading of the void in Cha's *Dictée*, presented in her essay "Poised on the In-between: A Korean American's Reflections on Theresa Hak Kyung Cha's *Dictée*," I believe we can see the conceptual investments involved in interpreting this key idea. From the beginning of Kim's essay, she equates the void/emptiness with loss, lack, and abjection. She quotes the following passage from *Dictée*: "'It murmurs inside. It murmurs. Inside the pain of speech the pain to say. Larger still. Greater than is the pain not to say. . . . It festers inside. The wound, liquid, dust. Must break. Must void.'" Kim then comments:

> By changing "void" from a noun into a verb, Cha transforms the passive and receptive into the active and explosive. In *Dictée* neither the conquered land, nor the female body, nor the colonized individual began as "empty." Thus, although the mother is forbidden to speak her native language by the Japanese colonizers, who "inhabit you whole, . . . force their speech upon you and direct your speech only to them" (Cha 50), she cannot be totally silenced.[15]

For Kim, emptiness is understood within an economy of loss, as a state of forced silence, and therefore *Dictée*'s strength lies in its transformation of emptiness, a condition forced upon the individual by various ideological and hegemonic forces, into an "active and explosive" assertion of self, individuality, and subjective self-expression.

In this reading, emptiness is an unnatural condition ("the colonized individual did not begin empty"), and therefore represents the telos of imperialism, conquest, and domination consummated in the loss of self, voice, subjectivity, freedom, and ultimately life. This reading of the void draws upon a Fannonian description of colonialism's destruction of "local cultural originality," since Kim writes that "the colonized individual" did not "begin as 'empty,'" but that colonialism attempts to empty the colonized. For Kim, following Fanon, being colonized by a language radically alters one's consciousness. As Fannon argues, "To speak . . . means above all to assume a culture, to support the weight of a civilization."[16] Speaking an imperial language (French or English, or in Cha's mother's case, Japanese) means that one is coerced into accepting the collective consciousness of the French, British/American, or Japanese. Since these cultural values are internalized (or "epidermalized"), creating a disjunction between one's racialized body and consciousness, a description, in the tradition of Frantz Fanon, of the "void" therefore might propose an emptying of one's natural self/consciousness by way of its being replaced by a colonized consciousness.[17] Clearly, there is not a problem reading the "void" as the effect of hegemonic erasure of minority discourses, histories, and culture, for this is an absolutely key element in Cha's work, yet it becomes a problem when Cha's "void/emptiness" is understood within a metaphysical framework incapable of registering its complex theoretical, aesthetic, and even spiritual dimensions. When we return to explore the void as the site of displaced subjecthood, we will see that Kim's reading of "void" as a form of abjection will be reread as a vital rupture tied closely to ideas of shamanic possession and Daoist soteriology. But before we can return to these themes, it is necessary to explore more complex, heterocultural ideas of the void as they appear more widely in Cha's work.

The Void as Origin

To get a better understanding of the form and function of voiding in Cha's poetics, it would be helpful to start at the end of *Dictée*. As with other works, like *Exilée* and *Étang*, which will be discussed later, *Dictée* ends with a gesture toward Daoist notions of emptiness/void. This time, however, she does so more explicitly, by including a Daoist chart, or 圖 (*tu*, which I will refer to as a diagram), that traces the universe's cosmogonic origins from (and back toward) the void/emptiness:

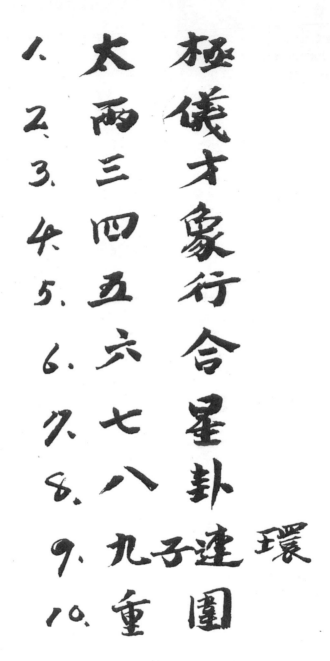

FIGURE 5.2. Image of a Daoist cosmogonic chart, or 圖 (tu), which traces the universe's origins from (and back toward) the One: void/emptiness. From Cha, *Dictée*, 154; © Regents of the University of California. Published by the University of California Press.

The Chinese text that appears on page 154 of *Dictée* (Figure 5.2) appears without identification of any kind and can be translated as 太极, *taiji* ("great ultimate"), 两仪 *liangyi* (*yin/yang*: heaven "yang-yi" and earth "yin-yi" from the *Yijing*), 三才 *sancai* (天 heaven, 地 earth, 人 man), 四象 *sixiang* (the four groups of seven constellations of the twenty-eight "lunar mansions" in Chinese cosmology: 青龙—black dragon, 白虎—white dragon, 朱雀—rose finch, and 玄武—black warrior, which can be read as East, West, South, North), 五行 *wuxing* (five elements 金 metal, 木 wood, 水 water, 火 fire, 土 earth), 六合 *liuhe* (can mean "universe" or the six directions (cardinal + up and earth-down), 七星 qixing (the seven stars of the big dipper—斗星), 八卦 *baguo* (eight trigrams), 九子连环 *jiuzilianhuan* (nine interlinked points), 重 圆 *chongyuan* (repeating circles). Interestingly, nineteen pages later we find an unnumbered list of approximate translations.

Tai-Chi First, the universe

Leung Yee	Second, Yin and Yang
Sam Choy	Third, Heaven, Earth and Humans
Say Cheung	Fourth, the Cardinals, North, South, East, West
Ng Hang	Fifth, the five elements, Metal, Wood, Water, Fire, Earth
Lok Hop	Sixth, Four cardinals and the Zenith and Nadir
Chut Sing	Seventh, seven stars, the Big Dipper
Bat Gwa	Eight, the Eight Diagrams
Gow Gee Lim Wan	Ninth, Unending series of nines, or nine points linked together
Chung Wai	Tenth, a circle within a circle, a series of concentric circles[18]

While readers and critics alike point to the inclusion of multiple languages and diagrams like the one above primarily as examples of *Dictée's* heterogeneous linguistic and graphic composition, the content and origin of these portions of the text have not been critically addressed. The diagram draws from Daoist cosmogony, inner alchemy (内丹, *neidan*), and the hybrid philosophical movement of Neo-Confucianism, and I will be concentrating on its relationship to Daoist *neidan*, since it is this discourse that weaves through Cha's work more generally. Beginning in the seventh century CE, *neidan* began as a movement away from the

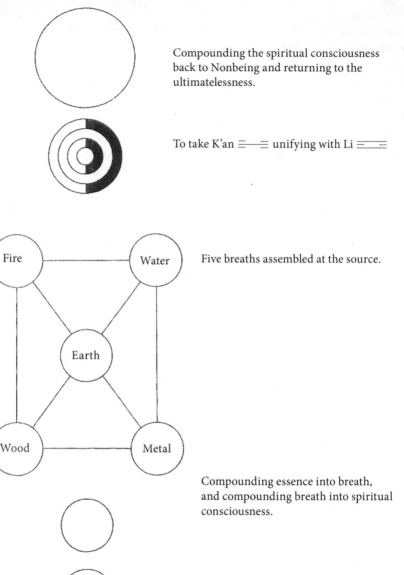

Compounding the spiritual consciousness back to Nonbeing and returning to the ultimatelessness.

To take K'an ☵ unifying with Li ☲

Five breaths assembled at the source.

Compounding essence into breath, and compounding breath into spiritual consciousness.

The Gate of the Dark Femininity

FIGURE 5.3. Chang Chung-Yuan translates *taijitu* as "chart of ultimateless-ness," which is both a cosmogonic narrative (the origin of the universe of differentia from the One) and offers a way to conceive returning from differentia back to the One. Based on material from Chang, *Creativity and Taoism*, 167.

interior visualization practices that dominated earlier forms of Daoist meditation (which used visualization as a means of ecstatic flights into celestial spheres). This new movement focused on emptying the self as a means of "unifying with the Dao." Isabelle Robinet writes, "Whereas in [the earlier forms of Daoism] Shangqing techniques 'oblivion,' the halting of thought, was only a conditional state, a break with the ordinary world, it now became a technique in its own right and accompanied speculations on the reality of the world and nothingness. . . . Deliverance came to mean liberating the spirit from all concepts and all ideas of gain and loss, so that there would remain nothing, not even the absence of anything [void]."[19] This vision of a radical *wuwo* (emptied self) follows from a far more radical take on *wuwei* than that which Yip proposes, in order to arrive at an unmediated experience of "the real."[20]

The diagram above does not come from Cha's primary source book for things Daoist, Chang Chung yuan's *Creativity and Taoism*,[21] from which she includes quotes throughout her MFA thesis, "Paths" (which will be discussed in detail at a later point), yet this list is quite similar to a diagram that she would have encountered in Chang's book.[22]

This diagram in Figure 5.3 (known as the *taijitu*) was constructed by Zhou Dunyi, based on the *wujitu* (diagram of the Great Void) first associated with the Daoist hermit Chen Tuan (906 CE–89 CE), who is said to have carved it on a cave wall in Hua Mountain near Xi'an.[23] When read from the top down, as Cha's numeration would suggest, it describes the origin of the universe in the terms presented in chapter 42 of the *Daodejing*:

道生一 ， 一生二 ， 二生三 ， 三生萬物
    Tao engenders One;
    One engenders Two;
    Two engenders Three;
    Three engenders the ten thousand things.[24]

Here, we begin with the undifferentiated "Source," variously referred to as 太一 (*taiyi*, Great One), 太極 (*taiji*, Great Ultimate), 混沌 (*hundun*, Primordial Chaos), or 前天 (*qiantian*, Primordial Heavens)—or even *xu*, the Void, which is often figured as pure undifferentiated potentiality that is the foundation of being, its origin and its destination. The second phase, presented as *yin/yang* in Cha's diagram, is represented in Chang's diagram by the complementary binary of the trigrams for fire and water central to inner/alchemical representations of the transformative permutation of *yin* and *yang* in all phenomena. The third phase in Chang's diagram skips the triad of Heaven/Earth/Humans as well as the fourth phase, which refers to calendric cosmology and moves straight to the fusion of the five phases in the configuration given in one of the two most important diagrams of Daoist ritual and alchemy, the *houtu* map.[25] Cha's diagram continues to provide correlative pairings of numbers with foundational elements of Daoist cosmogony: the sixth reveals Daoist cosmological schemata of directions; the seventh refers to the stars of the Big Dipper (北斗, literally, "northern bushel"), which is a fundamental component of Daoist private and public rituals of renewal; the eighth gives us the 八卦 (*bagua,* eight trigrams); the ninth refers to the so-called "magic square," a sudoku-like numeric grid derived from the other principal Daoist diagram, the *Lo Shu;*[26] and, finally, the tenth offers "a circle within a circle, a series of concentric circles." The circle also ends Chang's diagram, and is in fact a central element in inner-alchemical textuality and practice.

The circle often illustrates the absolute, or illumination, an idea tied to the concept of the cycle, a form of time capable of being reversed. Since linear time inevitably leads toward decay and death, Daoist alchemical language takes the circle as an alternative model of temporality through which an adept is able to "climb back up the path of time"—an image, Isabelle Robinet reminds us, that "is dear to interior alchemy, to find once more the Source from which he springs." Robinet explains that the circle helps articulate the way in which Daoists envision the world, as that which is always in the process of appearance and disappearance: "the cycle represents not only the constant repetition of cycles but also a return to the point of departure as the adept thus takes up life all over again." She continues, "The cyclical process occurs in stages and, in a time quite apart from linear time, a cyclical and achronic time during which the materials on which the adept works (lead and mercury, or body, breath, spirit, etc.) are progressively deepened, purified, exalted, in an upward moving, widening spiral that culminates in the universal and the ultimate truth and finally permits escape from the cycle of life and death."[27] It is not a coincidence that both Chang's and Cha's diagrams end in circles; the fact that Cha repeats the tenth phase of her diagram on the following page is also worth noting, since it in effect enacts its meanings. The diagram ends:

Tenth, a circle within a circle, a series of concentric circles

and is then reiterated, this time enfolded by white space above and below.

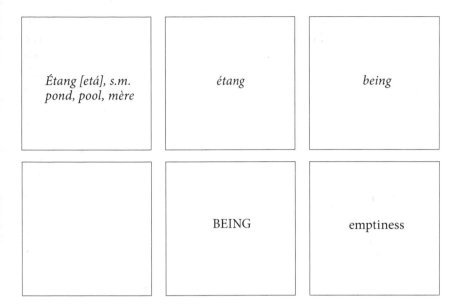

FIGURE 5.4. "Étang," by Theresa Hak Kyung Cha (1978). © 1993 Regents of the University of California. Published by the University of California Press.

Tenth, a circle within a circle, a series of concentric circles.[28]

Cha's line emerges
from the blank page,
it becomes—from and (of) emptiness,
as it expands (or contracts) toward beginning again.

This reading of Cha's use of white space is not arbitrary, since she explicitly links white spaces to theoretically invested notions of emptiness, as in her poem "Étang," printed on a series of cards (see Figure 5.4).[29]

The French word *étang* means "pond or pool," but Cha adds *mère*, meaning "mother or source," which also rhymes with *mer*, "sea," thus creating a fabric of interspliced meanings that suggest a watery femininity. Thus, the cards, in order, read "étang," "being," [blank card], "BEING," and "emptiness." The poem works its way from the *yin* source figured here as both watery and female (both attributes of *yin*), to "being," to an empty card, to "BEING," and finally to "emptiness." Cha's revised definition figures pondness as the source of being, but a pond manifests itself by way of its non-being (as a vessel, a pond that has not been dug remains unmanifested, for a pond must be empty before it can house its own becoming). In "Étang" emptiness is figured most intensely as the unmarked white space of an empty page.

This charged investment in whiteness appears throughout Cha's work and can be found in *Dictée* as well: "She opens the cloth again. White, Whitest of beige. In the whiteness, subtle hues outlining phoenix from below phoenix from above facing each other in the weave barely appearing. Disappearing into whiteness."[30] Whiteness here invokes a vocabulary of ephemerae, ranging from fog and mist, to the vagueness of distance characteristic of "ghost painting" exemplified in paintings like Chen Rong's famous *Nine Dragons,* which depicts dragons (rather than a phoenix) emerging and disappearing into the color and fold of the clouds that enshroud and unveil them.[31] In the work "Earth," we find the following passage:

> Nirvana
> this white sheet
> empty within
> being middle   balance
> become   in
> the color word fold
> paper
> seed and transmitter
> without one but all[32]

This whiteness, like the whiteness into which Cha's phoenix and Chen Rong's dragons emerge and disappear, is a theoretically and aesthetically rich condition: "The screen fades to white";[33] "In whiteness beyond matter. Sight. Speech."[34]

The Void as Entrance/Destination

I would like to return to the circles at the "ends" of Cha's and Chang's diagrams because these circles require us to do so. In Chang's *Daoism and Creativity,* he offers a reading of his diagram in which the end becomes its beginning. Chang describes how in practice a Daoist adept, through meditation, moves from the bottom circle—the gate of Dark Femininity, which in inner-alchemical discourses is also called "obtaining the aperture" and refers to the space between the kidneys that is the starting point of alchemical cultivation and refinement.[35] From the aperture the adept moves upward through the circles to the origin in the Great Void. In other words, Chang reveals that the diagram, far from being a mere description of or elaboration upon the Daoist cosmogony found in the *Daodejing*, is actually a step-by-step guide backward through time (again envisioned as a cycle precisely for this purpose of temporal reversal) toward a mergence with primordial non-being. Due to both the progressive nature of Chang's diagram and his description, it is necessary to quote him at some length:

> The diagram consisted of several tiers of circles describing the process of meditation. The first tier (the bottom row in the illustration) was a circle labeled, in Lao Tzu's expression, The Gate of Dark Feminity, which is the Foundation of Heaven and Earth. The next tier is another circle, illustrating the process of compounding *ching* [*jing* 精] (essence) into *ch'i* [*qi* 氣] (breath), and then into *shên* [*shen* 神] (spirit). *Ching, ch'i, and shên* are the fundamental concepts of meditative breathing, as we already explained. In other words, this tier shows how the energy from the lowest center of the body is transformed into the circulation of breath and is further transformed into spiritual consciousness. The following, or middle, tier of the diagram consists of the five elements: fire wood at the left; metal and water at the right; earth in the middle. They symbolize the five movers in the lesser circulation, which ultimately reach the grand circulation. The fourth tier shows the unification of *k'an* and *li* in the form of a circle, which is divided into *yin* and *yang*. The fluctuation of *yin* and *yang* in the grand circulation lead to *shên,* or spiritual consciousness. The tier at the top of the drawing shows the compounding of *shên* back to *hsü,* or non-being. Thus all things return to *wu chi,* or ultimatelessness. The spiritual consciousness is the ultimate of the individual, and non-being is the ultimatelessness.[36]

Read as a meditative guide then, Cha's own alchemical diagram, following the logic of Chang's, begins with the tenth "circle" and proceeds backward toward "ultimatelessness"—in Cha's "Tai Chi," the great ultimate, a condition of space/time often referred to as "prior heaven," which contains the binary of *yin* and *yang* before its proliferation into its correlative states. Cha mobilizes this sentiment: "Before Heaven. Before birth and before that. Heaven which in its ultimate unity includes earth within itself. Heaven in its ultimate generosity includes within itself, Earth. Heaven which is not Heaven without Earth (inside itself)."[37] The end of *Dictée* becomes a new beginning. The cycle continues; the process is always in the midst of be-

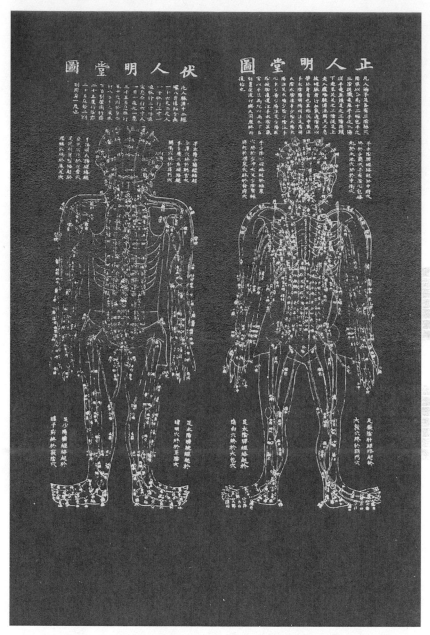

FIGURE 5.5. Acupuncture points. From Cha, *Dictée*, 63, © Regents of the University of California. Published by the University of California Press.

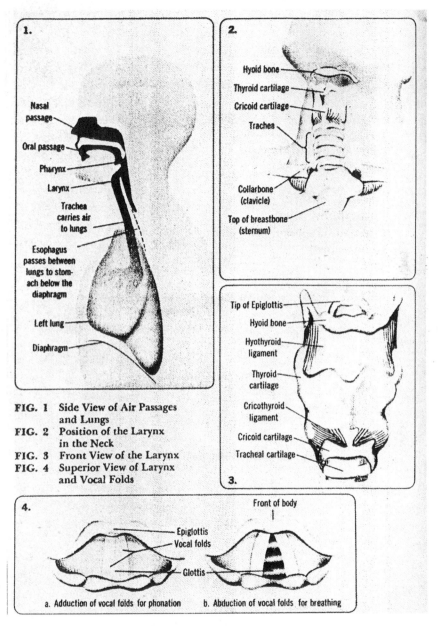

FIGURE 5.6. Modern anatomical diagram of vocal organs. From Cha, *Dictée*, 74, © Regents of the University of California. Published by the University of California Press.

ginning again. "Tenth, a circle within a circle, a series of concentric circles" is no longer a reduplication of the finale, but a new page, a reignition.[38]

Yet this is not the only diagram Cha (or Chang) offers her readers, as she uses both traditional acupuncture charts and more modern anatomical illustrations (see Figures 5.5 and 5.6). While the two diagrams are not depicting the same things, it is important to notice that both juxtapose concrete anatomical displays with discourses centered upon the circulation of breath in the service of entering the void. This strange combination of visual and linguistic texts is peculiar to inner-alchemical textuality: many inner-alchemy manuals/texts include concrete anatomical or cosmological diagrams set against often abstract and cryptic directions, guiding the adept into labyrinthine meditations on emptiness.[39] Cha, too, juxtaposes her diagram with lines that appear to guide the reader into or through deeper realizations of emptiness. Directly preceding her diagram Cha writes:

> Phrases   silent
> Paragraph silent
> Pages and pages a little nearer
> To movement
> Line
> After line
> Void to the left to the right.
> Void the words.
> Void the silence.[40]

At a later point, Cha again appears to be working in the mode offered by Chang's description of Daoist meditation (or just as likely her *taiji chuan* instructors) and offers again what appears as a guided meditation switching between descriptive and imperative voices. She writes:

> Colors faintly dust against your vision.
> Erase them.
> Make them again white. You Re dust.
> You fade.
> Even before they start to take hue
> Until transparent
> into white they vanish
> white where they might impress
> a different hue. A shadow.
> Touch into shadow slight then re turn a new

shape enter again into deeper shadow
becoming full in its mould.
Release the excess air, release the space between
the shape and the mould
Now formless, no more a mould.[41]

In this passage Cha takes the reader through various states of visualization where the adept/reader is led to move beyond sensory perceptions to various states of non-being. Color—to white, then from shadow, the adept is guided toward a "re turn a new" by way of filling the shadow's empty mould, which is itself passed beyond, by way of releasing "the excess air," to become formless. Again we return, by way of breath and visualization, to an origin in the void's "ultimatelessness." So as we explore the possible function of the void in Cha's work, it is important to bring with us distinctly positive associations around the void, not indigenous to Western metaphysics. Only then will we be able to embrace an ambivalence forged from both the negative violent connotations associated with void as loss and void as generative origin, for in the context of shamanic possession it is difficult to see the voided self as purely abject or wholly libratory, but rather as somewhere in between, rich with unique and radical possibilities.[42]

"The artist's path is that of a medium"

Now that we have complicated the void in Cha's work, revealed that it is a site of possible abjection, but also liberation vis-à-vis Daoist alchemical language and practice, it is possible to explore the void in Cha's work as a complex site of self-emptying. First, we will look at how Cha adopts not only Barthes's well-known poststructuralist theories, as is usually argued, but also elements of his own "Daoist imaginary." After establishing the basic dimensions of this aggregate of Daoist-poststructuralist claims, we can explore increasingly radical enactments of shamanic emptying in Cha's work as she uses reading/writing as an alchemical agent through which the subject is emptied of the "expressive I."

At the center of Cha's Daoist-poststructuralist poetics lies Barthes's distinction between what he terms "lisible" and "scriptible," or "readerly" and "writerly," texts. Readerly texts, like a realist novel, assign readers the role of passive receiver of fixed, predetermined meanings, while "writerly" texts, in Barthes's words, provide

a perpetual present, upon which no consequent language (which would inevitably make it past) can be superimposed; the writerly text is ourselves writing, before the infinite play of the world (the world as function) is traversed, intersected, stopped, plasticized by some singular system (Ideology, Genus, Criticism) which reduces the plurality of entrances, the opening of networks, the infinity of languages.[43]

Clearly, Cha reads Barthes, as most do, to be primarily interested in liberating the "reader" from the passive reception of commodified meaning, as she writes in her introduction to her 1981 film theory anthology, *Apparatus* (which includes essays by Roland Barthes and Christian Metz among others): "Turn backwards and call upon the machinery that creates the impression of reality whose function, inherent in its very medium, is to conceal from its spectator the relationship of the viewer/subject to the work being viewed."[44] Even today, this focus on the liberation of the reader remains central to avant-garde language practice,[45] yet Cha, I would argue, is equally interested in liberating the writer as well. For her, Barthes's famous announcement of the "death of the author"[46] is more than a shift to the reader for meaning-production; it is a soteriological end, an escape for the writer from the tyranny of the "self" of the expressive "I." The first step of this shift of emphasis recasts the "plurality of entrances" opened up by the "writerly text" as a space of "interfusion between writer and reader," where "the viewer holds the position as the complement, an avenue through multiple interpretations, give multiple dimensions to the work . . . the renewal and regenerating process could be illimitable."[47] For Cha, the "writerly text" reveals that meaning is not the only thing co-created (or restored) with the audience, but that the very notion of being a writer/artist is forged within the dream of the audience, and is like Zhuang Zi's identity, forged of his dream, by way of his dream.

It is very likely that Cha's well-known phrase "the dream of the audience" is a direct reference to Zhuang Zi's dream, which she quotes in its entirety in her essay "Paths." "'Once I dreamt that I was a butterfly,'" Cha begins the quote,

> "fluttering here and there; in all ways a butterfly. I enjoyed my freedom as a butterfly, not knowing that I was Chou. Suddenly I awoke and was surprised to be myself again. Now how can I tell whether I was a man who dreamt that he was a butterfly, or whether I am a butterfly who dreams that she is a man? Between Chuang Chou and the butterfly, there must be differentiation. (Yet in the dream no differentiation takes place.) This is called interfusion of things."
> Chuang Chou (Ch. II)[48]

For Cha, Zhuang Zi's butterfly opens another means of perceiving how the writer and reader (artist/audience) occupy both subject and object positions simultaneously (something writing makes possible), wherein "a covenant, 'interfusion of subject and object is then finalized.'" Cha continues: "The artist's path is close to that of the alchemist in that his/her path is that of a medium. His/her vision belongs to an altering, of material, and of perception. Through this attempt, the perception of an audience has the possibility of being altered, of being presented a constant change, Re volution."[49] By situating the artist/artwork/viewer trichotomy within Zhuang Zi's notion of interdiffusion, Cha reaches for a Daoist discourse we have seen before—Lao-Zhuang—to forge a heterocultural discourse better suited to articulate the liberation of the writer. The writer is a writer within the dream of the audience, but the writer of the open text is not in a strict binary with the readers but the site of interdiffusion whereby the writer and reader are no longer separate, no longer violently singular, but released into the space of language together (co-inhabitants). She writes that "the artist given the gift of Medium, partaking in transformation processes captures eternal wonder. I cannot help but to express the overwhelming sensation that almost resembles a returning, an abandon, a salvation from the struggle of being human, to only the purest of pure."[50] What is this "overwhelming sensation" that almost resembles "a returning, an abandon . . . to only the purest of pure"? In Daoist soteriology, escaping to, or 步虚 ("walking" in the void), is, in the later inner-alchemical school of "complete perfection" (全真, *Quanzhen*), described as a space of 清净 (*qingjing*, "purity and stillness"), a state of "realization" that follows Daoist meditative practices (to realize this complete *wuwei*). To apply such explicitly Daoist terminology at this juncture may seem like an active/creative reading on my own part, except that the link between the emptied writer of "writerly texts" and *wuwei* can be traced back to Barthes's own turn toward Daoism. For late Barthes, the neutral ("le neutre") is recast as the Daoist concept of *wuwei*, as that which "baffles the paradigm"[51] and escapes the totalizing grammar of hegemonic ideologies. There is, here, an idea of the dead author become blank, void, neutral, and "freed" through "doing nothing," becoming "neutral." Interestingly, Barthes's Daoism, like Cha's, is informed by physiological practices of "inner alchemy," and he discusses on several occasions various Daoist techniques, like "embryonic breathing" and Daoist dietary practices, which aim at emptying the body, heart/mind, to "become an empty mirror."[52]

Also, it is interesting to note Cha's Daoist language set forth in "Paths" that describes the effect of a fully realized *wuwei* as "a returning, an abandon, a salvation from the struggle of being human, to only the purest of pure," which sounds remarkably similar to Barthes's own formulation as described by Trinh Minh-Ha: "Barthes seeks a certain suspension in his discourse, a suspension experienced as 'a blank which effaces in us the reign of codes' and as a regenerative place of rest."[53] Minh-Ha, again citing Barthes, states that, "for writing to be born, the writer is no longer, which does not mean that he/she withdraws, but he/she dies within himself/herself in order to exist simultaneously with the text."[54] Writing, it would seem, in Barthes's Daoist imaginary, or especially as it is refigured in Cha's, has become an immortal embryo, gestated through the inner alchemy of self-emptying and released into/by the "plurality entrances" to return to the undifferentiated infinity, void. The "death of the author" is not just the "birth of the active reader," but is the site of the liberated writer, who by emptying his or her "speech" of its "authorial presence" becomes "a perpetual present, upon which no consequent language (which would inevitably make it past) can be superimposed." The embryonic text has thus returned to the infinity that precedes time, to the "*taiji*" of Cha's alchemical/cosmogonic chart.

The figure a "return" does not stop here, however, as it conditions much of Cha's work that deals with exile in polymorphous permutations throughout. Yet this is not a return to a "homeland" or a "mother tongue," but a return to an "in-betweeness" that precedes "the infinite play of the world (the world as function)," which "is traversed, intersected, stopped, plasticized by some singular system (Ideology, Genus, Criticism)."[55]

In her performance piece "Exilée" (1980), Cha counts the minutes of a transnational flight between the Bay Area and South Korea while iterating the fact that the two places are always separated by a permanent "sixteen hours" of difference:

> Ten hours twenty two minuits
> Sixteen hours ahead of this time
> Ten hours twenty one minutes
> Sixteen hours ahead of this time . . . [56]

This performance piece highlights the untraversable distance fundamental to the diasporic experience in a way that calls to mind a line of separation, not unlike the terminator, which is continually moving in time but always marks the difference between light and dark, the shift from day and night across the globe. This reading of minutes passing yet inevitably marking a dichotomy of distance and difference is registered in Cha's distinctive code-switching since *minuits,* French for (plural) midnight(s), appears in the place of *minutes* throughout the text.[57] This

ambiguity suggests that at every interval, no matter how minute, distance follows, is always following, is always being marked.[58]
  Cha then writes:

> Backwards, from backwards from the back way back. to This. This
> phantom image/non-images
> almost non-images without images each ante-
> moment moment no more no more a moment
> a moment no duration no time. phantom no visible
> no name no duration no memory no reflection no echo.[59]

While Lawrence Rinder is right to point out that in this passage "any hope of closing the gap of physical distance is washed away in a flood of abnegation,"[60] I am not sure if his emphasis on a loss of hope is the only reading of Cha's movement toward total negation. Cha's passage poses a series of positions whereby states of being are revealed in the twilight of the terminator, crossing over the line between day and night, being and non-being. Here existents teeter on the rim of becoming, from "phantom and non-image" to "almost non-images," minutes pass into *midnights*. We watch as *backwards* brings time not to a stop but to "no time" and finally to a "no name," "no duration," "no memory," "no reflection," "no echo." Cha dissolves presences into non-presences, yet the language lingers, the words remain, emptied of their referents but lingering on the page. In the performance piece, these words are juxtaposed with Cha's verbal iteration of receding and immutable time and a gentle montage of images, including, most prominently, different cloud formations taken from above and within. The effect is a sense that negation follows the motion of virga rains, falling away in streaks without reaching the ground, a being groundless, a groundless being. The juxtaposition of these cloud images with Cha's "flood of abnegation" recalls archetypal Daoist imagery of cloud-traveling adepts walking the void (步虛). While it is not incorrect to read Cha's inability to transcend temporal and spatial boundaries of diaspora as a loss, the text's final negation can also be read as actualizing the rejuvenating potential of negation as rupture and, in a cosmogonic sense, return, if a return to the infinite plurality of languages/entrances, which is time and again figured as the middle, or the void, of in-betweeness, as in this passage from *Dictée*:

> Further, Further inside. Further than. To middle. Deeper. With-
> out measure. Deeper than. Without means of measure. To core. In
> another tongue. Same word. Slight mutation of the same. Undefin-

able. Shift. Shift slightly. Into a different sound. The difference. How it discloses the air. Slight. Another word. Same. Parts of the same atmosphere. Deeper. Center. Without distance. No particular distance from center to periphery. Points of measure effaced. To begin there. There. In Media Res.[61]

Void as Self-Emptying (Kenosis)

Cha figures this diasporic aporia as an emptying, "in Media Res," a "*tertium quid*," neither totally of its source nor of its destination, but a vessel, emptied of both.

Cha writes:

From A Far

What nationality
or what kindred and relation
what blood relation
what blood ties of blood
what ancestry
what race generation
what house clan tribe stock strain
what lineage extraction
what breed sect gender denomination caste
what stray ejection misplaced
Tertium Quid neither one thing nor another
Tombe des nues de naturalized
What transplant to dispel upon[62]

Following Rinder, Josephine Nock-Hee Park describes this allusion to *tertium quid* as a loss. Park writes that "in this grim vision of those who emigrate and assimilate, all that they possess is their bodies, shorn of 'house clan tribe stock strain.' Literally posited between these two nations and languages, however, is the phrase 'Tertium Quid,' pointedly written in Latin, which has a transnational existence in both English and French."[63] While Park is certainly just in her description of *tertium quid* as an experientially "grim" space as well as an interlinguistic space/signification, she does not explore this term's significance in Catholic (negative) theology, which takes this "neither one nor the other" as part and parcel with "kenosis." This negative Catholic kenosis, or "self-emptying," and Cha's Daoist notions of "void" through "self-emptying," weave together throughout

Dictée, and if critics were to explore this side of *tertium quid* in their work, it would be difficult to read this "in-betweenness" purely under the sign of abjection. Yet perhaps it is useful to think of loss and abjection as an element of liberation as well—but abjection as defined by Julia Kristeva.

Kristeva describes the abject as that which "draws me to the place where meaning collapses . . . what does not respect borders, positions, rules. The in-between, the ambiguous, the composite."[64] The abject, for Kristeva, functions as the underbelly of the symbolic, that which fundamentally challenges the self, draws it closer to the edge of subjectivity by revealing among other things the fundamental importance and impermanence of the body. Kristeva writes, "Abjection preserves what existed in the archaism of pre-objectal relationship, in the immemorial violence with which a body becomes separated from another body in order to be."[65] Since abjection first and foremost recalls the process whereby a child is differentiated from the mother, for Kristeva, this would explain how the main threat to the fledgling subject is his or her dependence upon the maternal body, and therefore abjection is fundamentally related to the maternal function, and this misplaced abjection accounts for the oppression of women within patriarchal cultures more generally.

If the Void is the site of abjection, the rupture of the self, the interdiffusion of subject and object, it may very well be experienced as a violence. And yet, redirected by Daoist terms and concepts, it could also become the "Gate of the Dark Femininity,"[66] the aperture through which one begins the process of transformation back to the great undifferentiated Void, which is the goal of Daoist soteriology. The moment of abjection, in fact, plays a central role in the matrilineal tradition of Korean shamanism as well, and Cha's integration of these elements marks a clear departure from Barthes's Daoist imaginary into something we can think of as wholly unique to her work. While many shamans working today have followed matrilineal lines of descent, most if not all of these lines, and most women not following such lines, were initiated into shamanic practice only after experiencing a traumatic event or illness. According to the Korean shamanism scholar Youngsook Kim Harvey, "spirits in search of human victims to possess are particularly attracted by those whose souls have been 'fractured' . . . by personal tragedies or exploitations others have caused them to suffer."[67] Common throughout the world, shamans often trace their decision to take up the trade to such moments of trauma. It is in this context of shamanic possession, channeling, and trance work that we may want to, at least in part, read Cha's many references to self-emptying.

While the Japanese ruthlessly attempted to eradicate shamanism from the Korean Peninsula during the decades of their occupation, shamanism found itself the object of ridicule and attack from Korean Christians after independence as well (shamanism is still underground in the Communist North). Yet Cha's work throughout *Dictée* restores the shamanic undercurrents of Christian ritual practice. Cha writes: "I receive God, all pure. Totally. For the Dwelling of God Housed in my body and soul must be clean."[68] A few pages earlier, we read a description of Mass that emphasizes the body's capacity to serve as a vessel for Christ:

> The Host Wafer (His Body. His Blood.) His. Dissolving in the
> mouth to the
> liquid tongue saliva (Wine to Blood. Bread to Flesh) His. The right
> side. Only
> visible on their bleached countenances are the unevenly lit circles of
> rouge and
> their elongated tongues. In waiting. To receive. Him. Waiting.
> Nearing, nearer
> and nearer to the altar of God.[69]

Cha's description of Mass coupled with the *Confiteor* offers a ritualized preparation of the body to become "the Dwelling of God." Later this theme of possession is imaged more viscerally when Cha describes not the kenosis of Jesus by way of his sacrifice in the sacrament of blood/ flesh, but the needle drawing the narrator's own blood: "One empty body waiting to contain. Conceived for a single purpose and for the purpose only. To contain. Made filled."[70] Here the syringe suggests the body, emptied at the origin for the purpose of housing the Other, which is in the ancient Hebrew worldview, like most shamanic worldviews, believed to be "in the blood." In 1215 the Fourth Lateran Council decreed that when the priest at the altar uttered the phrase "Hoc est corpus meum" (This is my body), the bread and wine were changed into the body and blood of Christ.[71] Many scholars link the Eucharist to prior shamanic rituals like that of the cult of Dionysis where the life energy of animals was consumed by way of the vehicle of blood.[72] While invoking the Catholic archetype of housing Christ through kenosis, or self-emptying, Cha's emphasis on the utility of the emptied body calls to mind the self-emptying associated with more Daoist notions of "housed emptiness."

The term "kenosis" is a helpful term to think through Cha's void, because of its connotative residues. Most sinologists refrain from using the term unless explicitly engaging in comparative religious studies.[73] The reason for avoiding this term in sinology is easy to understand: kenosis is a heavily invested term in Christian theology and brings with it a controversial career in Christology that would only detract from the specific Daoist concepts and practices being studied.[74] But Cha's *Dictée* is anything but a monocultural text. Fragmented Catholic themes, terms, imagery, and theology are woven into and through the text's multiple cultural, theoretical, historical, and Daoist themes.

I would argue that these literal moments of possession are figurations of the more theoretically invested notion of channeling multiple voices into (or from within) the displaced "I" that pervades Cha's poetics more generally. At the heart of the matter, subjecthood requires language. We speak, think, and dream in languages we understand, yet there are times when this may not be the case. The most prominent examples of "speaking the foreign" appear to arrive by way of religious practices. Religious practitioners partake in incantation, chanting, intoning, or reciting of sacred writings in languages that often do not consummate conventional semantic meanings for the practitioner. Roman Catholics often recite Latin liturgical texts without understanding Latin; Muslims often recite passages of the Koran without understanding Arabic (take the world's most populace Islamic nation, Indonesia, as a likely example); non-Hebrew-speaking Jews often recite passages of the Torah; and Buddhists chant mantras in Sanskrit without in many cases understanding Sanskrit. Some religious practitioners may imagine sound as a bridge to the sacred, which, as Jean-Luc Nancy writes, "signifies the separate, what is set aside, removed, cut off"—what he calls "the *distinct*."[75] Yet I do not believe a recitation of an unknown language can actually form a bridge to the "totally distinct,"[76] as religious recitations may not be viewed as truly "speaking the foreign," since the ritual supplies meanings to the speaker that allows the speaker to "author," or at least understand, the vocalizations as an expressive, devotional, or faith act (as would the occasion of glossolalia, or "speaking in tongues"). It is far beyond the scope of this chapter to discuss the possibility of "speaking/reading the foreign" in religious practice. Instead, Cha offers a different occasion of speaking the foreign, which bears upon this study of the "void" in her work more generally, namely, the voiding/kenosis enacted by dictation, or *dictée*.

The term "dictation" has three principal meanings: (1) The pronouncing of words in order to be written down. (2) Authoritative utterance or prescription; the exercise of dictatorship. (We can see how these definitions reinforce the idea of dictation being a form of interpellation and indoctrination resulting in a violent loss of subjecthood, yet the term in the French refers more specifically to another process.) (3) The transcribing of a dictated passage of a foreign language. In this sense, *dictée* is both transcription and transliteration. In fact, transliteration is listed in the *Oxford English Dictionary* as the second meaning of transcription, with the third being "a transfer, assignment (of a debt or obligation) = L. *transcriptio*." It is this particular combination of an interlinguistic attendance, or obligation, that I would like to focus on.

The most common place to find instances of interlinguistic dictation is in the countless foreign-language classrooms across the globe. I recall early in my study of Chinese going through my language textbooks and transliterating the Chinese characters so that I could recite the text in class the following day. And, of course, every test included dictation, where I had to write down (both in characters and, at times, in transliterated/Romanized Chinese) the words or sentences the teacher spoke. I often spoke (and much more often heard) words and even full sentences that I did not yet understand. Nevertheless, a student is graded by how well he or she pays attention to the specific sounds and textures of a language, even when it is still semantically unavailable. In both the religious and secular instances of this "speaking the foreign" still foreign, we find a linguistic exercise where the "speaker" is not the person physically "speaking." In a truly remarkable inversion of the relationship between language and subjecthood, dictation, transliteration, transcription, and recitation of languages still foreign, the subject is emptied of its "I-ness" and becomes the addressee, even when "speaking." In Julia Kristeva's *Language of the Unknown*, she offers a diagram that may help clarify this point (see Figure 5.7).

Kristeva writes: "Each speaking subject is both the addresser and the addressee of his own message, since he is capable of emitting a message and deciphering it at the same time, and in principle does not emit anything he cannot decipher."[77] She continues, "One can thus see that the circuit of linguistic communication established in this way leads us into the complex realm of the subject, his constitution in relation to his other."[78] Of course, I am most interested in the fact that translingual *dictée* does not follow this "constitution of the subject in relation to the other," but in fact reveals the "kenosis of the subject in relation to the other," since the student, speaking back, or transcribing/trans(l)iterating the foreign, entails a divestment, a total "acquiescence to the messenger. Acquiesce, to and for the complot in the Hieratic tongue. Theirs. Into Their tongue."[79] For Cha, *dictée* requires this total acquiescence to the hidden, cryptic, and yet sacred foreign (complot).

If we applied Kristeva's dialectical formulation to *dictée,* the teacher

FIGURE 5.7. "Communication diagram." Based on material from Kristeva, *Language*, 8.

would act as the addressor (and his or her own addressee) by speaking a sentence still semantically unavailable (for the teacher) to the student, the addressee. The student (addressee) then must map the aural textures of the message by way of resubmitting the message without having understood it (by either a verbal or orthographic iteration), an act I would venture is as close to speaking the foreign one will find. The message, for the student, is purely vocative (address). Speaking takes place only at a mechanical level and withholds its "complot." The message remains, itself "from afar," and as such speaks from "on high." If, according to Kristeva, the abject is that which disrupts the divide between self and other, speaking the foreign is the language of abjection, but also Zhuang Zi's dream of interdiffusion. Studies of the peculiar states of consciousness accessed by shamans and mediums when in the trance state are inconclusive and beside the point,[80] since the potential of the void in Cha's work is not reducible to such trances, but is instead a framework to view alternative ways of speaking and writing that do not return the world to the subject by reconstituting the bifurcation of subject/object but dissolves the I in the alkahest of another's speech.

Perhaps more interesting still is the fact that *Dictée* invites readers to experience a form of translingual kenosis. As Juliana Spahr points out, the ideal reader of Cha would need to be able to read six different languages in order to find the work fully semantically available, but such a reader would still face the hybrid or pidgin moments, fragments, and dislocations of the text's formal disjunction. Spahr writes:

> The issue of readers' potential alienation has to be located in their own ingenuity. Readers who lack mastery of all six languages in *Dictée* have a number of options: they can simply ignore the sections that are not readily interpretable to them; they can translate the text themselves with the assistance of a dictionary or someone who knows the language; or they can go out and learn the language and return to the text at a later date (I am ignoring here options

that reject the reading process altogether, like throwing the book down in disgust, just because these options are always available when reading any book).[81]

Interestingly, Spahr does not mention the possibility that the reader may actually "read" the foreign text without understanding its meaning, even though this is the one possibility most in line with the actual practice of *dictée*. If we take the void, and kenosis, as ultimately a colonialization of subjectivity, such a practice may seem counterproductive, as it would in Derrida's account of Levinas's desire for a language of pure address without "content" (a "saying" without a "said," or a language without a "phrase"), which Derrida argues would make the reader into a slave. He writes: "What would a language without phrase, a language which would say nothing, offer the other? Language must give the world to the other, *Totality and Infinity* tells us. A master who forbids himself the phrase would give nothing."[82] Understood in the terms Derrida gives us, a language without content cannot be seen as a valuable or viable notion, but in my reading such a practice may be "productive"—capable of producing new, interesting, and perhaps more ethical outcomes—for two reasons. First, the act of mouthing, mimicking, enunciating without understanding allows the reader to experience language as an addressee, without recourse to the power to reposition oneself as the addressor (one who understands and exerts some authorial intention over meaning-making). Such an experience, as harmless or as harmful as it my seem, may offer readers insight into both ideological voiding (forced dictation "emptying" of one's selfhood, as Elaine Kim points to) as well as Daoist voiding (escape from the subject's claims to power over the otherness—*ziran*—of the phenomenal world and the self, through its continual recourse to biased knowledge claims). The second reason why this practice may be "productive" in an appreciation of *Dictée* is the fact that it also forces the reader to become more aware of the corporeal basis of language—the tongue fumbling against the wrong teeth, the awkward misbalance of underdeveloped and overdeveloped muscles and reflexes (in relationship to non-native languages). Cha's short video "Mouth to Mouth" (1975) shows a mouth "mouthing" the consonant initials of the Korean alphabet, *hangul*, which reveals the link between muscle, breath, and the written word. Such an experience may reveal something about the relationship between the oscular and the graphemic/orthographic conditions central to Cha's treatment of language and voice. If, as Levinas argues, "it is not I who resist the system, as Kierkegaard thought; it is the other," then the experience of losing subjecthood near its very origin (where the self manifests as a speaking subject), if only for brief moments in the void, may offer a genuinely unique contribution to contemporary discussions of metaphysical ethics. To return to Derrida's critique of purely vocative speech, it is not the Other as master that ethics must worry about, but the "I." Yet the "I" loses its power to command the Other (its claim to mastery) while retaining its obligation to address it, all without recourse to the habitual grammars of "self-expression." In this sense, the void, or the voided self, takes on yet another layer of possible meanings in Cha's work. Not only is Cha liberated by the interdiffusion within the dream of the audience (via the writerly text), but she is offered another avenue of existence altogether. Barthes writes: "We cannot speak, and surely not write, without being subject to one of these modes: either affirming, or denying, or doubting, or questioning. But cannot the human subject have another desire: to suspend his utterance without however, abolishing it."[83] It would seem Cha found two avenues for realizing such a "housed emptiness" (emptiness housed in something that is not consumed by its emptiness but "holds" it in one way or another): both writerly texts and foreign-language dictation offer some degree of this "neutral speech."

Both Barthes's idea of ideological "neutrality" and Cha's kenotic dictation are foreshadowed by the beginning of Barthes's seminal *Empire of the Signs* where he speculates on the radical potential of "knowing" or "speaking" a language foreign to the speaker. He writes:

> The dream: to know a foreign (alien) language and yet not to understand it: to perceive the difference in it without that difference ever being recuperated by the superficial sociality of discourse, communication or vulgarity; to know, precisely refracted in a new language, the impossibility of our own; to learn the systematics of the inconceivable; to undo our own "reality" under the effect of other formulations, other syntaxes; to discover certain unsuspected positions of the subject in utterance, to displace the subject's topology; in a word, to descend into the untranslatable, to experience its shock without ever muffling it, until everything Occidental in us totters and the rights of the "father tongue" vacillate—that tongue which comes to us from our fathers and which makes us, in our turn, fathers and proprietors, of a culture which, precisely, history transforms into "nature."

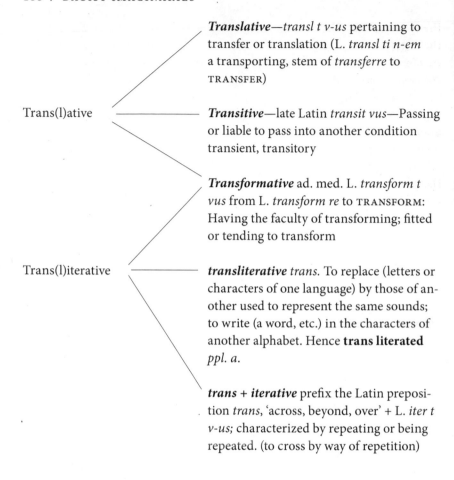

Translative—transl t v-us pertaining to transfer or translation (L. *transl ti n-em* a transporting, stem of *transferre* to TRANSFER)

Transitive—late Latin *transit vus*—Passing or liable to pass into another condition transient, transitory

Transformative ad. med. L. *transform t vus* from L. *transform re* to TRANSFORM: Having the faculty of transforming; fitted or tending to transform

transliterative trans. To replace (letters or characters of one language) by those of another used to represent the same sounds; to write (a word, etc.) in the characters of another alphabet. Hence **trans literated** *ppl. a.*

trans + iterative prefix the Latin preposition *trans,* 'across, beyond, over' + L. *iter t v-us;* characterized by repeating or being repeated. (to cross by way of repetition)

Trans(l)ative

Trans(l)iterative

FIGURE 5.8. "Trans(l)ative/Trans(l)iterative," a diagram I constructed after a class taught by Myung Mi Kim in 2003, SUNY Buffalo.

Alchemy as a Transformative Poetics

By playing with the orthography of the two principal media of inter-linguistic processes, I hope to foreground that both translation and trans-literation imagine a *trans* of "equivalency" between different semantic or aural material. Yet no traversal has taken place, only a transversal, or trans-formation. If translations posit the possibility of transference in an ultimate sense, then all languages must "still" originate from a single, static, Adamic, or originary, tongue. Otherwise translation posits shades of approximations ranging from one pole of the literal "word-by-word" translation to the "paraphrase." Yet machine translation continues to learn the hard way that language does not come to meaning by constellations of the denotative potentialities of words alone, but within syntax and the constantly shifting contingencies of culturaly conditioned interpretive networks.

Cha is, of course, unfaithful to the metaphysics of equivalency and disrupts naturalized expectations regarding both the processes of trans(l)-ation and trans(l)iteration. She is not looking for Benjamin's "pure language," but reveals how all translation is transformation, as is all transcription and transliteration. By enclosing the "l" in each term in parentheses, I hope to destabilize each term's normative use-values and bring into question their unique claims.[84] In so doing, I hope to highlight instead the degree to which each term can come to suggest another process less determined by a metaphysics of equivalency. Cha uses Daoist language to register a metaphysics of transformation as fundamental, and reveals in her poetics that all trans- (movement across, beyond, over) entails new formations. Cha is quick to point out in "Paths" that the transformative nature of language and art also holds the prospect of self-transformation. Cha begins that essay with an introduction to alchemy:

> Alchemical elements used by Alchemists could be most commonplace: water, air, fire, earth, etc. They simply exist, as space, as time exists, almost unnoticeably. The Alchemist with the utmost care and precision. [sic] (water collected from dew settled on leaves . . .) He enters a covenant with these elements, with the intention not of imposing upon these materials, not so much to transform and shape them according to his will, but during the unfolding of this pact, these elements will be the ones to transform his soul. He will work on them, with them, without any distinction as he works on his soul.[85]

Passages like this one clearly mark a desire by Cha to fuse her poststructural theory with another kind of language, one that shifts emphasis to personal liberation, through a certain kind of art-making ("writerly"). And while Cha's "transpacific imaginary" remains resolutely polyvalent and heterogeneous, I have chosen to mark one aspect of this "imaging," as such, as a trans(l)ative, trans(l)iterative, alchemical kenosis. Isabelle Robinet may help illuminate the nature of Cha's use of language as an alchemical medium when she states: "Alchemical language exists on two levels. It is both a language, with its own vocabulary [elements, transformations, etc.], and a use of this language—a meta-language—that both renders the language effective and at the same time indicates its death by going beyond it."[86] Both movements of alchemical language appear to be crucial to Cha's productions as she works through the ideological interpellations of the diasporic exilée to find 清净 (*qingjing*, "purity and stillness") waiting at the beginning and end of becoming and losing one's selfhood. As a final point, I would like to suggest that Cha's adoption of this libratory reading of "void" contains within it a direct challenge to the victim/ oppressor dialectic that bypasses the "recuperation of voice" offered by Elaine Kim's reading *Dictée*. If, as Althusser argues, "individuals are always already subject" because we are "subject to" and "made into subjects by" hegemonic ideologies,[87] then Cha's reimagining of an emptied subject position can, by way of an alchemy, transform ideological interpellation (much like Korean shamanism has transformed the trauma of other forms of abjection) into something quite different from subjecthood or victimhood—into an emptied, neutral space of infinite play, eternally resistant to ideological commodification.

By tracing the Daoist-oriented networks through which Cha has, in large part, come to her notions of "this infinite void," it is my hope that her readers will not only see a new dimension of *Dictée*, but the fecund nature of Cha's poetics of emptiness more generally. Could Cha's "void," which can be thought of at least in part as the result of violent ideological interpolation, offer a philosophical, spiritual, and ethical idea of an altered/ emptied self free from both the threat of hegemonic subjugation and the need to subordinate otherness as a means of constructing an autonomous "I" (which merely reproduces the logic of subjugation one is attempting to critique)? As a rhetorical question, I want to let the pressure of not knowing its answer press one to see the value of addressing the Daoist elements of Cha's poetics. After all, without them, we are left with less to work with, and perhaps less to learn from.

While I have stressed from the beginning of this book the importance of reading heterocultural literature with reading frames as hybrid as the texts being read, in the case of *Dictée* criticism, these frames have not been hybrid enough. Of course, this is a truly formidable task. Lisa Lowe is correct when she states that "it is impossible to reduce *Dictée* to a single classification or preoccupation, for it resists such determination."[88] And it is my hope that my reading does not close down the palimpsestical nature of the text's multiple registers by authoring a "Daoist" or "shamanic" version or interpretation of the work, but simply allows these aggregates to rise into view. Given the text's many cultural, political, and historical layers, the omission of these textual conditions may have seemed insignificant, yet I hope to have shown that the reverse is true.

Epilogue

*Imagine a narrow path paved with blocks of granite, leading from
checkered rice-fields spreading to the horizon in three directions into some
foothills whose nearby summits mask loftier peaks beyond. The path is so
narrow that one expects it to peter out among the rocks, and there are no
signposts to indicate that it leads anywhere in particular; but now and
then we come upon sheer walls of rock on which, blurred by the rain of
centuries, have been chiseled poems in huge characters faithfully modeled
on the calligraphy of bygone scholars famed for their skillful brushstrokes.*
—BLOFELD, FROM THE INTRODUCTION TO RED PINE'S COLD MOUNTAIN

After reading *Cold Mountain*, Red Pine's collection of translations of
Han Shan's poetry in the early to mid-1980s,[1] the American minimalist
painter Brice Marden set about creating a series of paintings that marked
a sea change from the geometric minimalism he is usually known for. In
a series of paintings entitled *Cold Mountain Series (Han Shan)*, Marden
offers us a purely visual representation of Han Shan's poems. The charac-
ter-like forms in his paintings are not Chinese characters, but their non-
semantic shadows. These forms undulate in and out of focus, as if peer-
ing out from behind moving cloudbanks. The paintings are beautiful;
they reveal the artist's deep commitment to his material and a desire to
find a visual form that suggests both the natural setting of Cold Moun-
tain (characters climbing like vines across the canvas's rock face) and
the emptiness he sees animating Han Shan's poems. In several pieces of
the *Han Shan* series, Marden enacts this emptying by scraping the paint
off some of the lines, and in others by painting over them with paint
the same color as the canvas, giving the effect that the character-like
forms are passing into and out of being. Fluid lines appear and disap-
pear as if the canvas were undifferentiated Mind, and the character-like
forms, empty of referential meanings, appear as thoughts on the verge of
cognition.

When Marden opened Red Pine's translations of the poet Han Shan,
he entered into the intertextual world of a romantic transpacific imagi-
nary (not so unlike the one we witness in Tony Barnstone's translation
with which I began this study). By traveling into John Blofeld's descrip-

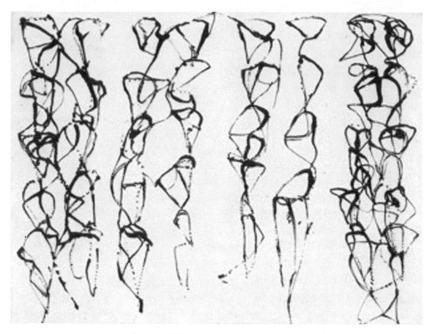

FIGURE E.1. Brice Marden, *Cold Mountain Series, Zen Study 3* (Early State). 1990. Etching and lift ground aquatint, printed in black plate: 20 11/16 x 27 3/16"; sheet: 27 3/8 x 35 1/4". Publisher: the artist, New York. Printer: Jennifer Melby, New York. Edition: 3. Linda Barth Goldstein Fund. (432.1990) Museum of Modern Art, New York, NY, U.S.A. © 2009 Brice Marden / Artists Rights Society (ARS), New York, Digital Image © The Museum of Modern Art / Licensed by SCALA / Art Resource, NY.

tion of Cold Mountain in the book's preface, he also entered into a major transpacific thoroughfare of American poetics as well. Even though Blofeld had not himself been to Cold Mountain in person, he opens before Marden a landscape of orientalized/exoticized beauty and mystery.[2] Over several pages, Blofeld enthusiastically pulls his reader into thick forests, by rustling animals and gushing rivers, limpid streams, and across bridges with names like "Bridge to the Sea of Clouds." Here Marden is hurriedly passed by Daoist monks, who climb the high walls "undulating like a dragon's back with the contours of the ground" without laboring for breath before finally reaching the temple where the reader is met by "smiling mystics offering us a place to rest and dinner composed from mountain fare." It is in this strange "Orient" that Marden found inspiration for his paintings; it is here he encountered the "sheer walls of rock on which, blurred by the rain of centuries," ancient poems were chiseled. Perhaps Marden's own transpacific imaginary is chiseled into those same imagined stones.

Marden's paintings are translations that proceed through mimicry, yet translators can only mimic what they believe to be "on the other side." Like so many of the translators we have discussed, Marden's translations mimic the visual content of the calligraphic originals as well as the particular epistemology he sees animating the poetry itself. His paintings are nearly a perfect embodiment of Wai-lim Yip's poetics of emptiness, since the Chinese poem (or the suggestion of one) finally reveals Yip's language of pure transparency. Language has "moved out of the way" to let nature reveal itself without "epistemological elaborations." The poem, no longer burdened by thoughts or sounds, becomes its own referent; the signifiers are finally one with their signifieds (or at least the paintings seem to offer this).

Marden's paintings are also an interesting cognate of Gary Snyder's poetic vision, or visionary poetics. If the work of Chinese poets like Han Shan is, as Gary Snyder argues, to see "the world without any prism of language, and to bring that seeing into language," Marden has taken us a step closer to the nirvanic perspective so often apophatically gestured to by Han Shan himself. No longer burdened by language, the onlooker is free to "see" what lies beyond it. And apparently behind the paint lies emptiness. In a sense, Marden's *Han Shan* paintings are a fitting place to conclude this project since they seem to form a pool at the end of the streams described by both Yip and Snyder. In the course of this work, I have endeavored to presence some of the bends and disturbances along the way. Principal among these disturbances is this stream's elision of cosmological formalism, its distrust and disinterest in Chinese poetry's nuanced *prosodic* textures, its intricate yet bold soundings. Yet if Marden's paintings are the telos of a major stream of American poetics of emptiness, then the stream has, in an important sense, left the sound of poetry behind.

It would be a shame to think that these silent, carved rocks, or the paintings they have inspired, represent the telos of the transpacific imaginary, however. I do not simply mean to emphasize the hypermimetic silence of the paintings, but also the limitations of Blofeld's imaginative universe that, at least in part, inspired them. What may have struck Blofeld and his readers as sublimity in his description of *Han Shan* now strikes us as reified surfaces complicit in the othering of Asian cultural discourses into romantic caricatures. Even if Yip's and Snyder's desire to reach outside language is haunted by the success of Marden's paintings, their poetics cannot be reduced to Blofeld's *Han Shan*. While Orientalism, in Said's pejorative sense, is, and will likely remain, an important element of the transpacific imaginary, it is my hope that this book's attendance to the wide scope, historical depth, aesthetic complexity, and theoretical rigor of the heterocultural productions discussed, reveals not the thin caricatures of distant otherness but the multiphasic transformations of East Asian philosophy and poetics in twentieth-century American poetry.

The Orientalism of Blofeld's transpacific imaginary serves as a common example of why the Buddho-Daoist elements of American poetry and poetics have not been taken seriously, and I would argue lends support to Rey Chow's current skepticism toward "the economy of idealized otherness."[3] Chow charged that because of the obstinate anti-theoretical methods of Area Studies, the present idealization of "otherness," popular in cultural studies more generally, presents us with a danger, because a turn toward non-Western cultures "espoused in the name of cultural studies could easily be used to refuse and replace rather than strengthen the theoretical modes of inquiry." As Chow sarcastically asserted, "Now we can go back to the study of indigenous cultures and forget all about 'Western theory'!"[4] For Chow and others, Transpacific Studies must first and foremost remain squarely within the methodological priorities and practices of Western literary criticism, rather than Area Studies, which is reflected in Rob Wilson's important charge to bring theoretical attention to "new cultural voices and undertheorized works struggling to emerge across troubled sites of cultural production."[5] I see this practice (and the desire that fuels it) as both extremely positive and ultimately helpful, yet there is another voice growing within (Cross-)Cultural Studies, a theoretically informed group of scholars who, nevertheless, question the rise of critical theory as a global standard of scholarly production and wonder if non-Western epistemological and hermeneutic systems may have a part to play in contemporary criticism.

Toward the end of his book *Orientalism and Religion: Postcolonial Theory, India, and 'The Mystic East,'* a text that employs a largely Foucaultian reading of Western Indology, Richard King disrupted his own privileged use of critical theory throughout his study to pose a provocative question:

> Why should theorists be limited by the Western framing of this debate? Consider, for instance, the example of Buddhist philoso-

phy. In ancient Buddhist thought there has been no postulation of an all-powerful deity nor of an immortal soul constituting our real and essential identity. The spat between the Church and the secular humanists did not occur. In contrast, Buddhist philosophy and practice is grounded upon a realization of the impermanent (*anitya*) and fluctuating nature of the self (*pratityasamutpada*) of all sentient beings as impermanent, multifaceted and "relational" processes.[6]

King goes on to argue that such a disruption "is motivated on my part by a concern to transgress the limits set up by the lacunae in much contemporary postcolonial theorization—as if the European framings of the debate were the only options available to the postcolonial critic." And he concludes, "The introduction of a variety of indigenous epistemic traditions is, in my view, the single most important step that postcolonial studies can take if it is to look beyond the Eurocentric foundations of its theories and contest the epistemic violence of the colonial encounter."[7] While I find King's argument very compelling as well, the problem with this gesture, and others like it, is that they usually come before or after a study that does not enact this "break" with Western theory in the slightest. King is, I believe, on to something, but his gesture remains just that.

Furthermore, Chow worries that suggestions made by scholars like King may lead critics to return to essentializing forms of nativism, and she has good reason to worry. There is little value in simply endorsing, for instance, a Sinocentric episteme over a Eurocentric one, since such structures of knowledge are inherently invested in state ideology (and undergird ethnic, cultural, or racial notions of superiority). With the dramatic rise of *guoxue* ("state studies," or the studies of Chinese classics) among the business and political classes in China, for instance, we see a shift from Marxist to Confucian rhetorical idioms beginning to take place.[8] And while this might have been appealing to the Tel Quel, who after their return from China in the mid-1970s lamented that "China is fully imbricated in an economic and political model that the West already *knows*,"[9] there is little doubt that Confucian ideology will offer the kind of "other logic" of which they dreamed. Instead, as we enter this "Pacific Era," the Chinese state's embrace of classical Chinese philosophy and aesthetics (which Sollers identified as being apposite with the French avant-garde's poststructuralist agenda) has been reintroduced as a function of state ideology, showcased during the stunning Olympic opening ceremony in Beijing (where there was not a single reference to Mao or the proletariat, but a headlong embrace of classical history, literature, aesthetics, and ritual). There is little doubt that elements of China's classical rhetoric and aesthetics will be repurposed to support PRC's state ideology, which will complicate its status as a "countercultural logic" in the Western poetic imagination due to its non-Western origins. Clearly, the heterocultural nature of the transpacific imaginaries discussed in this work have, within their historical contexts, succeeded in challenging traditional Western metaphysics, yet I would argue that future transformations of the poetics of emptiness will need to adapt to these changing geopolitical trends to remain relevant.

Interestingly, one of the most important facets of the poetics of emptiness that has kept it relevant to the present moment is perhaps the same thing that has kept it marginalized in literary criticism: its messiness—its decidedly unfixed, heterocultural nature. Buddhologists and sinologists, interested in the "primary texts," have not taken a great interest in what I have called the "transformations" of the "transpacific imaginary," which by still other names might be called the "distortions" of the "lay American dabbler" or some other dismissive marker. While I believe good scholarship should engage in compulsory self-reflexive analysis of how its political and ideological, even methodological, investments frame non-Western cultural discourses, this scholarly agenda is not the ultimate goal of the heterocultural poetry and poetics explored in this work. The texts read in this book willfully (and otherwise) interfuse and transform multiple cultural discourses in the hope of producing heterocultural idioms different from both the East Asian and Western discourses they draw upon and contribute to; they embrace poetics as a third space of cultural production—a *tertium quid,* to borrow a term favored by Theresa Hak Kyung Cha.

In light of this different intellectual and cultural agenda, I do not believe that we can dismiss the particular historical manifestations of the poetics of emptiness for the transhistorical/cultural brush with which they are often formulated. After all, the East Asian aggregates of American poetics will always be meaningful, regardless of the historical rigor of their articulation. The question is whether literary criticism will take up the challenge of engaging the multifarious, heterogeneous cultural discourses that condition these complex cultural productions. In this sense, what the work of Ernest Fenollosa, Gary Snyder, Wai-lim Yip, or Theresa Hak Kyung Cha makes accessible, a polymorphous and unstable transpacific imaginary, is perhaps more important than what they "distort or misrepresent" in a strict scholarly sense. While I believe that criticism must be able to address distortions made by both poets/translators and critics if they perpetuate systemic misrepresentations, it is just as important to note the metaphysical fiction that underlies notions of interlingual semantic fidelity itself. As Lydia Liu passionately argues following Jorge Borges, "It is the business of this industry [bilingual dictionaries] to make sure that one understands 'that languages are made up of equivalent synonyms.'"[10] Liu uses the examples of non-synonymous "translations," like the English word "self," or "individual," and the so-called Chinese "equivalents" *ji, wo, ziwo*, to underscore the very real incompatibility of the conceptual framework each term depends on for its meaning.[11] Therefore, it is important to track the transformations of meanings across linguistic (and cultural) systems but foolhardy to search for exact equivalents. In this light, one may be able to glimpse one of the more progressive elements of heterocultural poetry and poetics: it seeks to find new forms of perception, not equivalent ones.

Setting the metacritical context of this debate aside, there remains a practical question I am not sure Chow, King, or others have presenced: namely, how is one to "read" heterocultural texts animated by various cultural and epistemic discourses if one's interpretive frame is not "literate" in the discourses conditioning the text? Can the theorizing Chow and Wilson wish to bring to their "undertheorized" transpacific texts respond to the heterocultural discourses that inform them? At a practical level, how does a critic engage a term like "emptiness," with its heterogeneous signification across multiple epistemic and ontological traditions, as it appears in cultural productions as varied as those of Gary Snyder and Theresa Hak Kyung Cha? Interestingly, it may well have been Ezra Pound, in his *Cantos*, who has offered (or forced upon us) one of the best solutions to this quandary. As a poem that "contains history," the *Cantos* might be more generatively described as an intertext constructed out of far more languages, historical, mythical, and literary allusions, etc., than those his readers might bring to the text. Therefore, his readers are forced to investigate clues and follow leads, acquire new languages, and familiarize themselves with previously unknown (and/or ignored) texts in order to "read" the poem at all. Following this basic methodology, the poetics of emptiness under discussion here is an invitation to become more generous, curious, and ambitious readers than we might be without it. As I have mentioned earlier, heterocultural poetry offers readers the opportunity to develop reading frames as hybrid as the texts being read. Of course, this is an invitation to become other than what we were before interacting with them and is no small endeavor.

Given the need to expand beyond our habitual hermeneutic horizons, I did not see sufficient reasons to adopt Rey Chow's rejection of Asian studies as a repository for metacritical concepts (and historical/cultural contextual information) that we may need to attend to the heterocultural dimensions of this work. Yet the impetus of this work is not guided by the sole desire to include non-Western epistemic traditions in contemporary literary criticism either. As I believe this study has made very clear, Asian philosophical and aesthetic traditions are already interfused within American literary discourses, so it is up to critics to learn how to engage these heterocultural conditions, not to idealize them or lament the difficulty or impossibility of their introduction from a mythic "outside." It is my hope that this work will not defend Western theory from the "nativist" barbarians at the gate, or gesture fancifully to epistemological systems beyond it. After all, there is no gate, just as there is not something beyond it waiting to save Western scholarship from its provinciality. The outside is already here, in our poetry.

NOTES

Prologue: Transformations of a Transpacific Imaginary

1. Barnstone, "The Poem behind the Poem," 3.

2. Ibid., 4–5 (italics mine).

3. Ibid., 4. See also Geoff Waters's insightful essay, "Some Notes on Translating Classical Chinese Poetry," in the on-line publication *Cipher Journal*. Waters writes: "Liu wrote this poem after he was demoted in 815 to a minor post in the far southern town of Liuzhou, where he died a few years later. Liu's career had been in ruins since September 805, when the Shunzong Emperor abdicated suddenly after only six months on the throne. Shunzong had appointed the reformer Wang Shuwen to be Grand Councilor, temporarily ousting Wu Yuanheng and his powerful party. Wang, in turn, appointed a number of idealistic younger scholars to senior positions in his government, including Liu Zongyuan and Liu Yuxi. When Shunzong was forced out, Wang Shuwen fell and Liu Zongyuan's official career was effectively over. I see in this poem, beneath the striking visual, an ironic self-commentary: Liu was growing old, banished, alone, and wasting his talent far from Court, in a deep southern backwater town where snow never fell."

4. Yeh, "The Chinese Poem."

5. Lucas Klein offers a provocative reading of Liu's use of a technique called *aojue* 拗絕, which Klein defines as "roughly equivalent to either feminine rhymes or off-rhymes in English. Rhyming on three 'entering' tones—as they were called—the *rusheng* 入聲 no longer a part of standard Chinese, this poem cross-cuts against the grain of expected Tang poetry versification, leaning as it does on the clipped notes of *dzhiu ɛ t*, *mi ɛ t*, and *siu ɛ t*. The effect, no longer attainable without special training, would have been jarring to poetry readers of the day, signaling an undercurrent of disquiet beneath the otherwise tranquil scene of the poem" (see Klein, "Liu Zongyuan & Fishing in the Snow of Translation"). This reading suggests that Liu was not simply offering a scene of Buddho-Daoist "emptiness" in the abstract.

6. Yeh, "The Chinese Poem," 251.

7. I will discuss this point further in Chapter 4.

8. Wilson, *Reimagining the American Pacific*, 33.

9. Ibid., 31.

10. Huang, *Transpacific Displacement*, 3.

11. Ibid., 4. For Greenblatt's full argument, see his *Marvelous Possessions*, 99.

12. See Whorf, *Language, Thought, and Reality*.

13. Whorf, "An American Indian Model of the Universe," quoted in Yip, "The Use of 'Models' in East–West Comparative Literature," 17.

14. Yip, "The Use of 'Models' in East–West Comparative Literature," 17.

15. Ibid., 18.

16. Zong-qi Cai, *Configurations of Comparative Poetics*, 249–50.

17. Ibid., 250.

Introduction: The Poetics of Emptiness, or a Cult of Nothingness

1. Droit, *The Cult of Nothingness*, 9.

2. Loy, *Nonduality*.

3. See Loy, *A Buddhist History of the West*, for an interesting expansion of this idea.

4. This is not to say that "nothingness" is uniformly a binary construct in the West. In the final chapter of Ron Schliefer's book, *Intangible Materialism*, for instance, he offers a Peircean semiotic reading of such "nothingness" in relation to pain that replaces binarity with a Peircean triad: sensuousness (experience without "meaning" and hence "empty"); reference (indexicality); and meaning. The book also spends some time following the semiotics of "zero" (which I discuss in the following paragraph) as something more than "simply" nothing.

5. Hugo, *Les misérables*, pt. 2, bk. 7, chap. 6, http://www.gutenberg.org/etext/135.

6. A good example of the equation of evil to nothingness can be found in the writing of St. Augustine in particular (see Williams, "Insubstantial Evil"). There are instances in Western literature and negative theology where the opposite is posited, as in, for example, Yeats's short story "Where There Is Nothing, There Is God." See also Jin Y. Park's discussion of "nothingness" in the philosophy of Heidegger in "The Logic of Nothing and A-Metaphysics."

7. Heidegger wrote the "Letter on Humanism" in November, 1946, about three months after he cooperatively translated the *Daodejing* with the Chinese scholar, Paul Shih-yi Hsiao. See Paul Shih-yi Hsiao's essay "Heidegger and Our Translation of the Tao Te Ching," in *Heidegger and Asian Thought*, edited by Graham Parkes. Honolulu: University of Hawaii Press, 1987, 93–104.

8. See Derrida's early essay on Bataille and Hegel, "From Restricted to General Economy: A Hegelianism without Reserve."

9. It is important to note that this poem's lamentation of the lost center offers a different pathos than much of Yeats's other work.

10. Nietzsche, *The Genealogy of Morals*, 299. Slavoj Žižek comments on this negative view of nothingness: "In order to account for the nihilistic denial of the assertive will to life, Nietzsche, in *On the Genealogy of Morals*, introduced the well-known distinction between someone not willing anything at all and someone willing nothing itself." Nihilistic hatred of life is "a revolt against the most fundamental presupposi-

tions of life: yet it is and remains a will! . . . Rather than want nothing, man even wants nothingness" (Žižek , *The Ticklish Subject*, 107).

11. See Yeats's early short story "Where There Is Nothing, There Is God," in which he offers a negative theology in part drawn from his study of Irish occultism.

12. For an interesting discussion of the image *qua* negativity, see Calichman, "Nothing Resists Modernity."

13. Auden, *Collected Poems*, 247.

14. Fredmen, "Neo-Paganism, Buddhism, and Christianity," 203.

15. So the present study is not broadly focused upon different concepts of emptiness that have migrated (by way of heterocultural transformation) into American poetry, which would necessarily need to concentrate on the incredibly influential works of Phillip Whalen, John Cage, Jackson Mac Low, and Allen Ginsberg, for instance. But these poets, and many more (I will offer a longer list in a moment), do not come to their own poetics of emptiness through concepts of principally Chinese poetic and philosophical textuality, and therefore will have to be taken up at a later time.

16. *OED*, http://dictionary.oed.com/cgi/entry/50040044?query_type=word&queryword=zero&first=1&max_to_show=10&sort_type=alpha&result_place=1 (accessed 31 August 2007).

17. In verse 18 of the *Mūla*, Nāgārjuna writes:

Whatever is dependently co-arisen,
That is explained to be emptiness.
That, being a dependent designation,
Is itself the middle way.
(Nāgārjuna, *The Fundamental Wisdom of the Middle Way*, 48)

Jay Garfield, who translated Nāgārjuna's *Mūlamadhyamakakārikā*, comments: "These are the two truths: on the one hand they are conventionally existent and the things we say about them are in fact true, to the extent that we get it right on the terms of the everyday. . . . On the other hand, they are not (independently) existent. These two truths seem as different as night and day—being and non-being. But . . . their ultimate nonexistence and their conventional existence are the same thing—hence the deep identity of the Two Truths. And this is true because emptiness is not other than dependent-arising, and hence because emptiness is empty" (Garfield, *Empty Words*, 39).

18. While clearly leaving much to be desired, I will be using short dramatic dialogues for two reasons: first, because philosophical dialectics is an important rhetorical device in many schools of Buddhism; and second, because I believe that they work well to clarify points that might otherwise take a long time to develop through standard scholarly forms. I benefited early on from David Loy's use of this trope in his book *Nonduality: A Study in Comparative Philosophy*.

19. See *The Flower Ornament Scripture: A Translation of the Avatamsaka Sutra*.

20. Chapters 1 and 2 will explore Pound's deletions and discuss their relationship to Fenollosa's Buddhism in detail.

21. Drawing a distinction between the two schools, D. T. Suzuki writes in the introduction to his translation of the Lankavatara Sutra: "The Ālayavijñāna of the Yogācāra is not the same as that of Laṅkā and the Awakening of Faith. The former conceives the Ālaya to be purity itself with nothing defiled in it whereas the Laṅkā and the Awakening make it the cause of purity and defilement. Further, the Yogācāra upholds the theory of

Vijñaptimātra and not that of Cittamātra, which belongs to the Laṅkā, Avataṁsaka, and Awakening of Faith. The difference is this: According to the Vijñaptimātra, the world is nothing but ideas, there are no realities behind them; but the Cittamātra states that there is nothing but Citta, Mind, in the world and that the world is the objectification of Mind. The one is pure idealism and the other idealistic realism" (see Lirs*Ru website, http://lirs. ru/do/lanka_eng/lanka-intro.htm#introduction).

22. Tathāgatagarbha-inspired concepts, like the Tibetan concept of *rigpa,* may differ from one another in nuanced ways, but most point to a vast non-dual consciousness that undergirds all things.

23. See *Pruning the Boddhi Tree,* 3–29.

24. See the *Mahayana Mahaparinirvana-sutra.* The Nirvana Sutra argues that beings are embryonic Tathāgatas (thus-come ones, or "Buddhas," by virtue of the pervasiveness of the *buddha-dhātu,* Buddha-nature).

25. See Suzuki, *Lankavatara Sutra.*

26. Once again, W. B. Yeats is interesting to note in the context of cosmogony since in his early and intense study of Irish mythology and the occult he drew upon notions of "nothingness" informed by a similar pathos, one that sees nothingness as a generative monism, definitely different from Daoism but nonetheless interestingly similar in tone. For example, Yeats would define "nothingness" in terms of a "phaseless sphere," which Heather Marin traces to his friend AE's (George Russell's) book, *The Candle of Vision,* in which Yeats would come to find a description of a generative monist void/deity called "Boundless Lir": "In the beginning was the boundless Lir, an infinite depth, an invisible divinity, neither dark nor light, in whom were all things past and to be. There at the close of a divine day, time being ended, and the Nuts of Knowledge harvested, the gods partake of the Feast of Age and drink from a secret fountain. Their being there is neither life nor death nor sleep nor dream, but all are wondrously wrought together. They lie in the bosom of Lir, cradled in the same peace, those who hereafter shall meet in love or war in hate. The Great Father and the Mother of the Gods mingle together and Heaven and Earth are lost, being one in the Infinite Lir" (Russell, *The Candle of Vision,* 153). For a commentary that connects this passage to Yeats, see Martin, *W. B. Yeats,* 37.

27. Lao Zi, *Tao Te Ching,* 14.

28. Ibid., 42.

29. Ibid., 1.

30. Ibid., 40.

31. The term *ziran* appears in the *Daodejing,* 25: "*dao* follows the law of *ziran.*"

32. The term *wuwei* appears in chapter 63 of the *Daodejing* in the phrase "weiwuwei" 為無為, and the actual phrase "*wuwei*" shows up only three times in the inner chapters of the *Zhuangzi* but becomes a term of major philosophical and aesthetic import in and after Neo-Daoism.

33. This idea also parallels Michael Saso's description of "kenotic emptying of mind, heart, and emotions for the encounter with the Dao" (see Saso, *Blue Dragon, White Tiger,* 19; also, Saso, *Teachings of Master Chuang,* 225–33). Saso traces his notion of Kenotic practices to the *Zhuangzi Neipian.*

34. Lao Zi, *Tao Te Ching,* 16.

35. See "Keeping the One," a chapter in Schipper, *The Taoist Body,* 130–59.

36. The first volume in this series was published in 2009 and is entitled *The Emer-*

gence of Buddhist American Literature; there are more volumes forthcoming. See Storhoff, *Understanding Charles Johnson*, for another example of this expanding field.

37. See my essay "Listen and Relate: The Buddho-Daoist Poetics of Jackson Mac Low," which will appear in a forthcoming volume in the SUNY Press series on Buddhism and American Culture.

38. Sausy, "Fenollosa Compounded: A Discrimination."

39. From their conception, both the present volume and *The Chinese Written Character as a Medium for Poetry: A Critical Edition* were designed to complement one another. For example, for all of my citations to the original archival folders of Fenollosa's unpublished materials I have included the page numbers where these can be found in the *Critical Edition*, so that readers can easily move back and forth between the two published volumes. The introduction to the *Critical Edition* also offers a preview of the basic outline of my Buddhist reorientation of Fenollosa's famous essay, explored in the present work.

40. Alan Watts came to use this term to describe his loosely constructed Buddho-Daoist philosophical orientation. "Zennist," for Watts, therefore, is somewhat different from how I want to use it, but much of Watts's writing reveals "Zennist" reading habits, which interpret Chinese poetry, and even Daoism, through a hermeneutic influence by Zen (see Watts, *Tao*).

41. Emerson, "Nature."

1 / Emptiness in Flux: The Buddhist Poetics of Ernest Fenollosa's "The Chinese Written Character as a Medium for Poetry"

1. "Japan's Tribute to Fenollosa." *Boston Evening Transcript*, Dec. 24, 1920, A1.

2. See Hayot, "Critical Dreams." There is an updated version of this essay in Hayot, *Chinese Dreams*.

3. Ezra Pound, headnote to the 1936 edition of Fenollosa's *The Chinese Written Character as a Medium for Poetry*; Pound's note and the entire essay are reprinted in *The Chinese Written Character as Medium of Poetry: A Critical Edition*, 41–74.

4. Davie, *Articulate Energy*, 33.

5. Charles Olson discusses the CWC in his own poetry manifesto, "Projective Verse" (1950); see also his 1951 poem "The Gate and the Center."

6. Saussy, *Great Walls of Discourse and Other Adventures in Cultural China*, 38.

7. Kenner, *The Pound Era*, 158.

8. Ibid.

9. Huang defines "transpacific displacement" as "a historical process of textual migration of cultural meanings, meanings that include linguistic traits, poetics, philosophical ideas, myths, stories, and so on." I would like to preserve this sense of "transpacific textual migration" without necessarily limiting my exploration to the cultural studies emphasis that follows: "And such displacement is driven in particular by the writers' desire to appropriate, capture, mimic, parody, or revise the Other" (Huang, *Transpacific Displacement*, 3). Working through this overarching frame of mastery of Otherness, developed in the philosophy of Emanuel Levinas and carried on in the later work of Jacque Derrida, has saturated the hermeneutical habits of literary criticism to such an extent that other "reasons" for "transpacific displacement" are increasingly difficult to presence.

10. Kern, *Orientalism, Modernism, and the American Poem*, 7. Kern's use of this

"Adamic language" frame can also be found without a great deal of modification in Alexander Walsh's *Roots of Lyric: Primitive Poetry and Modern Poetics.*

11. Ibid., 7. If Kern means (which I believe he does) that there is little to no East Asian element in Fenollosa's thinking, he has far overextended himself, since he shows little to no interest in reading Fenollosa's own writing about Asia.

12. This is a point I will return to toward the end of the chapter.

13. Pound, *The Cantos,* 687. Pound would have come to this bias through the *Zizhi tongjian gangmu* 資治通鑑綱目 (A comprehensive mirror for the aid of government), by the eleventh-century Chinese historian Sima Guang. Pound read in Père Mailla de Moyriac's condensed French translation, *Hisoire genérale de la Chine,* names like "*bhud-foes*" and "*hochangs*" (Buddhists and monks), described as symptoms of societal decadence. Thank you to Haun Saussy for this point (and the quotation being annotated) (see Saussy, "Fenollosa Compounded," 19). I will return to Pound's particular "Confucian" interpretation of Fenollosa's essay at a later point in the chapter.

14. Also written in Chinese as 帝釋網 and 帝網 (see Soothill and Hodous, *A Dictionary of Chinese Buddhist Terms*).

15. While Fenollosa did not officially study Kegon Buddhism with a Kegon priest or scholar, he would have been familiar with "Indra's net" from the writing of his student and friend Kakuzo Okakura, who discusses this metaphor in his 1903 book *Ideals of the East.* Okakura writes, "For art, like the diamond net of Indra, reflects the whole chain in every link. It exists at no period in any final mould. It is always a growth, defying the dissecting knife of the chronologist. To discourse on a particular phase of its development means to deal with infinite causes and effects throughout its past and present. . . . We must pass in review the various phases of Confucian philosophy; the different ideals which the Buddhist mind has from time to time revealed" (Okakura, *The Ideals of the East, with Special Reference to the Art of Japan,* 9; again, gratitude to Haun Saussy for this reference).

16. Fenollosa, "The Chinese Written Language as the Medium for Poetry" [final draft, ca. 1906, with Pound's notes, 1914–1916], 97.

17. Ibid., 102.

18. Ibid., 103.

19. I will return to Pound's reading of Fenollosa after I explore the Buddhist epistemological and ontological undercurrents of Fenollosa's poetics.

20. On the political and intellectual conditions surrounding Fenollosa's university appointment, see Pyle, *The New Generation in Meiji Japan.*

21. While Fenollosa's ability to study under such a master was largely due to the drive to Westernize, it is important to note that Fenollosa helped both Kanô Hôgai (1828–88) and Hashimoto Gaho (1835–1908) reestablish themselves as major artists of the period. He even made Kanô Hôgai into a character embodying the synthesis of East and West in his epic poem "East and West."

22. In the course of these travels he was able to acquire a massive collection of Japanese art, which was purchased by the Boston Museum of Fine Arts.

23. For more information on Fenollosa's life, see his biography, *Ernest Fenollosa: The Far East and American Culture,* written by Lawrence Chisolm. See also Cohen, *East Asian Art and American Culture*; Yamaguchi, *Fenollosa*; and Fenollosa, Murakata, and Houghton Library, *The Ernest Fenollosa Papers* (the published version of Fenollosa's papers deposited at the Houghton Library, Harvard University).

24. Snodgrass, *Presenting Japanese Buddhism to the West*, 2.

25. Fenollosa, "Contemporary Japanese Art," 580.

26. See Snodgrass, *Presenting Japanese Buddhism to the West*, 32; and the *Japan Weekly Mail* for January 30, 1892, for an original account of this assertion.

27. For representations of this art, see the catalogue of an exhibition held at the Tokyo National Museum, April 3–May 11, 1997: "World's Columbian Exposition of 1893 Revisited." For an interesting connection between Japanese "modernism" and American "modernism" in architecture, see Nute, "Frank Lloyd Wright and Japanese Art"; Nute uncovers the fact that Lloyd's first employer was Fenollosa's first cousin, and speculates on how Japanese art theories would have entered Lloyd's own architectural ideas.

28. Snodgrass, *Presenting Japanese Buddhism to the West*, 33.

29. Ibid., 2.

30. Inoue, *Bukkyo katsuron*. This work is reproduced in the journal *Meiji bunka zenshu*, vol. 9, *Shukyo* (1954): 377–416. An English translation can be found in the appendix of Staggs, "In Defence of Japanese Buddhism," 398. See also Staggs, "Defend the Nation and Love the Truth"; and Snodgrass, *Presenting Japanese Buddhism to the West*, 142.

31. For an overview, see Jansen, "Modernization and Foreign Policy in Meiji Japan."

32. Fenollosa, "The Chinese Written Character as a Medium for Poetry: An Ars Poetica," with a Foreword and Notes by Ezra Pound [1918, 1936], 42.

33. Ibid., 75. Ezra Pound deleted the paragraph from which this quote was taken.

34. Fenollosa, "The Coming Fusion of East and West" [1898].

35. In his "Notes for a History of the Influence of China upon the Western World," Fenollosa situates his work within the context of European aggression in the settling of the Boxer Rebellion: "Through all my work in the East, I have felt it as a cold, sarcastic repression and scorn, on the part of Europeans. And it is this unfortunate prejudice against the most serious understanding of the East that is responsible for many tragic features in the present imbroglio at Peking" (174).

36. Fenollosa, "The Chinese Written Language as the Medium for Poetry" [final draft, ca. 1906, with Pound's notes, 1914–1916], 76.

37. Fenollosa, "The Coming Fusion of East and West" [1898], 155.

38. See "yellow peril" arguments like that found in Huntington, *The Clash of Civilizations and the Remaking of World Order*.

39. Fenollosa, "The Coming Fusion of East and West" [1898], 155.

40. See "Analysis and Synthesis," Ernest Francisco Fenollosa Papers, bMS Am 1759.2 (50), Houghton Library, Harvard University; "Idealism and Realism," Ernest Francisco Fenollosa Papers, bMS Am 1759.2 (36); and "Preliminary Lectures on The Theory of Literature: A Theory of Literature," in Fenollosa, Murakata, and Houghton Library, *The Ernest F. Fenollosa Papers*, 135–70.

41. Paul Carus also promoted this view; see Tweed, *The American Encounter with Buddhism*, 60–68. While Fenollosa held Western science as its most valuable asset to a global culture, he still viewed it with significant ambivalence.

42. Fenollosa gives a detailed account of Kang Yuwei's (1858–1927) attempts at East/West synthesis and political reforms in *Epochs of Chinese & Japanese Art* (V.II 21). Kang argued that China should imitate Meiji Japan in its program of reform, in-

cluding the adoption of a constitutional government. The Emperor Guangxu 光緒 (ruled 1875–1908) appointed Kang as the head of the government in June 1898, and Kang immediately began the "One Hundred Days of Reform," which issued edicts ranging from the inclusion of Western studies in all Chinese education, to reforms throughout the army and government. The edicts were implemented in only one province, however, and after only three months in power, a coup d'état returned authority to the conservative administrators led by the Empress Dowager.

43. *Seventh Report of the Class Secretary of the Class of 1874 of Harvard College. June 1889–June 1899* (Boston: Geo. H. Elis, 1899), 47, cited in Yutaka Ito, "*Words Quite Fail*," 199.

44. See Gompers, "Imperialism—Its Dangers and Wrongs." There were, however, many public figures like Andrew Carnegie, a classical isolationist fearing "European entanglement" who also opposed annexation for fear of race-mixing. Figures like David Starr Jordan, the founder of Stanford University, led the anti-miscegenation group, while the Anti-Imperialist League argued that an annexation would contradict the very republican and democratic foundations of the American system of government. Those arguing for annexation, like Kansas senator W. A. Peffer, argued along straightforward white supremacist lines for Anglo-Saxon world domination.

45. Fenollosa, "Coming Fusion," 155.

46. Ibid. What sets Fenollosa's apart from the positions of others, mentioned earlier, is his inversion of racial degeneracy theory, which took all forms of racial and cultural mixing as inherently "degenerative." Arthur Joseph de Gobineau, an early French race theorist, published his "Essay on the Inequality of Human Races" in 1854, in which he used anthropology, linguistics, and history to formulate a biologically determined theory of race that gave no opportunity for upward mobility, but saw all mixing as degenerate. Gobineau insisted that those races which remained superior were those that kept their racial purity intact—and that mixing would lead to "racial suicide" (Arthur de Gobineau, *The Inequality of Human Races*). Francis Galton, in a chapter from his book *Hereditary Genius* entitled "The Comparative Worth of Different Races," uses a grading scale to classify races by their "intelligence." Galton's genetic concepts of racial superiority became very popular in United States (and Europe). So, while as far back as 1691 some states had already banned all forms of interracial marriage, anti-"miscegenation" laws (itself a neologism of the mid- to late-nineteenth century meant to denote the negative, "degenerative" nature of race-mixing) gained a new pseudo-scientific legitimacy in the years of Fenollosa's writing. In his "Notes for a History of the Influence of China upon the Western World," Fenollosa explicitly compares Europeans' biased attitudes about Asia to Americans' racial attitudes: "Unfortunately, even today, we Westerners, for the most part, came to Asia, not to discover and welcome identities, but to impose our differences; and between the foreign residents of China and Japan and the natives there is almost as much of a caste feeling, as in our Southern states between the whites and the blacks. It is no mere missionary bias that leads us to undervalue their cultures, it is a solid jealousy of race and social prejudice" (199). So while Fenollosa fails to abandon the language of Social Darwinism, he does seek to use it against the Eurocentric grain of his period.

47. See Miller, *Benevolent Assimilation*.

48. See Nishida, "The Problem of Japanese Culture," 859; and Nishida, "Towards a Philosophy of Religion with the Concept of Pre-Established Harmony as Guide."

See also Sharf, "The Zen of Japanese Nationalism," in which the author discusses the works cited here. Finally, for a thorough discussion of Japanese Buddhism and imperialism/militarism in the mid-twentieth century, see Victoria, *Zen at War*; and Victoria, *Zen War Stories*.

49. See *Pruning the Bodhi Tree*.

50. While Kipling described the annexation of the Philippines as the "white man's burden," Fenollosa's own imperialism would be more accurately articulated through his "New Buddhist" orientation: a *"bodhisattva* burden" if you will.

51. The manuscript note is also described in Fenollosa, Murakata, Houghton Library, *The Ernest Fenollosa Papers*, 3:48.

52. "My position in America; a manifest of mission," manuscript note dated 1 May 1891, p. 1, Ernest Francisco Fenollosa Papers, bMS Am. 1759.2 (60), Houghton Library, Harvard University.

53. Ibid.

54. Ibid.

55. It is likely that Fenollosa is referring here to William James, *Principles of Psychology* (1890), since he uses terminology derived from James's discussion of music, which no doubt condition his views on the role of overtones in the production of harmony. See Saussy, "Fenollosa Compounded," 182–83n53, for a lengthy excerpt that compellingly links James's and Fenollosa's thinking on this point.

56. Fenollosa, "My position in America; a manifest of mission," manuscript note dated 1 May 1891, p. 1, Ernest Francisco Fenollosa Papers, bMS Am. 1759.2 (60), Houghton Library, Harvard University.

57. Tendai Buddhism is a major Sino-Japanese school of Mahayana Buddhism, named after Mount Tiantai in southeastern China, where its first monastery was established.

58. 中道實相 The reality of the "mean" is neither 有 substance (or existent), nor 空 void (or nonexistent), but a reality that is neither, which is to say, it is a "mean" between the two extremes of materialism and nihilism. This "mean" is found in a third principle between the two, suggesting a space beyond the categories of existence 有 and nothingness 無. This "mean" is 圓道—the perfect way (of the three principles of Tiantai) (see Soothill and Hodous, *A Dictionary of Chinese Buddhist Terms*, 398). For more on Tiantai, see Swanson, *Foundations of T'ien-T'ai Philosophy*.

59. The dialectical method argues that historical process, or the progress of the "spirit's" movement toward self-consciousness and freedom, manifests as a dialectic tension, as a result of mankind's limitations at each phase of history. This area of Hegel's thought has been often reduced (and grossly oversimplified) to a dialectical relationship of the categories of "thesis," "antithesis," and "synthesis." An idea contains a form of incompleteness that gives rise to the antithesis, a conflicting idea, and a third point of view, a synthesis, arises from this conflict. This synthesis overcomes the conflict by reconciling the truths contained in the thesis and antithesis at a higher level, but the synthesis, which is a new thesis, generates a new antithesis, and the process continues until truth is arrived at—which Inoue claims to have found in the Tendai "middle path."

60. Inoue, *Bukkyo katsuron: Joron*, 398. Inoue's revelation that Buddhism's "Middle Way" is superior to Western religion and philosophy took place in 1885, the same year that he graduated from Tokyo University, and the same year that Fenollosa

took Buddhist ordination. The fact that Fenollosa, who was nicknamed *daijin sensei* (teacher of great men), took his ordination in this year would have lent great support to Inoue's thesis that all Western philosophers would logically convert to Buddhism once they were properly introduced to Japanese Mahayana. On the other hand, Inoue's claim that Tendai doctrines were superior to all Western religion and philosophy would have also have bequeathed Fenollosa a unique status among both his Asian and Western peers.

61. "Remarks on Japanese Art in General," p. 8, Ernest Francisco Fenollosa Papers, bMS Am 1759.2 (84), Houghton Library, Harvard University.

62. Chisolm, *Ernest Fenollosa*, 131.

63. Fenollosa, *Epochs of Chinese & Japanese Art*, 145.

64. For more about Rhys Davis, the Pali Text Society, and colonialism, see Almond, *The British Discovery of Buddhism*.

65. For a discussion on how both the Buddhist and Christian delegates to the exhibition deployed Social Darwinism, see Snodgrass, *Presenting Japanese Buddhism to the West*, 2, 16, 20–21, 47, 61, 80.

66. Fenollosa, *Epochs of Chinese & Japanese Art*, 29.

67. Fenollosa, "The Chinese Written Character as a Medium for Poetry: An Ars Poetica," with a Foreword and Notes by Ezra Pound [1918, 1936], 46.

68. Ibid. Fenollosa makes a similar point in an earlier draft of the CWC: "For in nature, in a plant, for instance, all things are done at once, the flow of sap, the assimilation of nutriment, the bursting of leaves, the hardening of fiber and the coloring of petals, the storing of the seed essences, do not wait for our slow analyses, as separate groupings in successive time, but go on together, and what is more mutually affect one another. The abstraction of logic from the simultaneity and entanglement of forces, namely, all that which constitutes life; and so give us dead abstractions" ("Synopsis of Lectures on Chinese and Japanese Poetry," see *Critical Edition*, 110).

69. For an excellent discussion of *pratītya-samutpāda* (Pali: *praticca-samutpada*), see Garfield, *Empty Words*. For a discussion of "Indra's net" and the Avatāmsaka/Huayan/Kegon ("Flower Garland") school/*sutra*, see *The Flower Ornament Scripture: A Translation of the Avatamsaka Sutra*.

70. Fenollosa, ""Preliminary Lectures on The Theory of Literature," 156.

71. Whalen Lai makes this point in "Ch'an Metaphors."

72. This metaphor can be found in the Platform Sutra (see Yampolsky, *The Platform Sutra of the Sixth Patriarch*), and *Zen Words for the Heart: Hakuin's Commentary on the Heart Sutra,* among many other places. The Critical Buddhism movement in Japan during the late 1980s cited this metaphor as a prime example of "non-Buddhist" monism common to most contemporary Japanese Buddhism (see Noriaki, "Critical Philosophy versus Topical Philosophy").

73. Fenollosa, "The Chinese Written Character as a Medium for Poetry: An Ars Poetica," with a Foreword and Notes by Ezra Pound [1918, 1936], 46.

74. Ibid., 50. Following this line, it is difficult to believe that Fenollosa was philosophically invested in the idea of characters as pictures of things. Furthermore, he routinely criticizes the West for its valuation of photographic realism in art, since such work falsely purports to show the "whole truth" (see Fenollosa, *Epochs of Chinese & Japanese Art*; and additional quotes in "The Chinese Written Character as a Medium

for Poetry: An Ars Poetica," with a Foreword and Notes by Ezra Pound [1918, 1936], 45–46).

75. Fenollosa, "The Chinese Written Character as a Medium for Poetry: An Ars Poetica," with a Foreword and Notes by Ezra Pound [1918, 1936], 50.

76. Ibid., 52.

77. Ibid., 51.

78. *OED* online database.

79. Fenollosa, "The Chinese Written Character as a Medium for Poetry: An Ars Poetica" (see *Critical Edition*, 56).

80. Fenollosa, "Chinese and Japanese Poetry. Draft of Lecture I, Vol. 1," 27–29. The earlier drafts of the CWC often contain analogous passages to those found in the version edited and published by Pound. In this case, Fenollosa's earlier draft retained the clearest articulation of his argument (see "Chinese and Japanese Poetry. Draft of Lecture I. Vol. I," Ezra Pound Papers, box 99, folder 4218, Beinecke Library, Yale University); Fenollosa also discusses this point in even more detail in a lecture entitled "Analysis and Synthesis," where he states: "Our very language becomes analytic, and we think that we get accuracy as each word comes to express the smallest shred of thought . . . .But in this way we do not really exhaust all the relations of things to one another, we merely ignore some of them. Things are not related to one another merely in series, or classified and enumerated groups. Several things, thoughts, or feelings may be so related as mutually to modify one another; and this modification sometimes is of such a nature that a new whole or entity is produced out of the parts which have become transfigured by their new relation" (see "Lecture on Analysis and Synthesis," p. 2, Ernest Francisco Fenollosa Papers, bMS AM 1759.2 [50], Houghton Library, Harvard University).

81. This point will be taken up in greater detail in a moment.

82. "The Chinese Written Character as a Medium for Poetry: An Ars Poetica," (see *Critical Edition*, 56).

83. *The Selected Letters of Ezra Pound*, 49.

84. Pound, *ABC of Reading*, 19–23.

85. "In the spring or early summer of 1912, H.D. [Hilda Doolittle], Richard Aldington, and myself decided that we were agreed upon the three following principles:

1. Direct Treatment of the "thing," whether subjective or objective.

2. To use absolutely no word that does not contribute to the presentation.

3. As regarding rhythm, to compose in the sequence of the musical phrase, not in the sequence of the metronome. (*Literary Essays of Ezra Pound*, 3)

86. The original *Alalects* 13.3 reads: 子路曰："卫君待子而为政，子将奚先？"子曰："必也正名乎！"子路曰："有是哉，子之迂也！奚其正？"子曰："野哉，由也！君子于其所不知，盖阙如也。名不正，则言不顺；言不顺，则事不成；事不成，则礼乐不兴；礼乐不兴，则刑罚不中；刑罚不中，则民无所措手足。故君子名之必可言也，言之必可行也。君子于其言，无所苟而已矣。 Chinese text cited from http://zhongwen.com/lunyu.htm. Pound's translation is from *Confucius*, 29–31. Here Pound's other important Confucian term, sincerity, is linked into his linguistic project. Pound's translation of *cheng yi*, usually translated as "making one's thoughts sincere," becomes "sought precise verbal definition of their inarticulate thoughts," which reveals the mimetic theory of language that formed the basis of his translative practices.

87. Pound, *Confucius*, 249. See also Lan, *Ezra Pound and Confucianism*. Lan locates Fenollosa as a principal catalyst in Pound's positivism, citing (like a broken record) that Fenollosa sought "language derived mostly from the use of concrete images." And, therefore, "by equating the natural law with the visual in language, the true with the concreteness of images, Pound assigned to poetry the task of bringing words closer to things" (63). Lan's reading of Fenollosa mirrors Pound's in the *ABC of Reading*, which places a special emphasis on concrete images as precise things, which supposedly, for Fenollosa, provides a solution to the abstractions of Logic.

88. Lan, *Ezra Pound and Confucianism*, 46–47.

89. Cheadle, *Ezra Pound's Confucian Translations*, 65.

90. In his study, Lan points out that Western literary criticism casts Pound's Confucianism into an unfavorable light. He cites critics like Alicia Ostriker, who attributes Pound's turn from the Goddess-worshiping Greeks to the Patriarchy of Confucianism. For James Wilhelm, Confucianism was a turn away from religious tolerance, and for Leon Surrete, Pound's turn from Plato's republic to Confucian totalitarianism planted the seeds of Fascism. Yet Lan justly points out that Western literary critics have not engaged Confucian source materials, and therefore cannot help operating from a simplistic understanding of Confucianism, which should cast doubt upon their speculations. Lan, on the other hand, explores how Pound's interpretation of Confucianism differs significantly from the Confucianism discourses under discussion in "Confucian Studies" present and past. Yet Lan also criticizes Confucian scholars' reluctance to engage Pound for fear of his controversial (a euphemism) political and racial ideas and his infamy as an amateur sinologist (a distain only rivaled by that for Fenollosa) (see Lan, *Ezra Pound and Confucianism*, 7–8). See also Ostriker, "The Poet as Heroine," 35; Wilhelm, *Ezra Pound*, 24–27; and Surette, *Pound in Purgatory*, 74.

91. Fenollosa, "The Chinese Written Character as a Medium for Poetry: An Ars Poetica," with a Foreword and Notes by Ezra Pound (see *Critical Edition*, 45).

92. See Huang, *Transpacific Imaginations*, 143. The earliest printing of "In a Station of the Metro" is in the April 1913 issue of *Poetry*.

93. Ibid., 152.

94. Ibid. (Huang's emphasis).

2 / Patterned Harmony: Buddhism, Sound, and Ernest Fenollosa's Poetics of Correlative Cosmology

1. While I found this lecture during the summer of 2004, I had not transcribed more than a few pages until the summer of 2005, when I was able to return to Yale thanks to the generous support of Haun Saussy, who found funding for my project and also helped support the long hours of transcribing that followed, including helping me get past many of the most inscrutable words in the text.

2. Most of these texts have been transcribed, annotated, and published in *The Chinese Written Character as a Medium for Poetry: A Critical Edition*.

3. Page marked "Fenol" in Pound's hand. Ezra Pound Archive, box 99, folder 4423, Yale University Libraries, Beinecke Library.

4. See *The Chinese Written Character as a Medium for Poetry: A Critical Edition*.

5. See also William James's notions of "overtones" and "unity," in his *Principles of Psychology*.

6. Joseph Needham used this term to describe Chinese cosmological thought (see Needham, *Science and Civilization in China*, vol. 2, 277, 280–89).

7. The practice of translating Buddhist terms into existing Chinese term/concepts, *geyi* 格義, was used in the early transmission of Buddhist texts into China, but was later abandoned for the practice of transliteration.

8. The Huayan school chose the *Avatamsaka Sutra* (Ch: *Huayan jing*) for its foundation, which immediately located this school in distinct epistemological position vis-à-vis all previous schools, for the *Avatamsaka* describes the historical Buddhist moment of awakening itself, which means an epistemology based upon this sutra begins from a nirvanic, rather than samsaric perspective (which most traditional Buddhist schools emphasized in one form or another).

9. Lai, "Chinese Buddhist Causation Theories," 243. In addition to the influence of Chinese cosmogony, Lai argues that this movement toward harmonious becoming and spontaneous oneness can be traced back to a particular Chinese version of the *Prajnaparamita Sutra* translated by the great Kumarajiva. According to Lai, Kumarajiva's choice of the word 即是 (*jishi*) is the copula in "rūpam śūnyam eva" (form [is] empty only). Lai writes: "The Chinese word for is 'is'—namely, chi-shi [*jishi*]—is not required in Sanskrit in this instance. Apparently, the Buddhist usages such as samsāra is nirvāna or form is emptiness introduced a strength or magnitude of meaning (signifying symmetrical identity), perhaps not available in earlier usage of the Chinese *chi* [*ji*] A=B." Lai continues by discussing Nāgārjuna's strong efforts to negate and not to affirm: "That is, things neither come nor go, are neither the same nor different" (ibid., 253–54).

10. In Pound's edited version, this line reads: "Poetry surpasses prose especially in that the poet selects for juxtaposition those words whose overtones blend into a delicate and lucid harmony" (see Pound's appendix to Fenollosa's "The Chinese Written Character as a Medium for Poetry: An Ars Poetica" [with a Foreword and Notes by Ezra Pound, 1918, 1936], 60).

11. Clearly, we can see an echo of Keats's negative capability, but Fenollosa's explanation takes on explicit classical Chinese shadings.

12. Fenollosa, "Preliminary Lectures on The Theory of Literature: A Theory of Literature," 160.

13. This idea also parallels other Western interpretations of "Daoist" emptying. For example, Michael Saso's description of "kenotic emptying of mind, heart, and emotions for the encounter with the Dao" looks nearly the same as Fenollosa's description (see Saso *Blue Dragon, White Tiger*, 225–33). Saso traces his notion of kenotic practices to the *Zhuangzi Neipian*.

14. Fenollosa, "Chinese and Japanese Traits."

15. This idea is central to the poetics of emptiness developed by Wai-lim Yip discussed in Chapter 4.

16. Fenollosa, "Preliminary Lectures on The Theory of Literature: A Theory of Literature," 160–61.

17. Ibid., 161.

18. Ibid. I am reminded here of Denise Levertov's "Some Notes on Organic Form," from *The Poet in the World*, 7–13, in which Levertov speaks of the poet in similar terms, as a medium seeking out natural affinities and forms in nature.

19. Fenollosa, "Preliminary Lectures on The Theory of Literature: A Theory of Literature," 161.

20. Ibid.

21. Ibid., 160.

22. Owen, *Traditional Chinese Poetry and Poetics*, 19–20.

23. Ibid., 20.

24. Fan, *Wenxin diaolong zhu* 文心雕龍注 [Commentaries on *Wenxin diaolong*], 1.

25. Cai, *Configurations of Comparative Poetics*, 160.

26. See Liu Xie, *Book of Literary Design,* trans. Siu-kit Wong, Allan Chung-hang Lo, and Kwong-tai Lam.

27. Fan, *Wenxin diaolong zhu* 文心雕龍注 [Commentaries on *Wenxin diaolong*], 1–21.

28. Cai, *Configurations of Comparative Poetics,* 51.

29. Liu Xie, *Book of Literary Design*, trans. Siu-kit Wong, Allan Chung-hang Lo, and Kwong-tai Lam, 1. I have cited these translations, not for their fidelity to the original (for they are not), but for the closeness of their contemporary translation to Fenollosa's ideas at the turn of the century.

30. Liu, *Chinese Theories of Literature,* 16.

31. Fenollosa, "Preliminary Lectures on The Theory of Literature: A Theory of Literature," 145.

32. Ibid. It is unclear what the internal quote marks indicate here.

33. Ibid., 144.

34. Ibid. While we only find the term *wen/bun* used untranslated as harmony/synthesis in Fenollosa's lecture/essay "A Theory of Literature," one can find a discussion of *wen* and the origin of writing in notes taken during his studies with Professor Mori. Fenollosa writes, "Soketsu's (the language's founder) [Ch: Fu Xi or Bao Shi] skill in finding the true chord of nature was such that the heavens poured down grain, and the demons of night whine at it. The legend is as old as the characters, and scholars take it that the characters have a very deep essence in them, reaching to the essence of the universe and able to bring prosperity, or adversely, misfortune" Quoted by Huang, *Transpacific Displacement*, p. 38. A similar, albeit less dramatically presented account of writing's origin can be found in Xu Shen's postface to the *Shuowen jiezi* 說文解字, where he writes that Fu Xi, "looking up, contemplated the images (*xiang*) in the sky, and looking down, the markings (*fa*) on the earth. He observed the patterns (*wen*) on birds and animals and their adaptations to the earth. From nearby, he took hints from his own body, and elsewhere from other things. Then he began to make the 'eight trigrams' of the *Book of Changes,* to pass on the model symbols (*xianxiang*) to later times" (this translation of Xu Shen's *Shuowen jiezi* 說文解字 is from Gu, *Chinese Theories of Reading and Writing*, 85).

35. Fenollosa, "Preliminary Lectures on The Theory of Literature: A Theory of Literature," 144.

36. While it is easy to see why Fenollosa would be drawn to the binary opposition of *wen* and *luan*, I find it interesting that he fixates upon another binary opposition, between *wen* and *li*. After all, in his masterwork *Epoch's of Chinese & Japanese Art,* Fenollosa describes Zhu Xi's Neo-Confucian "synthesis" of the three teachings "the greatest intellectual feat accomplished by Chinese thought during the five millennia of its existence" (Vol. 2, 35).

37. Fenollosa always capitalizes "Ri."

38. Fenollosa, "Preliminary Lectures on The Theory of Literature: A Theory of Literature," 145.

39. Ibid., (Fenollosa's emphasis).

40. Yet Fenollosa's heterorcultural poetics does not stop at the limits of lexico-graphical expansion: he does not simply want to add *wen* to an abstract list of literary terms; he follows Liu Xie in arguing that the *Yijing* can be used to help perceive and manifest *wen* in one's daily life. For a further discussion of the transformations of the *guo*, see ibid., 147–49.

41. Fenollosa, "The Chinese Written Character as a Medium for Poetry: An Ars Poetica," with a Foreword and Notes by Ezra Pound (see *Critical Edition*, 54).

42. "The Chinese Written Language as a Medium for Poetry" (see *Critical Edition*, 95).

43. Fenollosa, "Chinese and Japanese Poetry. Draft of Lecture I. Vol. II" (see *Critical Edition*, 139).

44. Fenollosa, *Epochs of Chinese & Japanese Art*, Vol. 2, 5.

45. For Fenollosa this parallel between man and nature was wholly embodied by Chinese poetic form as extremely structured forms of parallelism, which I will return to in a moment (see Fenollosa, "Chinese and Japanese Poetry. Draft of Lecture I. Vol. II" [1903], *Critical Edition*, 138).

46. One of the most interesting things about Fenollosa's enthusiasm for correlative cosmology lies in how rarely this view has been shared by Western scholars in the twentieth century. While Joseph Needham, a Western scholar, finds value in the system(s) of "Chinese sciences," far more have viewed it with ambivalence, suspicion, or even distain: Émile Durkheim and Marcel Mauss argue it is a "primitive classification scheme," and Lévy Bruhl argues it is an example of "arrested development," "pre-logical thinking," and "balderdash." While Fenollosa's attempt to integrate correlative cosmology with his Tendai/Kegon epistemology reveals a rushed conflation on his part, the poetics he creates from this admixture is richly textured and totally unique (see J. J. Clarke, *The Tao and the West*, 68, 221; Durkheim and Mauss, *Primitive Classification*, 73–74; and Needham, *Science and Civilization in China*, 284–87).

47. For more on Yip's concept of "epistemological elaborations," see Chapter 4.

48. See Legge, *The Sacred Books of the East*, vol. 16, 424.

49. Ibid.

50. Ibid., 16:425.

51. Ibid.

52. This section of Fenollosa's translation notes is reproduced in Kodama, *American Poetry and Japanese Culture*, 66.

53. For more about this term see Bodman's dissertation, *Poetics and Prosody in Early Mediaeval China*, 262.

54. Ibid., 162.

55. Fenollosa describes the four tones as follows: "The open or even tone, which holds its sound on a musical level. The rising tone, which sounds something like a [*sic*] interrogative inflection; the falling tone, which is something like our inflection of pleading or negative assumption, and the closed tone, when the vowel sound was final-ly shut off by a consonant ending." It is important to note that the fourth of these tonal categories, "entering tones," are no longer present in modern Mandarin pronunciation

(a point I will return to in a moment, as Fenollosa takes this absence very seriously) ("Chinese and Japanese Poetry. Draft of Lecture I. Vol II" [see *Critical Edition*, 137]).

56. Ibid.

57. I have a Chinese essay on my style of translating (through mimicry) classical Chinese poetic form, entitled 夺胎换骨: 译诗存音, or "Evolving from Embryo and Changing the Bones: Translating the Sonorous," which is forthcoming in "外国文学研究" (*Foreign Literature Studies*). My first publication of this style of translation can be found in Stalling, "Five Variations of a Poem by Li Yu." Finally, this work will appear in my forthcoming book entitled *Yingelishi: Sinophonic English Poetry and Poetics* (under consideration).

58. A facsimile of this page of the manuscript is reproduced in *The Chinese Written Character as a Medium for Poetry: A Critical Edition*, p. 114, in the section of that work concerning Fenollosa's 1903 essay, "Synopsis of Lectures on Chinese and Japanese Poetry."

59. *The Chinese Written Character as a Medium for Poetry: A Critical Edition*, 104.

60. Fenollosa, "Chinese and Japanese Poetry. Draft of Lecture I. Vol. II," 132–33.

61. The usefulness of Chinese poetry appeared very differently to Ezra Pound, since he saw in it primarily a powerful alternative to formal Victorian verse forms. Pound is, therefore, correct when he reads the CWC as "a study of the fundamentals of all aesthetics," but he and Fenollosa differ considerably in their understanding of these fundamentals. The glue that has held Fenollosa and Pound together for nearly a century may reside in the simple fact that one of them edited and controlled the texts of the other. Fenollosa was, after 1908, dead, in the conventional sense as well as in the sense of Roland Barthes's "death of the author."

62. Taking his cue from Confucius's example of musical harmonies, the second half of the CWC discusses poetry in terms of a poetic synthesis that may have fueled Pound's formulation of the trinity: melopoeia, phanopoeia, and logopoeia. Fenollosa writes: "Looked at aesthetically, our own poetry can be thought of as made up of two planes or dimensions,—the elements of beauty that spring from the words regarded as thought, and the elements of beauty that spring from the words regarded as sound. Now the Chinese has both of these; but in it, the first is bound up with still another formal element, namely, the elements of beauty that spring from the words regarded as visible. Thus, Chinese poetry can be regarded as having three dimensions; like painting, with its line, its dark and light, and its color" (see Fenollosa, "Chinese and Japanese Poetry. Draft of Lecture I. Vol. II" [1903], 133).

63. Ibid., 131.

64. "Marpessa" first appeared in the *Poems* (1897) of Stephen Phillips (1868–1915). Fenollosa quotes two lines from Idas's address to Marpessa:

Not for this only do I love thee, but
Because Infinity upon thee broods;
And thou art full of whispers and of shadows.
Thou meanest what the sea has striven to say
So long, and yearnéd up the cliffs to tell;
Thou art what all the winds have uttered not,
What the still night suggesteth to the heart.   (Stephen Phillips, *Marpessa*, 25)

65. Fenollosa, "Chinese and Japanese Poetry. Draft of Lecture I. Vol. II" [1903], 130.

66. Ibid., 134.

67. (J.) Omakitsu: (Wang Wei, 王維), 699–761. The poem is unusual in having six characters per line, rather than the more typical five or seven. The original poem given here is quoted from Wang Wei *Wang Youcheng ji jian zhu* 王右丞集箋注 (Annotated Poetry of Wang Wei Minister of Works), 258.

68. I have altered the scansion only slightly to make the meter more clearly readable.

69. We will look at an example of the Chinese-inspired rhyme scheme later in the chapter.

70. "Quatrain" in Persian.

71. By "conceptual," I want to point to the "so-called conceptual poetry" of Kenny Goldsmith, for example, who in his book *Day* rewrites every word of a single edition of the *New York Times* as a book. The words, numbers, fonts, etc., may all be the same as the original, but his act of republishing them opens new ways of reading them. In this sense, Fenollosa wants to open new ways of reading texts that are "ready-made" insofar as their traditional English meters are already made, but philosophically banal (see Goldsmith, *Day*).

72. "Chinese and Japanese Poetry. Draft of Lecture I. Vol. II," 134.

73. Fenollosa stood outside this current, but the phonology of earlier phases of the Chinese language had been the object of intense research in the Chinese scholarly tradition (the eighteenth-century lexicographer Duan Yucai made essential contributions), but it was in the 1920s that an alphabetically-based phonetic system for ancient Chinese was elaborated by Bernhard Karlgren, using a variety of contemporary dialects, traditional rhyming dictionaries, and poetic texts themselves as evidence. Karlgren presented his results in his *Analytic Dictionary of Chinese and Sino-Japanese*. On Karlgren's studies in the light of later work, see Behr, "Odds on the Odes—How Old Chinese Became an (Almost) Natural Language in 1992." For an example of phonological recovery of Tang poetic art, see Stimson, "The Sound of a Tarng Poem."

74. See Karlgren, *Analytic Dictionary of Chinese and Sino-Japanese, 1923*.

75. "Chinese and Japanese Poetry. Draft of Lecture I. Vol. II," 134 . There is a certain tension between Fenollosa's argument that Sino-Japanese has preserved the fifth-century and later eighth- and ninth-century Chinese pronunciations, and his well-known (and erroneous) belief that Chinese is a largely non-phonetic language. If characters pointed to "relations among things themselves," rather than words, the Japanese (and Korean and Vietnamese, for that matter) would have used native words to pronounce all the characters, rather than attempting to preserve the Chinese sounds. The difference asserted between things and words is, of course, too simple to account for the history of linguistic contacts.

76. Fenollosa, *Epochs of Chinese & Japanese Art*, Vol. I, 41. In the posthumous publication of Fenollosa's book, Professor Petrucci notes that "'Go' signifies in Japanese 'Southern.'"

77. The word person 人, pronounced as *nin*, would come from this first wave of sound readings, from the Buddhist term for person, *ningen* 人間.

78. Fenollosa writes: "Again in the 8th and 9th Century, the sounds of Northern China were introduced in a 2nd wave of culture. Fortunately both of these systems of

sound have been preserved by the syllabary, for the former has persisted in Buddhist speech, the later as the official. We have then a key to measure the change of Chinese sounds, from the 5th C to the 9th—or at least from the South to the North" (Fenollosa, "Chinese and Japanese Poetry. Draft of Lecture I. Vol. II" [1903], 134–35).

79. Fenollosa, "Chinese and Japanese Poetry. Draft of Lecture I. Vol. II" [1903], 137.

80. Ibid., 135.

81. Fenollosa discusses Kukai's creation of the kana syllabary in *Epochs of Chinese & Japanese Art*, vol. 1, 146.

82. Siddham survives in East Asia where Tantric Buddhism persists—in places where, for example, Korean Buddhists still write seed syllables in a modified form of Siddham.

83. This is unclear because modern scholarship throws doubt upon Kûkai's influence over the creation of kana; the fact that Siddham remained in use in Tantric ritual in Japan indicates to me that Shingon would not need kana to do this as well.

84. Further evidence for the belief in the inherent power of esoteric sound can be found in Fenollosa's *Epochs*, in which he describes an esoteric practice using the "in" language and focus upon vocable mantric sounds (vol. 1, 156). Fenollosa also describes his own branch of Tendai at Miidera as being in the same vein as Kukai (vol. 1, 147).

85. "Landscape Painting and Poetry," Ezra Pound Papers, box 101, folder 4250, Beinecke Library, Yale University. As to the actual Romanized version of the kana, Fenollosa seems to have settled on one of the first systems to be developed, called the Hepburn system, which might well have come to Fenollosa's attention through his friend, student, and collaborator Okakura, who along with his brother Yoshisaburo (who served as Lafcadio Hearn's translator) learned English at their local Christian mission school, operated by Dr. James Hepburn who popularized this system of Romanization (see Okakura, *The Book of Tea*, 67).

86. Fenollosa describes this "*kei*" as "words of accent, at point of striking lute." "Landscape Painting and Poetry," Ezra Pound Papers, box 101, folder 4250, Beinecke Library, Yale University, p. 4.

87. Ibid.

88. Pound, "A Few Dont's by an Imagiste," 200–201.

89. "A Few Don'ts" originally appeared in *Poetry* in 1913 and then again in a collection of Pound's essays on poetry entitled "A Retrospect" in *Pavannes and Divagations,* 1918.

90. Mair and Mei, "The Sanskrit Origins of Recent Style Prosody," 394.

91. Shen Yue, *Songshu,* in Bodman, *Poetics and Prosody in Early Mediaeval China,* 134. The bracketed comments are Bodman's.

92. Qian, *Orientalism and Modernism,* 54.

93. Ibid., 28.

94. Fang, Preface to *The Classic Anthology Defined by Confucius,* x–xi.

95. Ibid., xi.

96. Ibid., xii. The transliteration reads:

| Kuan | kuan | tsü | kiu | tsai | ho | chy | chou |
| Yao | tiao | shu | nü | kün | tsy | hao | k'iu |

Ts'en	ts'y	hing	ts'ai	tao	yu	liu	chy
Yao	tiao	shu	nü	wu	mei	k'iu	k'iu
K'iu	chi	pu	te	wu	mei	sy	fu
Yu	tsai	yu	tsai	chan	chuan	fan	ts'e
Ts'en	ts'y	hing	ts'ai	tso	yu	mao	chy
Yao	tiao	shu	nü	chung	ku	lo	chy.

97. Ibid.

98. Ibid.

99. Charles Olson (*The Distances* [New York: Grove Press, 1960], 61–62) is cited in Sarra, "Whistling in the Bughouse," 11.

100. For further discussion of this point, see Cai, *Configurations of Comparative Poetics*, 38–40.

101. Ibid., 45–47.

102. Owen, *Traditional Chinese Poetry and Poetics*, 29.

103. Ibid.

104. Fenollosa, *Epochs of Chinese & Japanese Art*, vol. 1, 145.

105. Ibid., vol. 2, 3.

106. Ibid., vol. 1, 15.

107. Ibid., vol. 1, 19.

108. Owen, "Omen of the World," 83.

3 / Teaching the Law: Gary Snyder's Poetics of Emptiness

1. Snyder, *Mountains and Rivers without End*, 158.

2. Snyder, *The Real Work*, 21.

3. Snyder, *Riprap & Cold Mountain Poems*, 67.

4. See Faure, *Chan Insights and Oversights*, 211. See also Norton, "The Importance of Nothing." Norton also focuses on the way disjunction works soteriologically in Snyder's work, but I am more interested in exploring how this aspect of Snyder's work borrows from Zennist readings of classical Chinese poetry, not classical Chinese poetry as Norton, Snyder, and others have. The difference is, I believe, important to a critical reading of the heterocultural formation of "emptiness" more generally in Snyder's poetry and poetics.

5. Scalapino, Introduction to *Overtime*, by Philip Whalen, xviii. We can think of this as "wrecking" the dualistically organized mind.

6. Faure, *Chan Insights and Oversights*, 211. In a note Faure writes, "According to Wang Shizhen, this passage is based on an aphorism of the Chan master Dongshan Liangjie (807–869): 'A word that contains speech is a dead word; a word that no longer contains speech is a live word.'".

7. Snyder, Foreword to *A Zen Forrest, Sayings of the Masters*, comp. and trans. Soiku Shieematsu, viii.

8. Ibid., ix.

9. Also called the "turning point," *quan yu* (turning language), or *bu er zhiyan* (non-dual words).

10. Wright, *Philosophical Meditations on Zen Buddhism*, 103.

11. Cai, *Configurations of Comparative Poetics*, 285.

12. Snyder, *A Place in Space*, 5.

13. I want to emphasize, however, that this inversion is not simply reducible to a Romantic Western imposition on or an "external" homogenization of an exotic poetry and poetics, since this inversion has already taken place in traditional Zennist hermeneutic practices.

14. See Gu, *Chinese Theories of Reading and Writing*, 4–5.

15. "The Taste," in *Left out in the Rain*, 163.

16. Davie, *Poet as Sculptor*, 45.

17. Snyder, "We Wash Our Bowls in This Water," in *Mountains and Rivers without End*, 137–38.

18. Snyder, *Earth House Hold*, 129.

19. D. T. Suzuki usefully traces the Laṅkā to a book, found in the Dunhuang caves, called the "Record of Master and Disciple in [the Transmission of] the Laṅkā" (楞伽師資記), which identifies it with Guṇabhadra, the translator of the Sung, or four-volume, Laṅkā, and not with Bodhidharma, as is generally done by Zen historians. But there is another text found at Dunhuang, called "Record of the Succession of the Dharma-treasure" (歷代法寶記), which traces the Laṅkā back to Bodhidharma and not Guṇabhadra (see Suzuki, *The Lankavatara Sutra*, available online at http://lirs.ru/do/lanka_eng/lanka-nondiacritical.htm).

20. To simplify matters, I will use only the term *tathāgatagarbha*, rather than always using it along with the largely analogous term *Buddha-dhātu*. Furthermore, due to the rather esoteric notion of "gharba" as "womb-matrix," I will use the term "Buddha Nature," as it coincides with Snyder's poetics more seamlessly, and is not misleading when one considers the nearly apposite meanings of *Buddha-dhātu* and *tathāgatagarbha*.

21. *Pruning the Bodhi Tree*, 242.

22. I discuss this so-called "positive emptiness" on pages 13–17 of the introduction.

23. See Jason Lagapa's helpful essay, "Something from Nothing: The Disontological Poetics of Leslie Scalapino."

24. This is because this poem is thought to be his "enlightenment verse," a genre of writing said to be written at the moment of a poet's or teacher's awakening.

25. Dogen's essay is in Dogen, *Shōbōgenzō* (正法眼蔵).

26. While I cannot be certain, this teaching appears to be one of several sutras classed as *tathāgatagarbha* in nature.

27. Snyder, *Mountains and Rivers without End*, 137–38.

28. For definitions, see Soothill and Hodous, *A Dictionary of Chinese Buddhist Terms*. Also, there is an interesting dialogue in the journal *Connotations* that engages the issue of non-duality and water in Snyder's poem "The Canyon Wren" (see Chung, "Allusions in Gary Snyder's 'The Canyon Wren'"), but this essay should be read in the context of all of the articles about this issue that have been published in *Connotations* (see Whalen-Bridge, "Gary Snyder, Dôgen, and 'The Canyon Wren'"; Patke, Response to "Gary Snyder, Dôgen, and 'The Canyon Wren'"; and Whalen-Bridge, "My Poet Is Better than Your Poet: A Response to Rajeev Patke." The disagreement appears to be in the difficult nature non-duality takes in the poem and Whalen-Bridges's attempt to provoke non-dual mind forms by breaking down the subject/object, nature/man binaries through a discussion of non-human language reception.

29. Snyder, *Earth House Hold*, 57.

30. Many of Snyder's poems end with this retroactive unifying grammar: the poem "Wave" ends in the positive emptiness "of my mind"; the poem "Song of the Slip" ends in the expression "make home in the whole"; in "Kai, Today" Snyder ends with the single word "sea," and so on.

31. See Parkinson, "The Poetry of Gary Snyder," 616–32; the work is also cited in Altieri, *Enlarging the Temple*, 166.

32. Altieri, *Enlarging the Temple*, 136–37.

33. While Altieri is right to point out this difference, I find it odd that he implicitly endorses Snyder's unity over modernist tension as if the lack of tension necessarily leads to an ego-less work.

34. Ibid., 137.

35. About a year after composing this section, I found a poem/koan similar to the one Ben-Ami Scharfstein describes briefly in his introduction to *The Sound of the One Hand* (see Scharfstein, "Zen: The Tactics of Emptiness," 26).

36. And while usually one only talks about doing away with "distinctions," "discriminations," and "dualities," I think that one should feel at liberty to use the term "difference" here, in light of the fact that the "monistic" ontology that undergirds this view of emptiness delegitimizes the ontological status of anything separate or different from itself. We are led to believe that such distinctions are caused by mind, and thus are not uncaused, not separate from the monism that gives rise to them.

37. Interestingly, in the next chapter we explore a poetics of emptiness that attempts to challenge dualism by running in the opposite direction (by privileging the autonomous otherness of differentia). And yet both of these strategies present theories of language wholly discordant with contemporary literary criticism, which complicates their critical reception today.

38. "Practitioners of Reality," a symposium with Norman Fischer, Michael McClure, and Leslie Scalapino, held at Stanford University, March 2003.

39. This argument is often very heated, with both sides polemically attacking the other as being either non-Buddhist (Hindu) or nihilistic, depending on what definition of emptiness one ascribes to.

40. While now quite old, one of the best essays tying Snyder's poetry to Romanticism is "Gary Snyder's Turtle Island: The Problem of Reconciling the Roles of Seer and Prophet," by Charles Altieri .

41. Snyder, *Riprap and Cold Mountain Poems*, 46.

42. Snyder, *The Gary Snyder Reader*, 526.

43. Ibid., 524.

44. Snyder, *The Real Work*, 178.

45. For an in-depth analysis of ocular rhetoric in Zen and other Mahayana schools, see McMahan, *Empty Vision*.

46. Snyder, "Reflections on My Translations of the T'ang Poet Han Shan," 233.

47. Ibid.

48. Snyder, *The Real Work*, 39.

49. Snyder, *The Gary Snyder Reader*, 94.

50. Perelman, "Poetry in Theory." Perelman critiques Snyder's poetics as being "anti-theoretical" and "a-historical," citing Snyder's poem "What You Should Know to Be a Poet," as a prime example:

all you can about animals as persons.
the names of trees and flowers and weeds.
names of stars, and the movements of the planets
and the moon
your own six senses, with a watchful and elegant mind.
at least one kind of traditional magic:
divination, astrology, the book of changes, the tarot;
dreams.   (Ibid., 163)

"The poem," Perelman continues, "is crisply efficient in laying out the elements and ethics of the counterculture of the sixties. The book the poet needs to study is the natural world, enlarged by shamanism to include the supernatural" (163). Perelman then goes on to argue that "[while] the stoicism of the Zen stance can be valuable; nevertheless I find this poem, as a social representative of poetry, quite a problem. Perhaps some of my difficulties stem from the title. Would this be easier to take if it were called 'WHAT YOU NEED TO KNOW'? For a poem that wants to impart knowledge about the world as a whole, there are two main blank spots, both of them theoretical. 'To be a poet' you apparently don't need to know anything about poems or poetics, and you don't need to know anything about theory. . . . This poem seems constituted by an a-historical, antitheoretical stance: the know-nothing armchair bureaucrat, dilettante, intellectual, the *theorist* who has never bucked hay is the target of the poem's lecture" (163). Perelman is right, insofar as Snyder's poetics is ahistorical and the *theorist* is the target of Snyder's lecture—and Dale Wright's definition of "American Romantic Zen" as an "openness to cultural and historical ideas quite other than their own" is clearly applicable here, but I am not sure we can call Snyder's work "anti-theoretical," since this would imply that theory lies wholly within the domain of Perelman's (or our) own critical orientation. The list of "natural" phenomena and "elegant mind" speaks to/through particular cultural idioms informed by specific philosophical discourses, which must be explored if we are to offer a heterocultural reading of Snyder's transpacific elements.

51. See Kitarō, "The Problem of Japanese Culture," 859; and Nishida, "Towards a Philosophy of Religion with the Concept of Pre-Established Harmony as Guide." See also Sharf, "The Zen of Japanese Nationalism," who cites these works in his discussion. The question, however, is how one comes to define this direct apprehension.

52. Eshleman, "Imagination's Body and Comradely Display," 233.

53. Snyder, *The Gary Snyder Reader*, 544.

54. See Yampolsky, *The Platform Sutra of the Sixth Patriarch*. For more general discussion of Zen sutras, and the Platform Sutra in particular, see the more recent text by Dale Wright, *The Zen Canon*, at pp. 70, 89, and 150.

55. This connection between sound and enlightenment recalls a number of sutras and Chinese poems, including poems by both Su Shi and Han Shan that I will discuss later when we explore the soteriological dimensions of aurality in Zen poetics.

56. Yet the hagiographical approach to Snyder's work has been increasingly challenged by far more critical voices, like that of Timothy Gray in his groundbreaking work, *Gary Snyder and the Pacific Rim: Creating Counter-Cultural Community*. While this work is not particularly interested in reading Snyder's work through a critical Buddhist framework, it does situate him in a richly (and "thickly") textured

historical context informed by the transpacific critical orientation of Rob Wilson and others.

57. Chow, *Ethics after Idealism*, xviii.

58. See Michael Castro's important study, *Interpreting the Indian: Twentieth Century Poets and the Native American*. Castro devotes a chapter to a study of Snyder's Native American appropriations and interests and revisits the historical period that saw a reaction against ethnopoetics and Snyder's work *Turtle Island*. While Jerome Rothenberg left his Native American translations and anthologies behind to explore his Jewish "roots," Snyder concentrated more than ever on the transpacific dimension of his poetics.

4 / Language of Emptiness: Wai-lim Yip's Daoist Project

1. The original publication date of *Zhongguo shi xue* was 1992; an expanded edition was published by Renmin Wenxue Chubanse in 2006.

2. Yip's English work began with his landmark retranslation of the poems collected in Ezra Pound's canonical *Cathay,* and grew to include an important anthology of classical Chinese poetic forms, entitled *Chinese Poetry,* and numerous critical essays published between the late 1960s and the late 1990s. Celebrated as one of the Ten Major Modern Chinese Poets by the Taiwan Ministry of Education, he was recently honored at the 7th Triennial Congress of the Chinese Literature Association, in conjunction with the publication of *The Complete Works of Wai-lim Yip* by Anhui Educational Press.

3. Yip, "Aesthetic Consciousness of Landscape in Chinese and Anglo-American Poetry," 101.

4. The term *ziran* appears in the *Daodejing*, verse 25: "*Dao* follows the law of *ziran*." And the term *wuwei* appears in chapter 63 of the *Daodejing*, in the phrase *weiwuwei* 為無為. The actual term "*wuwei*" shows up only three times in the inner chapters of the *Zhuangzi*, but becomes a term of major philosophical and aesthetic import in and after Neo-Daoism.

5. Yip, "Aesthetic Consciousness of Landscape in Chinese and Anglo-American Poetry," 102. Regardless of the Daoist precedents for Yip's interpretation of this koan, situated in his American context, his formulation strikes a decidedly Romantic tone. The invocation of childlike innocence and immediacy to nature, followed by the obfuscation of the adult mind, followed in turn by the possibility for a return to a pure seeing, could have (and indeed has) been written about Wordsworth's "Intimations Ode." For an affirmation of the Romantic vision of the ode, see the classic new critical essay by Cleanth Brooks, "Wordsworth and the Paradox of the Imagination," chapter 7 in Brooks's *The Well-Wrought Urn*; and for an interpretation of the ode as a poetics of loss, see Jerome McGann's "Wordsworth and the Ideology of Romantic Poems," chapter 8 of his *The Romantic Ideology*.

6. We could also read this koan through the notion of interdiffusion, like (Kegon) Huayan Buddhism's "Indra's net," which sees all phenomena as single jewels in an infinite net where each jewel reflects every other. In this case, the first stage is in error, for overemphasizing the identities of single jewels (mountains or tea bowls), just as the second places too much emphasis on the "wholeness" of the interdependent net itself (at the expense of each jewel's intrinsic uniqueness), while the third recognizes that the mountains are both the net and the jewels, so they can keep their "conven-

tional designations" without losing sight of their interdiffusion (Ch: *shishi wuai*, JA: *jijimuge*).

7. Lin, "Yip Wai-lim: A Poet of Exile," 112.

8. Yip captures his sense of exile by alluding to Cai Yan's "18 Beats on a Barbarian Reed Pipe," a poem Maxine Hong Kingston chose, a decade later, for the ending of her work, *The Woman Warrior*.

9. Yip and Pound, *Ezra Pound's Cathay*, 7.

10. For a list of all the steps, see ibid., 7–8.

11. Recall that in Chapter 3, Snyder saw soteriological potential in the couplet's abrupt shift in focus from the social, human world to the "other time" of the "grass growing wild," through "turning language" that shakes the reader's mind from its normative patterns, allowing a more direct experience of the transience of human affairs than what might be available through discursive language. Yip also values the abrupt "turning" of the lines, but, as we will see in a moment, he locates a very different governing set of philosophical values behind it.

12. Yip and Pound, *Ezra Pound's Cathay*, 18.

13. Ibid.

14. Ibid.

15. Ibid., 19.

16. In the ninth "Osiris" article of 1912, Pound describes words as electrified cones charged with the power of tradition (see Kenner, *The Pound Era*, 238).

17. Chang, *Creativity and Taoism*.

18. Yip does not reference Chang's work, but given the fact that Chang is articulating a view of Chinese poetry available in the Chinese tradition, Yip simply bypasses him and references a similar variety of source texts from Chinese philosophy, poetics, and poetry. The dates of publication are also important to keep in mind. While Chang Chung-yuan's *Creativity and Taoism: A Study of Chinese Philosophy, Art, and Poetry* was first published by Julian Press in 1963, due to its popularity it was reissued by Harper Torchbooks in 1970, which would have been during the time of Yip's shift toward an explicit Daoist poetics. The point I would like to make is not one of originality, and certainly not plagiarism, but that an important precedent in the "Daoist" transpacific imaginary reveals itself more fully in Yip's work.

19. Chang, *Creativity and Taoism*, 175.

20. Ibid., 176, 178.

21. See Venuti, *The Translator's Invisibility*; Niranjana, *Siting Translation*.

22. Yip, Prologue to *Diffusion of Distances*, 1.

23. See the journal *Alcheringa*, which was published from 1970 to 1980 and originally edited by Dennis Tedlock and Jerome Rothenberg (Rothenberg left in 1976 to found the *New Wilderness Letter*). Archival issues of the journal can be found at http://www.durationpress.com/archives/ethnopoetics/alcheringa/alcheringa.pdf.

24. Yip, Prologue to *Diffusion of Distances*, 2.

25. This autobiography was solicited by Pennywhistle Press for a new publication of Yip's selected English poetry, but has still not been published. The quote here is used with the permission of the author.

26. Yip, "The Use of 'Models' in East–West Comparative Literature," 25.

27. Said, *Orientalism*, 3.

28. Ibid., 2.

29. See Whorf, *Language, Reality, Thought*.

30. Count Kuki Shûzô (九鬼周造) was a student of Heidegger, a friend of Sartre, and was in part raised by Okakura Kakuzō (岡倉覚三) (see *Kuki Shūzō: A Philosopher's Poetry and Poetics*). Kuki also wrote the first book-length study of Heidegger, Kuki Shūzō (九鬼周造). "Haideggā no tetsugaku (the Philosophy of Heidegger)."

31. The term "*Iki*" is an allusion to Kuki Shūzō's work *Iki no kôzô* (The structure of Iki), an inquiry into traditional Japanese aesthetics he wrote in the 1930s. It has been translated by John Clark as *Reflections on Japanese Taste: The Structure of Iki*, and by Hiroshi Nara in his book *The Structure of Detachment: The Aesthetic Vision of Kuki Shūzō*. The Japanese aesthetic term *iki* いき is often represented as 粋.

32. Heidegger, *On the Way to Language*, 4–5, quoted in Yip, "The Use of 'Models' in East–West Comparative Literature," 15. Lidia Liu quotes a different section of this text and, like Yip, appears to share much of Heidegger's skepticism toward cross-cultural communication (see Liu, *Translingual Practice*, 4–6). See also Nishida, "The Problem of Japanese Culture," 859; and Nishida, "Towards a Philosophy of Religion."

33. Yip, "Taoist Aesthetic," 18.

34. Yip quotes a series of Chinese literary figures to support his ideas throughout his work. These include Lu Ji 陸機 (b. 261–d. 303): "The mind is cleared to crystallize contemplation" 罄澄心以凝思; Su Kungtu: "Live plainly: wait in silence / It is here the Scheme is seen" 素處以默/ 妙機其微; Yan Yu: "The last attainment of poetry is entering into *shen* (spirit)" 詩之極致有一 曰入神; and Su Shi: "In the state of emptiness, one takes in all the aspects" 空故納萬境. All of these passages are cited in Yip, "Language and the Real-Life World," 75–76; and Yip, "Taoist Aesthetic."

35. Yip, "Syntax and Horizon of Representation in Classical Chinese and Modern American Poetry," 50.

36. Yip, "Language and the Real Life World," 65.

37. Yip, "Syntax and Horizon of Representation in Classical Chinese and Modern American Poetry," 40.

38. Ibid. (Yip's emphasis).

39. Ibid.

40. Yip does praise English for its narrative strengths, but this strength is not coupled to an ontological strength, like his arguments of "*wuyan*" are.

41. Yip's bifurcation of language into these two types is itself present within the classical Chinese definition of particles as "empty words" (*zhuzi*), and the simple fact that they are used sparingly in classical poetry does seem to validate Yip's own devaluation, again revealing Yip's fidelity to his reading of the Chinese poetic tradition itself. François Cheng would disagree with this devaluation of empty words, however, citing that their very emptiness gave them a metaphysical/cosmological function within the poems in which they are used (see Cheng, *Chinese Poetic Writing*).

42. Yip, "Syntax and Horizon of Representation in Classical Chinese and Modern American Poetry," 50.

43. Ibid.

44. Ibid.

45. Fredman, "Neo-Paganism, Buddhism, and Christianity," 202.

46. Yip, "Syntax and Horizon of Representation in Classical Chinese and Modern American Poetry," 48.

47. Yip, "Language and the Real-Life World," 65. The bulk of Yip's criticism gestated in the late 1960s to mid-1970s, and his own poetic production can be included in the "tradition" of Donald Allen's *New American Poetry*, which set itself against the then still entrenched New Critics and T. S. Eliot. In this context, Yip tends to privilege what Lazlo Géfin calls the "ideogrammic stream" (imagist-objectivist-Black Mountain) as a break from so-called "traditional" Western poetics. I am using the term "traditional" since Yip himself does in pointing to the work of the "New Critics," which focused on earlier forms of scansion and thematic analysis, as opposed to the poetry and criticism gathered together under the heading of "New American Poetry." Therefore, we might extend the similarities between New American Poetry and Daoist poetics beyond their metaphysical claims, to the fact of their mutual "otherness" to what Yip considers "traditional Western poetics" (for a general discussion of this lineage of American poetry see Gefin, *Ideogram*).

48. Yip, *Chinese Poetry*, 231.

49. Yip, "Syntax and Horizon of Representation in Classical Chinese and Modern American Poetry," 62.

50. Ibid.

51. Ethnopoetics is less a school than a general term referring to the anthologizing work of Rothenberg, which focused on oral literatures like *Technicians of the Sacred* (1968) and *Shaking the Pumpkin: Traditional Poetry of the Indian North Americas* (1972), but which is most associated with the magazine *Alcheringa*, coedited with Dennis Tedlock from 1970 to 1976. Tedlock's many volumes of translations that attend to the aural (performative) condition of oral literature are central works in this movement.

52. The term "New American Poetry" is derived from Donald Allen's prophetic anthology *New American Poetry: 1945–60* (1960), which brought together poets associated with the San Francisco Renaissance, Black Mountain, the Beats, and the New York school as a challenge to the mainstream verse culture at the time anthologized in the *New Poets of England and America* (1962), edited by Donald Hall and Robert Pack. This broad challenge to the reign of New Criticism is, in the broad sense in which I am using it, "New American Poetry."

53. Yip, *Modern Chinese Poetry*, 77.

54. Ibid., xv.

55. Ibid., xvii.

56. See Chen Xiaomei, *Occidentalism*.

57. Yip, *Modern Chinese Poetry*, xix.

58. See Marjorie Perloff's *The Dance of the Intellect: Studies in the Poetry of the Pound Tradition* and *The Poetics of Indeterminacy: Rimbaud to Cage* for a discussion of the point.

59. For a good discussion of these differences, see Graham, *Poems of the Late T'ang*, 13–15.

60. For scholarship that moves past the confines of Lao-Zhang thought, see the work of Seidel, Kaltenmark, Girardot, Robinet, Kohn, Strickmann, Saso, Verellen, and Bokenkamp, etc., as well as Zheng Liangshu, Ge Zhaoguang, and Zong Lonxi, etc.

61. See Chapter 2.

62. Yip, *Chinese Poetry*, 130.

63. Yip chose not to render the later half of these lines as parallel, but they are in the original:

一視 喬 木 杪 .... tall trees twigs
仰 聆 大 壑 瀑　　.... big gully waterfall.

Yip does not hold the parallelism of the second half, but tries to make this up by placing extra emphasis on the first.

64. For Yip's translation, see *Chinese Poetry*, 145. I have benefited from Kang-I Sun Chang's analysis of the alternation between water and mountain scenery in his book *Six Dynasties Poetry* (see p. 53). Also, Cai Zong-qi's edited volume *How to Read Chinese Poetry* is a great source for more information about this poem and its correlative cosmological formal innovations. The Chinese poem follows:

於南山往北山經湖中瞻眺
謝靈運
朝旦 發陽崖
景落息陰崖
舍舟眺迴渚
停策依茂松
側逕既？窈窕
環洲亦玲瓏
視喬木杪
仰聆大壑瀑
石橫水分流
林密蹊絕蹤
解作竟何感
升長皆豐容
初篁苞綠籜
新蒲含紫？
海鷗戲春岸
天雞弄和風
撫化心無厭
覽物眷彌重
不恨莫與同
孤遊非情歎
賞廢理誰通

(Yip, *Chinese Poetry,* 144–45)

65. Interestingly, in David Hinton's recent book of translations of Xie Lingyun, he gives a wonderfully rich Daoist reading of Xie, but, like Yip, avoids mentioning anything about Xie's parallelism and correlative innovations, choosing instead to focus on largely the same elements of emptiness as Yip does (see Hinton, *The Mountain Poems of Hsieh Ling-yün*).

66. Yip, "Aesthetic Consciousness of Landscape in Chinese and Anglo-American Poetry," 130

67. For further discussion of these lines see Sun, *Pearl from the Dragon's Mouth*, 45, 180.

68. "Neo-Daoism" is a term indicating the second flowering of Daoist thought by a small but influential group of thinkers, such as Guo Xiang and Wang Bi. The movement is associated with the debate activity of "pure talk" (*qingtan*) 清談, and is further

linked to the so-called Seven Sages of the Bamboo Grove 竹林七賢, often depicted in paintings about the period (see Laing, "Neo-Taoism and the 'Seven Sages of the Bamboo Grove' in Chinese Painting"). For a more comprehensive study of Neo-Daoism, see Ziporyn, *The Penumbra Unbound.*

69. Cai describes how lines 11 and 12 signal how cosmic operations (*tiandao*) "reified in meteorological phenomena may bring about regeneration in the sphere of terristrial process (*didao*)" (Cai, *How to Read Chinese Poetry,* 133).

70. See Chang, *Six Dynasties Poetry,* 65; and for further reading see Liu, *The Literary Mind and the Carving of Dragons,* 369.

71. Bradbury, "The American Conquest of Philosophical Taoism," 30.

72. Ibid.

73. Yeh, "The Chinese Poem," 251.

74. See Kern, *Orientalism, Modernism, and the American Poem.* I discuss Kern's "Saidian" framing of American Modernism in Chapter 1.

75. For a brief discussion of "the territory of the—emptied—non-self" see Cai, *How to Read Chinese Poetry,* 126.

76. See Yip, "Daoist Aesthetic," 26; and Yip, "Language and the Real-Life World," 75.

77. See Liu, *The Art of Chinese Poetry*; and Liu, *Chinese Theories of Literature.*

78. Owen, Review of *Chinese Poetry,* by Wai-lim Yip.

79. Huntington, "Crossing Boundaries," 215.

80. Zong-qi Cai, *How to Read Chinese Poetry,* 227.

81. Blanchot, *Infinite Conversation,* 44.

82. Cai, *How to Read Chinese Poetry,* 228.

83. This is my own translation (which does not differ significantly from many others).

84. Yip, "Language and the Real-Life World," 71.

85. Ibid.

86. I say "endangers it" because in recent years Western literary criticism and philosophy has directly challenged truth-claims based upon vision and visual language. Michel Foucault's work provides one of the most sustained analyses of visual knowledge claims, showing that vision has dominated such claims throughout the West's history, and that the hegemony of vision has "real-life" implications for us all. His analysis, in *The Birth of the Clinic,* of the "cold medical gaze" of rationalistic science characterized by a scientist's gaze directed toward a corpse on a table, as well as his discussion, in *Discipline and Punish* (195–230), of the totalitarian gaze of the "panoptican," which represents the all-seeing gaze of social domination and control, have contributed to a general critical orientation of Western theory toward vision. This orientation can be seen in Edward Said's *Orientalism* and in the work of Johannes Fabian (*Time and the Other*), both of whom critique ocularcentrism's essentializing gaze that enables Orientalists and anthropologists alike to construct knowledge of the other. In her work *Speculum of the Other Woman,* Luce Irigaray connects the West's ocularcentrism to the power of the "male gaze" to construct and objectify gender across different power differentials. Given this general critical disposition toward vision as the basis of truth-claims, or the "real," it is difficult to accept Yip's heavily vision-oriented claims.

87. Ziporyn, *The Penumbra Unbound*, 66.

88. Ibid.

89. Ibid., 68.

90. Those strange things involve the abandonment of philosophical language for the psycho-physiological register of Daoist "inner alchemy," which describes the processes whereby adepts must manipulate various forms of energy within the body (semen and breath) up through the viscera to manifest the highest energy *"shen,"* which must itself be "stripped of its identity" if one is to return to the undifferentiated "Dao." Vision, it would seem, is a useful means toward disrupting discursive thought, but the authority accorded by vision must itself be disrupted, and this further disruption has historically taken place as physical practices within the public (ritual) and private (meditation) spaces of what Schipper has dubbed "the Taoist Body." While these practices often still employ poetic devices, they exist (often in the oral tradition) outside the confines of classical Chinese poetry and poetics as these are generally conceived.

91. Yip's work can be found in journals associated with the meteoric rise of *"guoxue"* (国学, or "Nation Studies," the study of classical Chinese thought) among the elite and growing middle class in China. Clearly, this movement is in large measure due to the fact that people are now able to study classical texts again, but it is also wrapped up in the search for a new political state ideology culled, at least in part, from classical Chinese language and culture. While Yip's "Daoist Project" can be seen as a powerful challenge to certain aspects of Western hegemonic discourses (and were absolutely necessary in the 60's, 70's, and 80's, in its present form it is less able to offer a compelling "counter-discourse to the territorializations of power" in China itself (see 国学 at http://www.guoxue.com/magzine/zgsgyj/zgsgyj2/tiyao2.htm).

92. See Sharf, "Who's Zen." See also Victoria, *Zen at War*; and Victoria, *Zen War Stories*.

93. Yip, "Pound and the Eight Views of Xiao Xiang," 25.

5 / Pacing the Void: Theresa Hak Kyung Cha's *Dictée*

1. Cha describes "A BLE W AIL" as follows: "In this piece, I want to be the dream of the audience. An environment, a curtain made from cheese cloth was hung, separating the performer's space and that of the viewer. The effect on the viewing of the performance is that of seeing through opaque-transparency. Inside the performer's space are lighted candles also reflected by pieces of mirror placed behind them, creating an oval shape area. The performer is wearing a white robe and 20 meters of black and red cloth underneath. The movements performed are divided into spaces that contain movement and space that are still. The sound and time are also divided into sound. silence parts." (Berkeley Art Museum/Pacific Film Archive #1992.4.32). In *Dictée*, Cha introduces the dress of Princess Pari as "a lightly woven smock which was also white [like the scarf], and the setting as 'an opaque screen' [where] from a distance the figure outlines the movement, its economy without extraneous motion" (167), and she later describes another setting where "through the paper screen door, dusk had entered and the shadow of small candle was flickering" (170).

2. Ashcroft, *Post-Colonial Transformation*, 75.

3. Cha studied the Guangping Yang style of *taiji* under the direction of Zhang Yizhong and his senior student Fu Tung Chen in Berkeley during the mid- to late 1970s.

Her teacher was the student of Kuo Lien Ying, the style's fourth-generation lineage holder. What is particularly noteworthy about this style of *taiji* is its incorporation of *bagua zhang* (eight-trigram palm) and *xingyi quan*, other Chinese internal martial arts that emphasize an understanding of Daoist philosophy and cosmology.

4. Cha quotes fairly extensively from both Chang Chung-yuan and Ekbert Fas on Daoism (as well as making a few references to Buddhism) in her MFA thesis, "Paths" (May 1978, p. 3, document no. 1992.4.165, Cha Collection, UC Berkeley Art Museum & Pacific Film Archive, available online at http://www.oac.cdlib.org/ark:/13030/tf296n989f/.

5. For an excellent text locating Barthes's interest in Daoism, see Barthes, *The Neutral, Lecture Course at the Collège de France.* See also Minh-Ha, "The Plural Void." This latter essay, while discussing Barthes, not Cha, details elements within Barthes's heterocultural imaginary that clearly appealed to Cha and offered a general theoretical orientation she both inhabits and exceeds by moving still further toward Daoist and shamanistic discourses in her work, a point heretofore not taken up by Cha scholars.

6. Hayot, *Chinese Dreams*, 170.

7. Ibid., 103–76.

8. Hayot describes Barthes's utopian China as a "blankness" that "refuses the Western episteme," a "blankness that does not reverse or negate, but defers" (ibid., 133). And while Hayot shows how Barthes tended to move away from his "utopian China" after returning from China along with other key figures in the Tel Quel circle, this idea of "blankness" is reconnected to China in the late 1970s through the Daoist concept of *wuwei* (see Barthes, *The Neutral,* 176–86; and Minh-Ha, "The Plural Void").

9. It is impossible to know if Cha would have heard Barthes speak on his Daoist reading of "the Neutral," but Barthes mentions having lectured on the subject in 1976 (see Barthes, *The Neutral,* 179).

10. The term "other logic" was used by figures of the Tel Quel circle like Philippe Sollers, who appears to primarily use the term to indicate the general field of discourses that center on "emptiness" (see Hayot, *Chinese Dreams*, 165).

11. A partial bibliography of recent Cha scholarship would include but not be limited to the following: Lowe, *Immigrant Acts*; Spahr, "Postmodernism, Readers, and Theresa Hak Kyung Cha's *Dictée*"; Huang, *Transpacific Imaginations*; Park, "What of the Partition"; Twelbeck, "Elle venait de loin"; Shih, "Nationalism and Korean American Women's Writing"; Guarino-Trier, "From the Multitude of Narratives . . . For Another Telling for Another Recitation"; Min, "Reading the Figure of Dictation in Theresa Hak Kyung Cha's *Dictée*"; Lee, "Suspicious Characters"; Frost, "In Another Tongue"; Grice, "Korean American National Identity in Theresa Hak Kyung Cha's *Dictée*"; and Bergvall, "Writing at the Crossroads of Languages."

12. Minh-ha, "The Plural Void," 33. Trinh T. Minh-ha's desire to link Cha's performance, at least implicitly, to Korean shamanism is corroborated by the number of critics who discuss, if only briefly, the inclusion in *Dictée* of the story of Princess Pari, the mythological founder of Korean shamanism. Yet these discussions have been limited to Cha's feminist revision of the Princess Pali myth along the lines of Maxine-Hong Kingston's revision of the mythic tale of Fa (Hua) Mulan. As important as it is to acknowledge the appearance of Princess Pari in the text, it is more important to interrogate the ways in which the vast network of interlocking images, language, concepts, themes, and untranslated religious documents work as a theoretical, philosophical, or even metaphysical matrix within the text. See, for example, Lee, "Princess Pari in

Nora Okja Keller's *Comfort Woman*"; and in a broader discussion, Lee, "Rewriting Hesiod, Revisioning Korea." Walter K. Lew also mentions this in his *Excerpts from, Diktē = Dikte* (alternatively written as ΔIKTH/DIKTE for DICTEE), 14–19; and see also Shih, "Nationalism and Korean American Women's Writing," 157.

13. In Minh-ha's wonderful lyric-essay "White Spring" (in which she describes *A BLE W AIL*), she time and again links Cha's work to references to Zen whose moments, taken in isolation, might appear as "Zennist" rather than Daoist (and of course there is a great deal of syncretism anyhow). But I believe that a more complete meditation on these East Asian philosophical elements within her work (which includes, most notably, shamanic notes discordant with Zen but not with Daoism) would tend to favor a distinctly Daoist orientation.

14. Shamanism is not something esoteric and rare in Korea but infuses everyday life for Christians and Buddhists alike. Today there are an estimated three hundred shamanistic temples within an hour of Seoul. So it is very reasonable to assume at least a passing familiarity with this discourse, and it is easy to see why Cha would have been drawn to its unique combination of Daoism and matrilineal Korean spirituality (see Sang-hun, "Shamanism Enjoys Revival in Techno-Savvy South Korea").

15. Kim, "Poised on the In-between," 18.

16. Ibid., 17–18.

17. Fanon, *Black Skin, White Masks*, 17–18.

18. Cha, *Dictée*, 173.

19. Robinet, *Taoism*, 202.

20. Unlike Yip, whose "emptied self" is posited as a way to directly apprehend of the "life world" unmediated by what he calls "epistemological elaborations," Cha appears to be less interested in this ontological world and more interested in voiding the "subject" in order to become neutral, totally neutral and thus free from ideological interpolation. This idea will be further explored later in the chapter.

21. Interestingly, Cha, while having derived her knowledge of Daoism from Chang's descriptions, chooses to focus on elements in Chang's work that he largely excludes from poetics. While Chang's "poetics of emptiness" offers a near exact prefiguration of Yip's, unlike Yip, Chang includes a chapter on *neidan*, in which he describes its evolution, defines the principal terms, and offers examples. Presumably, it is here that Cha becomes familiar with the tradition and its unique focus on the intersection of breath, body, and philosophical inquiry.

22. Chang, *Creativity and Taoism*, 166. The original diagram is discussed in Wang, "Zhou Dunyi's Diagram of the Supreme Ultimate Explained (Taijitu shuo)."

23. See Robin Wang, "Zhou Dunyi's Diagram of the Supreme Ultimate Explained."

24. Lao Zi, *Tao Te Ching*, 42.

25. The mythical Emperor of the East, Fu Xi, who discovered the diagram on the back of a dragonlike horse, created the *houtu*, which is composed of fifty-five dots; symbolic unification of the *yin* and *yang* elements of the five phases: wood, fire, earth, metal, and water, which is accomplished by assigning each a numerical value from 1 to 5 and combining two at a time to equal 5 in three different ways. This is called the "the unity of three 5's" (see Saso, *Blue Dragon, White Tiger*, 56–57, 77).

26. From this "map," one finds circular dots of numbers that were arranged in a three-by-three nine-grid pattern such that the sum of the numbers in each row, column, and diagonal was the same: 15.

27. Robinet, *Taoism*, 233–34.

28. Cha, *Dictée*, 175.

29. See "Étang" (1978), from the Cha Collection, UC Berkeley Art Museum & Pacific Film Archive, available online at http://www.oac.cdlib.org/ark:/13030/ tf9k4006pf/?brand=oac4. "Étang" was originally distributed by Line, of Berkeley, California. It is also published in Lewallen, *The Dream of the Audience*, 76–77.

30. Cha, *Dictée*, 113.

31. Little, *Taoism and the Arts of China*, 23.

32. Cha, *Dictée*, 49.

33. Ibid., 96.

34. Ibid., 159. Whiteness, of course, is also a color signifying mourning and death, and is also associated with the dress of Korean shamanism—and it also suggests a heavy influence from Barthes, whose privileging of the "white," "blank," "void" draws upon his Daoist imaginary (a point I will return to in a moment).

35. Wang, "Zhou Dunyi's Diagram of the Supreme Ultimate Explained (Taijitu shuo)," 312. See also Liu Zhongyu's essay, available at the Taoist Culture and Information Centre website (http://eng.taoism.org.hk), which Robin Wang cites on this point.

36. Chang, *Creativity and Taoism*, 165.

37. Ibid., 150–51.

38. Kristofer Schipper's describes this circular reversal, or what he terms a "counter cycle," when "the circulation of energies (*ch'i*) in the organism is also reversed. The generative succession of the Five Phase—Water produces Wood which produces Fire, et cetera—is now carried out in the opposite direction. The cycle of creation moves in reverse as well" (Schipper, *The Taoist Body*, 156).

39. For an example of this pairing, see Wong, *Cultivating Stillness*.

40. Cha, *Dictée*, 73.

41. Ibid., 128. For an example of the didactic rhetoric of classical Daoist guided meditation, see Kristofer Schipper's description of "embryonic breathing" exercises, in *The Taoist Body*, 157.

42. While books like Chang's may be the source for this particular kind of juxtaposition, this particular combination of physiological and philosophical language is a regular part of learning *qigong* and *taijichuan*, which again Cha practiced daily during the decade that led up to this work. It would be safe to assume that the guided meditative practices that would be a part of this practice would have granted Cha access to this distinctly Daoist alchemical convergence of the graphic and discursive, the corporeal/metaphysical, that we see arising at different moments throughout Cha's work.

43. Barthes, *S/Z*, 5. In the late 1970's and 80's, Barthes's insistence on writerly textual production has been taken up by the poet-critics of the so-called LANGUAGE school, and Barthes's critique of "readerly" texts can be seen, only slightly reformulated, in Charles Bernstein's notion of "frame lock," which he defines as "an insistence on a univocal surface, minimal shifts of mood either within paragraphs or between paragraphs, exclusion of extraneous or contradictory material, and tone restricted to the narrow affective envelope of sobriety, neutrality, objectivity authoritativeness, or deanimated abstraction" (Bernstein, "Frame Lock," 92).

44. Cha, Preface to *Apparatus*, i.

45. See Hejinian, "The Rejection of Closure."

46. For Barthes, "the goal of literary work (of literature as work) is to make the reader no longer a consumer, but a producer of the text" (Barthes, *S/Z*, 4).

47. Cha, "Paths," MFA thesis, May 1978, p. 2, document no. 1992.4.165, Cha Collection, UC Berkeley Art Museum & Pacific Film Archive, available online at http://www.oac.cdlib.org/ark:/13030/tf296n989f/.

48. Ibid.

49. Ibid., 1.

50. Ibid., 6.

51. Barthes, *The Neutral, Lecture Course at the Collège de France*, 176.

52. Ibid., 182.

53. Minh-Ha, "The Plural Void," 45. In many ways, this essay on Barthes articulates the Parisian avant-garde pacific imaginary that preconditions much of Cha's poststructuralist Daoism, even though Cha's poetics takes it further both in terms of Daoist alchemy and in its folk-shamanic traditions.

54. Ibid.

55. Cha "Paths," 5; Barthes, *S/Z*, 5.

56. Cha, "Exilée," 141.

57. I am indebted to Lawrence Rinder's essay "The Plurality of Entrances, the Opening of Networks, the Infinity of Languages" (15–16) for this point, and for locating this piece as well.

58. In Cha's piece "Awakened in the Mist," she works with this transformation of light into dark into light as the lights in the room of the performance come in and dissolve out as she recites "Everything is light, everything is dark . . . everything feels light, everything feels dark."

59. Cha, "Exilée," 143.

60. Rinder, "The Plurality of Entrances, the Opening of Networks, the Infinity of Languages," 16.

61. Cha, *Dictée*, 157.

62. Ibid., 20.

63. Park "What of the Partition," 217.

64. Kristeva, *The Powers of Horror*, 4.

65. Ibid., 10.

66. Chang, *Creativity and Taoism*, 166.

67. See Harvey, *Six Korean Women*, 238. I found this source through Lee, "Princess Pari in Nora Okja Keller's *Comfort Woman*."

68. Cha, *Dictée*, 17.

69. Ibid., 13.

70. Ibid., 64.

71. See Jacob, *Six Thousand Years of Bread*, 162.

72. See Stutley, *Shamanism, An Introduction*, 31. Dionysis is also a figure that interests Barthes, especially within the context of negative theology (see Barthes, *The Neutral, Lecture Course at the Collège de France*, 59).

73. Saso, *Blue Dragon, White Tiger*, 19. Saso, a Jesuit monk, uses Catholic theological terminology to establish a contrast between what he terms the "kataphatic (mind-heart filling) religion of the masses" and "the apophatic (emptying) spirituality of the Taoist recluse" (ibid., 21).

74. The term "kenosis" denotes the belief that the Son of God "emptied himself" of his divine powers in order to become fully human as the Jesus of Nazareth. Theologians who support this doctrine appeal to a reading of Philippians 2:5–8: "Let this mind be in you, which was also in Christ Jesus: Who, being in the form of God, thought it not robbery to be equal with God: but made himself of no reputation, and took upon him the form of a servant, and made in the likeness of men: And being found in fashion as a man, he humbled himself, and became obedient unto death, even the death of the cross." Kenotic Christology, which was originally championed in Lutheran debates of the sixteenth century, and later revived in the nineteenth century to reinterpret classical doctrines of incarnation, gave its adherents a powerful example of God's self-sacrificing nature. It is this idea of God's own "self-emptying" that is taken up in Eastern Orthodoxy, which locates God's kenosis in its Christian cosmogony whereby the cosmos is manifested by way of God self-emptying. For Orthodox Catholics, Roman Catholics, and Protestants, however, "kenosis" offers a powerful ethic which requires Christians to "empty themselves" by way of sacrifice. Yet "kenosis" has also had a controversial history in Christology, because Paul's pronouncement that Jesus emptied himself of his divinity to become "fully human" raised troubling questions regarding the nature of Jesus's incarnation. Principal among these, controversies surround the term "*tertium quid*," which refers to the belief of the followers of Apollinarism, or Apollinarianism, proposed by Apollinaris of Laodicea (ca. 310–ca. 390), who argued that Christ was neither human nor divine, but a combination of both, a third thing: Jesus's mind was divine, while his body was thoroughly human. This notion of Jesus as a "third thing" conflicted with established views of the Holy Trinity: in the Western Church, the Holy Spirit arrives "in procession" (*processio*) from the Father and the Son; in the Eastern Church, the Holy Spirit arrives from the Father *through* the Son.

75. Nancy fully develops this idea of "the *distinct*" in *The Ground of the Image* (New York: Fordham University Press, 2005), 1–14.

76. Nancy, *The Ground of the Image*, 1.

77. Exceptions would include vocalizations associated with Tourette's, for instance.

78. Kristeva, *Language*, 8.

79. Cha, *Dictée*, 18.

80. However, it is interesting to think about Tourette's syndrome, as cursing, for example, remains in almost all cases of aphasia as a subcortical activity, which suggests an origin from outside the realm of the linguistic constitution of the subject (see Schleifer, "The Poetics of Tourette Syndrome").

81. Spahr, "Postmodernism, Readers, and Theresa Hak Kyung Cha's *Dictée*," 7.

82. Derrida, "Violence and Metaphysics," 147.

83. Roland Barthes, *Alors la Chine?* (Paris: C. Bourgois, 1975), 13–14, cited in Minh-Ha, "The Plural Void," 45.

84. The term "trans(l)ative" appeared in the title of a course I took with Myung Mi Kim at SUNY Buffalo in 2003. Under Myung's guidance, we teased out some of the possibilities of this term, paying close attention to the "transitive" nature of the "translative" process.

85. Cha, "Paths," MFA thesis, May 1978, p. 3, document no. 1992.4.165, Cha Collection, UC Berkeley Art Museum & Pacific Film Archive, available online at http://www.oac.cdlib.org/ark:/13030/tf296n989f/.

86. Robinet.
87. Althusser, *Lenin and Philosophy and Other Essays*, 119.
88. Lowe, *Immigrant Acts*, 36.

Epilogue

1. From an April 2005 interview, Marden writes: "I was working with calligraphy, and looking at a lot of Chinese calligraphy. Getting poems by chance, I found the Red Pine translation at a bookstore. It has the Chinese characters and the translations in it. It was that form that I picked up on—four couplets, and five or ten characters per couplet. In the beginning I did drawings using the form that the poems take in the Chinese, then I started joining image and calligraphy, using the shape of the poem as a skeleton. I'm becoming more and more interested in the ideas of the Tao and of Zen. The Cold Mountain poems are very much about that" (see http://pquintas.typepad.com/ciprina/interviews). Also, it is interesting to note that Marden first encountered Han Shan in the 1960s through Snyder's translations (see Richardson, *Brice Marden*, 51; also, Liu Chiao-Mei, "The Wall," 212).

2. See Wright, *Philosophical Meditations on Zen Buddhism*. Wright reenters Blofeld's transpacific imaginary through a self-reflexive reading practice, in which he (1) relates a personal account of having come to his study of Buddhism through the textual bridges built by Blofeld; (2) explains how his early study of Zen Buddhism sought a transcendence of language and thought; and (3) describes his own awakening in the transcendental mode of Blofeld's descriptions. But Wright's decidedly poststructuralist re-reading of Blofeld's scholarship reveals a different vision of language's role in "enlightenment" today. Unlike Yip's view of language as the primary obfuscator of the real, or Snyder and Blofeld's instrumentalist view of language, Wright offers a view of language best described as "conditional." For Wright, there is no outside of language, because language "conditions" even its own transgression (as with Snyder's phrase "without any prism of language"). Wright's re-reading of Blofeld is a work of significant theoretical and practical value (it stays close to the textual conditions of Blofeld's invention of "Huang Po" and offers rich historical details to both complicate and liberate "Huang Po" from his own invention). Nevertheless, the certainty with which Wright proceeds to apply poststructuralist interpretations of Zen textual practices, determining their potential epistemological dimensions, leaves me a little uneasy. While liberating Huang Po from Blofeld's Romantic Orientalism, he has, perhaps, too tightly contained Blofeld's transpacific imaginary under too narrow a sign. Implicit in Western literary criticism's deployment of deconstructive readings is a search for truth—a more correct reading. And while often such re-readings are "better," in the sense that they are more textured, open, and capable of further meaning productions, this is not always the case. Wright's analysis is a bit too theoretically "clean," containing too few loose ends to be chucked back into translation's alchemical furnace.

3. Chow, *Ethics after Idealism*, 13.
4. Ibid., 6.
5. Wilson, *Inside Out*, 1.
6. King, *Orientalism and Religion*, 199.
7. Ibid.

8. See Annping Chin's "The Newest Mandarins," *New York Times,* December 16, 2007.

9. Hayot, 150.

10. Liu, *Translingual Practice,* 4. See also Borges, *Twenty-four Conversations with Borges, Including a Selection of Poems,* 51.

11. Liu, *Translingual Practice,* 7–8.

BIBLIOGRAPHY

Archival Sources

Ernest Francisco Fenollosa Papers (MS Am 1759–1759.4). Houghton Library, Harvard University, Cambridge, MA

"Étang." 1978. Document no. 1992.4.27.

Ezra Pound Papers, Beinecke Library, Yale University, New Haven, CT

Theresa Hak Kyung Cha Collection, 1971–1991, UC Berkeley Art Museum & Pacific Film Archive, Berkeley, CA

"Paths." MFA thesis, May 1978. Document no. 1992.4.165.

Published Sources

Abe, Masao. *Zen and Comparative Studies: Part Two of a Two-Volume Sequel to "Zen and Western Thought."* Edited by Steven Heine. Honolulu: University of Hawai'i Press, 1997.

Almond, Phillip C. *The British Discovery of Buddhism.* Cambridge: Cambridge University Press, 1988.

Althusser, Louis. *Lenin and Philosophy and Other Essays.* Translated by Ben Brewster. New York: Monthly Review Press, 2001.

Altieri, Charles. *Enlarging the Temple.* Lewisburg, PA: Bucknell University Press, 1979.

———. "Gary Snyder's Turtle Island: The Problem of Reconciling the Roles of Seer and Prophet." *boundary 2*, vol. 4, no. 3 (1976): 761–78.

Ashcroft, Bill. *Post-Colonial Transformation.* London: Routledge, 2001.

Auden, W. H. *Collected Poems: Auden.* New York: Vintage, 1991.

Barnstone, Tony. "The Poem behind the Poem: Literary Translation as American Poetry." In *The Poem behind the Poem: Translating Asian Poetry*, edited by Frank Stewart, 773–819. Port Townsend, WA: Copper Canyon Press, 2004.

Barthélemy Saint-Hilaire, Jules. *Le Nyaya*. "(Authenticité du *Nyaya*. Analyse du Nyaya. Appréciation de la doctrine du *Nyaya*)." *Mémoires de l'Académie Royale des Sciences Morales et Politiques de l'Institut de France*, vol. 3. Paris, 1841.

Barthes, Roland. *S/Z: An Essay*. Translated by Richard Miller. New York: Hill and Wang, 1974.

———. *The Neutral, Lecture Course at the Collège de France (1977–78)*. Translated by Rosalind E. Krauss and Denis Hollier. New York: Columbia University Press, 2005.

Behr, Wolfgang. "Odds on the Odes—how Old Chinese became an (almost) natural language in 1992." Book presentation paper for BMBF workshop "Foundations of Excellence in East Asian Studies," http://www.ruhr-uni-bochum.de/gpc/behr/HTML/Excellence.htm.

Bergvall, Caroline. "Writing at the Crossroads of Languages." In *Telling It Slant: Avant-Garde Poetics of the 1990s*, edited by Mark Wallace and Steven Marks, 207–23. Tuscaloosa: Alabama University Press, 2002.

Bernstein, Charles. "Frame Lock." In *My Way: Speeches and Poems*, 90–99. Chicago: Chicago University Press, 1999.

Blanchot, Maurice. *The Infinite Conversation*. Minneapolis: University of Minnesota Press, 1993.

Blofeld, John. Preface to *The Collected Songs of Cold Mountain*, translated by Red Pine. Revised and expanded ed. Port Townsend WA: Copper Canyon Press, 2000.

Bodman, Richard Wainwright. "Poetics and Prosody in Early Medieval China: A Study and Translation of Kukai' 'Bunkyo Hifuron.'" Ph.D. diss., Cornell University, 1978.

Boodburg, Peter. *Selected Works of Peter A. Boodberg*. Berkeley: University of California Press, 1979.

Borges, Jorge. *Twenty-four Conversations with Borges, Including a Selection of Poems*. Interviews by Roberto Alifano, 1981–1983, conversations translated by Nicomedes Suárez Araúz, Willis Barnstone, and Noemí Escandell; poems translated by Willis Barnstone, Jorge Luis Borges and Nicomedes Suárez Araúz; photographs by Willis Barnstone. Housatonic, MA: Lascaux Publishers, 1984.

Bradbury, Steve. "The American Conquest of Philosophical Taoism." In *Translation East and West: A Cross-Cultural Approach*, edited by Cornelia N. Moore and Lucy Lower, 29–41. Honolulu: University of Hawai'i, 1992.

Bridge, John Whalen. "The Sexual Politics of Divine Femininity: Tārā in Transition in Gary Snyder's Poetry." *Partial Answers* 5, no. 2 (2007): 219–44.

Brook, Timothy. "Rethinking Syncretism: The Unity of the Three Teachings and Their Joint Worship in Late-Imperial China." *Journal of Chinese Religions* 21 (Fall 1993): 13–44.

Brooks, Cleanth. "Wordsworth and the Paradox of the Imagination." In *The Well-Wrought Urn*. 1949, 101–23. Reprint, New York: Harcourt Brace, 1956.

Buddhaghosa. *The Path of Purification: Visuddhimagga*. Translated from the Pali by Bhikkhu Ñāṇamoli. 1st BPS Pariyatti ed. Onalaska, WA: BPS Pariyatti Editions, 1999. [Originally published 1956]

Busch, Heinrich. "The Tung-lin Academy and Its Political and Philosophical Significance." *Monumenta Serica* 14 (1949): 1–163.

Buswell, Robert E., Jr. *Cultivating Original Enlightenment*. Honolulu: University of Hawai'i Press, 2007.

Cage, John. "Lecture on Nothing." In *Silence: Lectures and Writings,* 109. Middletown, CT: Wesleyan, 1961.

Cai, Zong-qi. *Configurations of Comparative Poetics*. Honolulu: University of Hawai'i Press, 2002.

——, ed. *How to Read Chinese Poetry*. New York: Columbia University Press, 2008.

——. Prologue to *Chinese Aesthetics,* edited by Zong-qi Cai. Honolulu: University of Hawai'i Press, 2004.

Calichman, Richard F. "Nothing Resists Modernity: On Takeuchi Yoshimi's 'Kindai Towa Nanika.'" *Positions: East Asia Cultures Critique* 8, no. 2 (2000): 317–48.

Carroll, John B., ed. *Language, Thought, and Reality: Selected Writings of Benjamin Lee Whorf*. Cambridge, MA: Technology Press of the Massachusetts Institute of Technology, 1997, 1956.

Castro, Michael. *Interpreting the Indian: Twentieth Century Poets and the Native American*. Norman: University of Oklahoma Press, 1991.

Cha, Theresa Hak Kyung. Preface to *Apparatus: Cinematographic Apparatus,* edited by Theresa Hak Kyung Cha, i–ix. New York: Tanam Press, 1980.

——. *Dictée*. New York: Tanam Press, 1982.

——. "Exilée." In *Hotel*. New York: Tanam Press, 1980.

Chang, Chung-Yuan. *Creativity and Daoism: A Study of Chinese Philosophy, Art, and Poetry*. New York: Harper Colophon, 1963.

——. *Creativity and Taoism: A Study of Chinese Philosophy, Art, and Poetry*. New York: Julian Press, 1962.

Chang, Kang-I Sun. *Six Dynasties Poetry*. Princeton, NJ: Princeton University Press, 1986.

Chaves, Jonathan. "The Expression of Self in the Kung-an School: Non-Romantic Individualism." In *Expressions of Self in Chinese Literature,* edited by Robert Hegel and Richard C. Hessney, 123–50. New York: Columbia University Press, 1985.

Cheadle, Mary Paterson. *Ezra Pound's Confucian Translations*. Ann Arbor: University of Michigan Press, 1997.

Chen, Hongyin Julie. "Cross-Cultural Comparison of English and Chinese Metapragmatics in Refusal." Ph.D. diss., Indiana University, 1996.

Ch'en, Yu-shi. "The Literary Theory and Practice of Ou-yang Hsiu." In *Chinese Approaches to Literature*, edited by Adele Rickett, 67–97. Princeton, NJ: Princeton University Press, 1978.

Chen Xiaomei. *Occidentalism: A Theory of Counter-Discourse in Post-Mao China*. Lanham, MD: Rowman and Littlefield, 2002.

Cheng, François. *Chinese Poetic Writing*. Translated by Donald A. Riggs and Jerome P. Seaton. Bloomington: Indiana University Press, 1982.

Chiao-mei, Liu. "The Wall: Reshaping Contemporary Chinese Art." In *Chinese Walls in Time and Space: A Multidisciplinary Perspective*, edited by Roger Des Forges, Thomas Burkman, Liu Chiao-mei, and Haun Saussy. Ithaca, NY: Cornell East Asian Program, 2009.

Chin, Annping. "The Newest Mandarins." *New York Times*, December 16, 2007.

The Chinese Written Character as a Medium for Poetry: A Critical Edition. Ernest Fenollosa and Ezra Pound; edited by Haun Saussy, Jonathan Stalling, and Lucas Klein. New York: Fordham University Press, 2008.

Chisolm, Lawrence. *Ernest Fenollosa: The Far East and American Culture*. New Haven, CT: Yale University Press, 1963.

Chou, Chih-p'ing. *Yuan Hung-tao and the Kung-an School*. Cambridge: Cambridge University Press, 1988.

Chow, Rey. "Ethics after Idealism." *Diacritics* 21, no. 1 (1993): 3–22.

———. *Ethics after Idealism*. Bloomington: University of Indiana Press, 1998.

———. "How (the) Inscrutable Chinese Led to Globalized Theory," *PMLA* 116 (January 2001): 69–74.

———. "In the Name of Comparative Literature." In *Comparative Literature in the Age of Multiculturalism*, edited by Charles Bernheimer, 107–16. Baltimore: Johns Hopkins University Press, 1995.

———. *Primitive Passions: Visuality, Sexuality, Ethnography, and Contemporary Chinese Cinema*. New York: Columbia University Press, 1995.

———. "Where Have All the Natives Gone?" In *Contemporary Postcolonial Theory: A Reader*, edited by Padmini Mongia, 122–45. London: Arnold, 1996.

———. *Women and Chinese Modernity: The Politics of Reading between West and East*. Minneapolis: University of Minnesota Press, 1991.

Chung, Ling. "Allusions in Gary Snyder's 'The Canyon Wren.'" *Connotations* 12, no. 1 (2002/2003): 83–92.

Clarke, J. J. *The Tao and the West: Western Transformations of Taoist Thought*. London: Routledge, 2000.

Cohen, Warren. *East Asian Art and American Culture*. New York: Columbia University Press, 1992.

Conze, J. D. "Buddhist Prajna and Greek Sophia." *Religion* 5, no. 2 (1975): 160–67.

Cleary, Thomas, trans. *Rational Zen: The Mind of Dōgen Zenji*. Boston: Shambala, 1993.

Cook, Frances H. *Sounds of Valley Streams: Enlightenment in Dōgen's Zen, Translation of Nine Essays from Shōbōgenzō* . Albany: SUNY Press, 1989.

Coward, Harold. *Derrida and Indian Philosophy*. Albany: SUNY Press, 1990.

Dai Kan-Wa jiten 大漢和辭典 (Great Chinese-Japanese dictionary). Compiled by Morohashi Tetsuji 諸橋轍次. 13 vols. Tokyo: Taishūkan Shoten 大修館書店, 1943 (vol. 1); 1955–1960 (vol. 1 rev. and vols. 2–13).

Daodejing. Translated by D. C. Lau. Harmondsworth, U.K.: Penguin Books, 1963.

Davie, Donald. *Articulate Energy: An Inquiry into the Syntax of English Poetry*. London: Routledge & Paul, 1955.

———. *Poet as Sculptor*. New York: Oxford University Press, 1964.

DeFrancis, John. *The Chinese Language: Fact and Fantasy*. Honolulu: University of Hawai'i Press, 1984.

DeMartion, Richard. *Sources of Japanese Tradition*. Compiled by Ryusaku Tsunoda, Wm. Theodore de Bary, and Donald Keene. New York: Columbia University Press, 1958.

Derrida, Jacques. "From Restricted to General Economy: A Hegelianism without Reserve." In *Writing and Difference*, 317–50. Chicago: University of Chicago Press, 1978.

———. *Of Grammatology*. Translated by Gayatri Chakravorty Spivak. Baltimore: Johns Hopkins University Press, 1976.

———. "Violence and Metaphysics: An Essay on the Thought of Emmanuel Levinas" [1964]. In *Writing and Difference*, 97–192. Chicago: University of Chicago Press, 1978.

Dōgen. *Shōbōgenzō: Zen Essays*. Translated by Thomas Cleary. Honolulu: University of Hawai'i Press, 1986.

Droit, Roger-Pol. *The Cult of Nothingness*. Translated by David Streight and Pamela Vohnson. Chapel Hill: University of North Carolina Press, 2003.

Dumoulin, Heinrich. *Zen Buddhism: A History*. Vol. 1, *India and China*, and Vol. 2, *Japan*. New York: Macmillan, 1988.

Durkheim, Émile, and Marcel Mauss. *Primitive Classification*. Translated from the French and edited with an introduction by Rodney Needham. Chicago: University of Chicago Press, 1963.

Emerson, Ralph Waldo. "Nature" (1836). In *The Collected Works of Ralph Waldo Emerson: Nature, Addresses, and Lectures*, 8–11. Cambridge, MA: Harvard University Press, 1971.

Eoyang, Eugene Chen. *The Transparent Eye: Reflections on Translation, Chinese Literature, and Comparative Poetics*. Honolulu: University of Hawai'i Press, 1993.

Eshleman, Clayton. "Imagination's Body and Comradely Display." In *Gary Snyder: Dimensions of a Life*, 231–42. San Francisco: Sierra Club Books, 1991.

Fabian, Johannes. *Time and the Other: How Anthropology Makes Its Object.* New York: Columbia University Press, 1983.

Fan, Wenlan. *Wenxin diaolong zhu* 文心雕龍注 [Commentaries on *Wenxin diaolong*]. Beijing: Renmin wenxue chubanshe, 1958.

Fang, Achilles. Preface to *The Classic Anthology Defined by Confucius,* by Ezra Pound, i–xix. Cambridge, MA: Harvard University Press, 1954.

Fanon, Frantz. *Black Skin, White Masks.* New York: Grove, 1967.

Fass, Ekbert. *Toward a New American Poetics.* Santa Barbara, CA: Black Sparrow Press, 1978.

Faure, Bernard. *Chan Insights and Oversights: An Epistemological Critique of the Chan Tradition.* Princeton, NJ: Princeton University Press, 1993.

Fenner, Peter. *The Ontology of the Middle Way.* Boston: Kluwer, 1990.

Fenollosa, Ernest. "Chinese and Japanese Poetry. Draft of Lecture I. Vol. II." 1903. Reprinted in *The Chinese Written Character as a Medium for Poetry: A Critical Edition,* 126–43.

———. "Chinese and Japanese Traits." 1892. Reprinted in *The Chinese Written Character as a Medium for Poetry: A Critical Edition,* 144–52. Originally published in the *Atlantic Monthly,* June 1892, 769–74.

———. "Chinese Ideals." Nov. 15th 1900. Reprinted in *The Chinese Written Character as a Medium for Poetry: A Critical Edition,* 166–73.

———. "The Chinese Written Character as a Medium for Poetry: An Ars Poetica." With a Foreword and Notes by Ezra Pound. 1918, 1936. Reprinted in *The Chinese Written Character as a Medium for Poetry: A Critical Edition,* 41–74.

———. "The Chinese Written Language as the Medium for Poetry." Final draft, ca. 1906, with Pound's notes, 1914–1916. Reprinted in *The Chinese Written Character as a Medium for Poetry: A Critical Edition,* 75–104.

———. "The Coming Fusion of East and West." 1898. Reprinted in *The Chinese Written Character as a Medium for Poetry: A Critical Edition,* 153–65. Originally published in *Harper's New Monthly Magazine,* December 1898, 115–22.

———. "Contemporary Japanese Art: With Examples from the Chicago Exhibit." *Century Illustrated Magazine,* August 1893, 577–81.

———. *East and West: The Discovery of America and Other Poems.* New York: Thomas Y. Crowell, 1936.

———. *Epochs of Chinese & Japanese Art; An Outline History of East Asiatic Design.* London: Heinemann; New York: Frederick A. Stokes, 1921. [Originally published 1912]

———. "Notes for a History of the Influence of China upon the Western World." In Fenollosa, Murakata, and Houghton Library, *The Ernest Fenollosa Papers: The Houghton Library, Harvard University,* 3:171–227.

———. "Preliminary Lectures on The Theory of Literature: A Theory of Literature—Higher Normal School, Tokio, Jan. 25th' 98," 3:115–62 in Murakata, *The Ernest Fenollosa Papers.*

———. "Synopsis of Lectures on Chinese and Japanese Poetry." 1903. Reprinted in *The Chinese Written Character as a Medium for Poetry: A Critical Edition*, 105–25.

Fenollosa, Ernest, Akiko Murakata, and Houghton Library. *The Ernest Fenollosa Papers: The Houghton Library, Harvard University.* 3 vols. Tokyo: Museum Press, 1987.

Fenollosa, Ernest, and Ezra Pound. *The Chinese Written Character as a Medium for Poetry.* [Foreword and Notes by Ezra Pound.] London: S. Knoff, 1936.

———. *The Chinese Written Character as a Medium for Poetry.* [Foreword and Notes by Ezra Pound.] San Francisco: City Lights Books, 1964.

Fields, Rick. *How the Swans Came to America, How the Swans Came to the Lake: A Narrative History of Buddhism in America.* Boston: Shambhala, 1981.

The Flower Ornament Scripture: A Translation of the Avatamsaka Sutra. Translated from the Chinese by Thomas Cleary. 3 vols. Boulder, CO: Shambhala Publications, 1984.

Foucault, Michele. *The Birth of the Clinic: An Archaeology of Medical Perception.* Translated by Alan Sheridan. New York: Vintage, 1973.

———. *Discipline and Punish: The Birth of the Prison.* Translated by Alan Sheridan. New York: Vintage, 1979.

Fredman, Stephen. "Neo-Paganism, Buddhism, and Christianity." In *A Concise Companion to Twentieth-Century American Poetry,* edited by Stephen Fredman, 191–211. Oxford: Blackwell Publishers, 2005.

Frost, Elizabeth. "'In Another Tongue': Body, Image, Text in Theresa Hak Kyung Cha's *Dictée.*" In *We Who Love to Be Astonished: Experimental Women's Writing and Performance Poetics,* edited by Laura Hinton and Cynthia Hogue, 181–92. Tuscaloosa: University of Alabama Press, 2002.

Fung Yu-lan. *A Short History of Chinese Philosophy.* Edited by Derk Bodde. New York: Free Press, 1966, ©1948.

Gadamer, Hans-George. *Truth and Method.* London: Sheed and Ward, 1998.

Galton, Francis, Sir. *Hereditary Genius: An Inquiry into Its Laws and Consequences.* London: Macmillan and Co, 1869.

Garfield, Jay. *Empty Words: Buddhist Philosophy and Cross-Cultural Interpretation.* Oxford: Oxford University Press, 2002.

———. Introduction to *The Fundamental Wisdom of the Middle Way: Nāgārjuna's Mūlamadhyamakakārikā.* Oxford: Oxford University Press, 1995.

Gefin, Laszlo. *Ideogram.* Austin: University of Texas Press, 1982.

Gelpi, Albert. "The Genealogy of Postmodernism: Contemporary American Poetry." *The Southern Review* 26 (Summer 1990): 517 41.

Giles, Paul. *Virtual Americas: Transnational Fictions and the Transatlantic Imaginary.* Durham, NC: Duke University Press, 2002.

Gobineau, Arthur, comte de. *The Inequality of Human Races.* New York: G. P. Putman's Sons, 1915.

Goldsmith, Kenny. *Day.* New York: The Figures, 2003.

Gompers, Samuel. "Imperialism—Its Dangers and Wrongs." In *Republic or Empire? The Philippine Question,* edited by William Jennings Bryan et al. Chicago: Independence, 1899.

Graham, A. C. *Poems of the Late T'ang.* New York: Penguin, 1970.

Gray, Timothy. *Gary Snyder and the Pacific Rim: Creating Counter-Cultural Community.* Iowa City: University of Iowa Press, 2006.

Greenblatt, Stephen. *Marvelous Possessions: The Wonder of the New World.* Chicago: University of Chicago Press, 1991.

Grice, Helena. "Korean American National Identity in Theresa Hak Kyung Cha's *Dictée.*" In *Representing Lives: Women and Auto/Biography,* edited by Alison Donnell and Pauline Polkey, 43–52. New York: St. Martin's Press, 2000.

Gu, Ming Dong. "Aesthetic Suggestiveness in Chinese Thought: A Symphony of Metaphysics and Aesthetics." *Philosophy East and West* 53, no. 4 (October 2003): 490–513.

———. *Chinese Theories of Reading and Writing.* Albany: SUNY Press, 2005.

Guarino-Trier, Jennifer. "'From the Multitude of Narratives . . . For Another Telling for Another Recitation': Constructing and Re-Constructing *Dictée* and *Memory/all echo.*" In *Screening Asian Americans,* edited by Peter Feng, 253–72. New Brunswick, NJ: Rutgers University Press, 2002.

Hamilton, James. "East-West Borrowings via the Silk Road of Textile Terms." *Diogenes* 43, no. 3 (1995): 25–33.

Hakuin. *Zen Words for the Heart: Hakuin's Commentary on the Heart Sutra.* Translated by Norman Wadell. Boston: Shambhala, 1996.

Harvey, Youngsook Kim. *Six Korean Women: The Socialization of Shamans.* St. Paul, MN: West, 1979.

Hayot, Eric. *Chinese Dreams: Pound, Brecht, Tel Quel.* Ann Arbor: University of Michigan Press, 2003.

———. "Critical Dreams: Orientalism, Modernism, and the Meaning of Pound's China." *Twentieth Century Literature* 45, no. 4 (Winter 1999): 511–33.

Heidegger, Martin. *On the Way to Language.* Translated by Peter D. Hertz. New York: Harper and Row, 1971.

Hejinian, Lyn. "The Rejection of Closure." In *Language of Inquiry,* 40–58. Berkeley: University of California Press, 2000.

Herbert, Kevin. "The Silk Road: The Link between the Classical World and Ancient China." *Classical Bulletin* 73, no. 2 (1997): 119–24.

Hinton, David. *The Mountain Poems of Hsieh Ling-yün.* New York: New Directions, 2001.

Hobson, Geary. *The Remembered Earth: An Anthology of Contemporary Native American Literature.* Albuquerque, NM: Red Earth Press, 1979.

Hoffman, Yoel, trans. *The Sound of One Hand.* New York: Basic Books, 1975.

Hogan, Patrick Colm. "Ethnocentrism and the Very Idea of Literary Theory." *College Literature* 23, no. 1 (1996): 1–14.

Hopkins, Jeffrey. *Meditation on Emptiness*. London: Wisdom Publication, 1983.

Hsiao, Paul Shih-yi. "Heidegger and Our Translation of the Tao Te Ching." In *Heidegger and Asian Thought*, edited by Graham Park, 93–104. Honolulu: University of Hawai'i Press, 1987.

Huang, Yunte. *Transpacific Displacement: Ethnography, Translation, and Intertextual Travel in Twentieth-Century American Literature*. Berkeley: University of California Press, 2002.

———. *Transpacific Imaginations: History, Literature, Counterpoetics*. Cambridge, MA: Harvard University Press, 2008.

Hugo, Victor. *Les Misérables* [1862]. Project Gutenberg, EText-No. 135, http://www.gutenberg.org/etext/135.

Hui Hai. *The Zen Teaching of Instantaneous Awakening*. Translated by John Blofeld. Leicester, U.K.: Buddhist Publishing Group, 1987.

Hunt, Anthony. *Genesis, Structure, and Meaning in Gary Snyder's "Mountains and Rivers Without End."* Reno: University of Nevada Press, 2004.

Huntington, C. W, Jr., with Geshé Namgyal Wangchen. *The Emptiness of Emptiness: An Introduction to Early Indian Mādhyamika*. Honolulu: University of Hawai'i Press, 1989.

Huntington, Rania. "Crossing Boundaries: Transcendents and Aesthetics in the Six Dynasties." In *Chinese Aesthetics: The Ordering of Literature, the Arts, and the Universe in Six Dynasties*, edited by Zong-qi Cai, 191–222. Honolulu: University of Hawai'i Press, 2004.

Huntington, Samuel. *The Clash of Civilizations and the Remaking of World Order*. New York: Simon & Schuster, 1996.

Inoue, Enryō. *Bukkyo katsuron: Joron*. Tokyo: Testusgaku Shoin, 1887.

Irigaray, Luce. *Speculum of the Other Woman*, translated by Gillian G. Gill. Ithaca, NY: Cornell University Press, 1985.

Ito, Yutaka. "'Words quite fail': The Life and Thought of Ernest Francisco Fenollosa." Ph.D. diss., Rutgers University, 2002.

Jacob, H. E. *Six Thousand Years of Bread: Its Holy and Unholy History*. New York: Lyons and Burford, 1944.

James, William. *Principles of Psychology*. (1890). Frederick H. Burkhardt, general editor; Fredson Bowers, textual editor; Ignas K. Skrupskelis, associate editor. 3 vols. Cambridge, MA: Harvard University Press, 1981.

Jansen, Marius B. "Modernization and Foreign Policy in Meiji Japan." In *Political Development in Modern Japan*, edited by Robert Ward, 149–88. Princeton, NJ: Princeton University Press, 1968.

Jullien, François. *Le détour et l'accès: Stratégies du sens en chine, en gréce*. Paris: Grasset, 1951.

Kang, Laura Hyun Yi. *Compositional Subjects*. Durham, NC: Duke University Press, 2002.

Kao, Yu-kung. "The Aesthetics of Regulated Verse." In *The Vitality of the Lyr-*

ic Voice: Shih Poetry from the Late Han to the T'ang, edited by Shuen-fu Lin and Stephen Owen, 332–85. Princeton, NJ: Princeton University Press, 1986.

Karlgren, Bernhard. *Analytic Dictionary of Chinese and Sino-Japanese.* Paris: Geuthner, 1923.

Kennedy, George. "Fenollosa, Pound, and the Chinese Characters." *Yale Literary Magazine* 126, no. 5 (1958): 24–36.

Kenner, Hugh. *The Pound Era.* Berkeley: University of California Press, 1971.

Kern, Robert. *Orientalism, Modernism, and the American Poem.* Cambridge: Cambridge University Press, 1996.

Kim, Elaine. "Poised on the In-between: A Korean American's Reflection on Theresa Hak Kyung Cha's *Dictée.*" In *Writing Self, Writing Nation: A Collection of Essays on "Dictée" by Theresa Hak Kyung Cha,* edited by Elaine Kim and Norma Alarcón, 3–30. Berkeley: Third Woman Press, 1994.

Kim, Youngsook. *Six Korean Women: The Socialization of Shamans.* St. Paul, MN: West, 1979.

King, Richard. *Orientalism and Religion: Postcolonial Theory, India, and 'The Mystic East.'* London: Routledge, 1999.

Kingston, Maxine Hong. *The Woman Warrior.* New York: Vintage, 1989.

Kitarō, Nishida. "The Problem of Japanese Culture." Translated by Masao Abe and Richard DeMartion. In *Sources of Japanese Tradition,* edited by Ryusaku Tsunoda, Wm. Theodore de Bary, and Donald Keene, 857–72. New York: Columbia University Press, 1958.

Klein, Lucas. "Liu Zongyuan & Fishing in the Snow of Translation." *Cipher Journal,* http://www.cipherjournal.com/html/liu_zongyuan.html.

Kodama, Sanehide. *American Poetry and Japanese Culture.* Hamdon, CT: Archon Books, 1984.

Kristeva, Julia. *Language: The Unkown.* Translated by Anne M. Menke. New York: Columbia University Press, 1989.

———. *The Powers of Horror.* New York: Columbia, 1982.

Kroll, Paul. "Body Gods and Inner Vision: The Scripture of the Yellow Court." In *Religions of China in Practice,* edited by Donald Lopez, 149–65. Princeton, NJ: Princeton University Press, 1996.

Kuki Shūzō (九鬼周造). "Haideggā no tetsugaku" (The Philosophy of Heidegger). Tokyo: Iwanamishoten (岩波書店), 1933.

———. *Kuki Shūzō: A Philosopher's Poetry and Poetics.* Translated and edited by Michael F. Marra. Honolulu: University of Hawai'i Press, 2004.

———. *Reflections on Japanese Taste: The Structure of Iki.* Translated by John Clark; edited by Sakuko Matsui and John Clark. Champaign-Urbana: University of Illinois Press, 2007.

Lagapa, Jason. "Something from Nothing: The Disontological Poetics of Leslie Scalapino." *Contemporary Literature* 47, no. 1 (2006): 30–61.

Lai, Whalen. "Chinese Buddhist Causation Theories: An Analysis of the Sinitic Mahayana Understanding of Pratitya-samutpada." *Philosophy East and West* 27, no. 3 (July 1977): 241–64.

———. "Ch'an Metaphors: Waves, Water, Mirror, Lamp." *Philosophy East and West* 29, no. 3. (July 1979): 243–53.

Laing, Ellen Johnston. "Neo-Taoism and the 'Seven Sages of the Bamboo Grove' in Chinese Painting." *Artibus Asiae* 36, nos. 1–2 (1974): 5–54.

Lan, Feng. *Ezra Pound and Confucianism: Remaking Humanism in the Face of Modernity*. Toronto: University of Toronto Press, 2005.

Lao Zi. *Tao Te Ching*. Translated by Stephen Addiss and Stanley Lombardo. Cambridge: Hackett Press, 1993.

Lapsley, Robert, and Michael Westlake. *Film Theory: An Introduction*. Manchester, U.K.: Manchester University Press, 1989.

Lee, Kun Jong. "Princess Pari in Nora Okja Keller's *Comfort Woman*." *Positions: East Asia Cultures Critique* 12, no. 2 (2004): 431–56.

———. "Rewriting Hesiod, Revisioning Korea: Theresa Hak Kyung Cha's *Dictée* as a Subversive Hesiodic Catalogue of Women." *College Literature* 33, no. 3 (Summer 2006): 77–99.

Lee, Robert. *Orientals: Asian Americans in Popular Culture*. Philadelphia: Temple University Press, 1999.

Lee, Sue-Im. "Suspicious Characters: Realism, Asian American Identity, and Theresa Hak Kyung Cha's *Dictée*." *Journal of Narrative Theory* 32, no. 2 (Summer 2002): 227–58.

Leed, Jacob. "Gary Snyder, Han Shan, and Jack Kerouac." *Journal of Modern Literature* 11, no. 1 (March 1984): 185–93.

Legge, James. *The Sacred Books of the East*. Vol. 16. Oxford: Clarendon, 1899.

Levertov, Denise. *The Poet in the World*. New York: New Directions, 1973.

Levinas, Emanuel. *Otherwise than Being: or, Beyond Essence*. Translated by Alphonso Lingis. The Hague: Nijhoff, 1981.

———. *Totality and Infinity*. Translated by Alphonso Lingis. Pittsburgh: Duquesne University Press, 1969.

Lew Walter K. *Excerpts from, Diktē = Dikte: For Dictée (1982)*. Seoul: Yeul Eum, 1992.

Lewallen, Constance. *The Dream of the Audience: Theresa Hak Kyung Cha (1951–1982)*. With essays by Lawrence R. Rinder and Trihn T. Min-ha. Berkeley: University of California Berkeley Art Museum and University of California Press, 2001.

Li, Wai yee. "The Rhetoric of Spontaneity in Late-Ming Literature." *Ming Studies* 35 (August 1995): 32–49.

Lin, Julia C. "Yip Wai-lim: A Poet of Exile." In *Essays on Contemporary Chinese Poetry*. Athens: Ohio University Press, 1985.

Little, Stephen. *Taoism and the Arts of China*. Chicago: Art Institute of Chicago; Berkeley: University of California Press, 2000.

Liu, James J. Y. *The Art of Chinese Poetry*. Chicago: University of Chicago Press, 1962

———. *Chinese Theories of Literature*. Chicago: University of Chicago Press, 1975.

Liu, Lydia H. *Translingual Practice: Literature, National Culture, and Translated Modernity: China, 1900–1937*. Stanford, CA: Stanford University Press, 1995.

Liu, Ming-wood. *Madhyamika Thought in China*. Leiden: E. J. Brill, 1994.

Liu Xie. *Book of Literary Design*. Translated by Siu-kit Wong, Allan Chung-hang Lo, and Kwong-tai Lam. Hong Kong: Hong Kong University Press, 1999.

———. *The Literary Mind and the Carving of Dragons*. Translated by Vincent Yu-chung Shi. Rev. ed. Hong Kong: Chinese University Press, 1983.

Liu, Zhongyu. Essay Available at the Taoist Culture and Information Centre website http://eng.taoism.org.hk.

Looking East: Brice Marden, Michael Mazur, Pat Steir. Exhibition and Catalogue by John Stomberg; additional essay by Catherine L. Blais. Seattle: University of Washington Press, 2002.

Lopez, Donald. *Elaborations on Emptiness*. Princeton, NJ: Princeton University Press, 1996.

Lowe, Lisa. *Immigrant Acts: On Asian American Cultural Politics*. Durham, NC: Duke University Press, 1996.

Loy, David. *A Buddhist History of the West: Studies in Lack*. Albany: SUNY Press, 2002.

———. *Nonduality: A Study in Comparative Philosophy*. New Haven, CT: Yale University Press, 1988.

Lusthaus, Dan. *Buddhist Phenomenology: A Philosophical Investigation of Yogacara Buddhism and the Ch'eng Wei-shih lun*. London: Routledge, 2002.

Lynn, Richard John. "Alternate Routes to Self-Realization in Ming Theories of Poetry." In *Theories of the Arts in China*, edited by Susan Bush and Christian Murck, 317–40. Princeton, NJ: Princeton University Press, 1983.

———. "Orthodoxy and Enlightenment: Wang Shih-chen's Theory of Poetry and Its Antecedents." In *The Unfolding of Neo-Confucianism*, edited by W. T. deBary, 217–69. New York: Columbia University Press, 1975.

Magliola, Robert. *Derrida on the Mend*. West Lafayette, IN: Purdue University Press, 1984.

The Mahayana Mahaparinirvana-sutra: A Complete Translation from the Classical Chinese Language in 3 Volumes. Annotated and with full glossary, index, and concordance by Kosho Yamamoto. Ube City, Japan: Karibunko, 1973–75.

Mahdihassan, S. "Alchemy, Chinese versus Greek, an Etymological Approach: A Rejoinder." *American Journal of Chinese Medicine* 16, nos. 1–2 (1988): 83–86.

———. "A Comparative Study of Greek and Chinese Alchemy." *American Journal of Chinese Medicine* 7, no. 2 (1979): 171–81.

———. "Comparing Yin/Yang, the Chinese Symbol of Creation, with Ouroboros of Greek Alchemy." *American Journal of Chinese Medicine* 17, nos. 3–4 (1989): 95–98.

Mair, Victor H., and Tsu-Lin Mei. 1991. "The Sanskrit Origins of Recent Style Prosody." *Harvard Journal of Asiatic Studies* 51, no. 2 (December): 375–470.

Martin, Heather. *W. B. Yeats: Metaphysician as Dramatist*. Gerrards Cross, U.K.: Colin Smythe, 1986.

Martins Janeira, Armando. *Japanese and Western Literature: A Comparative Study*. Rutland, VT: C. E. Tuttle, 1970.

Masuzawa, Tomoko. *The Invention of World Religions*. Chicago: University of Chicago Press, 2005.

McCort, Dennis. *Going beyond the Pairs: The Coincidence of Opposites in German Romanticism, Zen, and Deconstruction*. Albany: SUNY Press, 2001.

McGann, Jerome. "Wordsworth and the Ideology of Romantic Poems." In *The Romantic Ideology: A Critical Investigation*, 81–92. Chicago: University of Chicago Press, 1983.

McMahan, David L. *Empty Vision: Metaphor and Visionary Imagery in Mahayana Buddhism*. London: Curzon, 2002.

McNiece, Ray, and Larry Smith, eds. *America Zen: A Gathering of Poets*. Huron, OH: Bottom Dog Press, 2004.

Meyer, Steven. *Irresistible Dictation: Gertrude Stein and the Correlations of Writing and Science*. Stanford, CA: Stanford University Press, 2001.

Miao, Ronald, and Marie Chan, eds. *Studies in Chinese Poetry and Poetics*. San Francisco: Chinese Materials Center, 1978.

Miller, Lucien. "East-West Literary Relations: The 'Wisdom' of the East." In *Masterworks of Asian Literature in Comparative Perspective: A Guide for Teaching*, edited by Barbara Stoler Miller, 526–38. Armonk, NY: Sharpe, 1994.

Miller, Stuart. *Benevolent Assimilation: The American Conquest of the Philippines, 1899–1903*. New Haven: Yale University Press, 1982.

Min, Eun Kyung. "Reading the Figure of Dictation in Theresa Hak Kyung Cha's *Dictée*." In *Other Sisterhoods: Literary Theory and U.S. Women of Color*, edited by Sandra Kumamoto Stanley, 309–24. Urbana: University of Illinois Press, 1998.

Miner, Earl Roy. *Comparative Poetics: An Intercultural Essay on Theories of Literature*. Princeton, NJ: Princeton University Press, 1990.

———. *The Japanese Tradition in British and American Literature*. Princeton, NJ: Princeton University Press, 1958.

Minh-ha, Trinh T. "The Plural Void: Barthes and Asia." Translated by Stanley Gray. *SubStance*, Issue 36, vol. 11, no. 3 (1982): 41–50.

———. "White Spring." In *The Dream of the Audience: Theresa Hak Kyung Cha*

(1951–1982), by Constance M. Lewallen, with essays by Lawrence R. Rinder and Trihn T. Minh-ha. Berkeley: University of California Berkeley Art Museum and University of California Press, 2001.

Mitchell, Frank. *The 17 Horse Songs of Frank Mitchell, Nos. X–XIII*. Edited by Jerome Rothenberg; total translations from the Navaho Indian; with images by Ian Tyson. London: Tetrad Press, 1969.

Morton, W. Scott. "No Plays and Greek Tragedy: A Preliminary Comparison." *American Asian Review* 4, no. 1 (1986): 44–60. Originally published in *International Congress of Orientalists (29th: 1973: Paris, France)*. Paris: The Congress, 1973, 2:87–91.

Nāgārjuna (2nd cent.). *The Fundamental Wisdom of the Middle Way: Nāgārjuna's Mūlamadhyamakakārika*. Translation and commentary by Jay Garfield. Oxford: Oxford University Press, 1995.

Nan, Hui-Chin. *The Story of Chinese Zen*. Translated by Thomas Cleary. Boston: Charles E. Tuttle, 1995.

Nancy, Jean-Luc. *The Ground of the Image*. New York: Fordham University Press, 2005.

Nara, Hiroshi. *The Structure of Detachment: The Aesthetic Vision of Kuki Shūzō, with a Translation of "Iki no kôzô."* Honolulu: University of Hawai'i Press, 2004.

Needham, Joseph. *Science and Civilization in China*. Vol. 2. Cambridge: Cambridge University Press, 1956.

Nietzsche, Friedrich. *The Genealogy of Morals*. Translated by Francis Golffing. New York: Anchor Books, 1956.

Niranjana, Tejaswini. *Siting Translation: History, Post-Structuralism, and the Colonial Context*. Berkeley: University of California Press, 1992.

Nishida Kitarō. "The Problem of Japanese Culture." Translated by Masao Abe and Richard DeMartion. In *Sources of Japanese Tradition*, compiled by Ryūsaku Tsunoda, Wm. Theodore de Bary, and Donald Keene, 857–72. New York: Columbia University Press, 1958.

———. "Towards a Philosophy of Religion with the Concept of Pre-Established Harmony as Guide." Translated by David A. Dilworth. *Eastern Buddhist*, n.s., 3, no. 1 (1970): 19–46.

Noriaki, Hakamaya. "Critical Philosophy versus Topical Philosophy." In *Pruning the Bodhi Tree*, edited by Jamie Hubbard and Paul Swanson. Honolulu: University of Hawai'i Press, 1997.

Norton, Jody. "The Importance of Nothing: Absence and Its Origins in the Poetry of Gary Snyder." *Contemporary Literature* 28, no. 1 (Spring 1987): 41–66.

Nute, Kevin. "Frank Lloyd Wright and Japanese Art. Fenollosa: The Missing Link." *Architectural History*, no. 34 (1991): 224–30.

Okakura, Kakuzo. *The Book of Tea*. 1906. Available online at La Alameda Press, http://www.laalamedapress.com/bookoftea2.pdf.

———. *The Ideals of the East, with Special Reference to the Art of Japan.* London: J. Murray, 1903.

Olson, Charles. "The Gate and the Center" [1951]. In *Collected Prose*, by Charles Olson, edited by Donald Allen and Benjamin Friedlander, 169. Berkeley: University of California Press, 1997.

———. "Projective Verse." In *The Poetics of the New American Poetry*, edited by Donald Allen, 147–57. New York: Grove Press, 1973.

Ostriker, Alicia. "The Poet as Heroine: Learning to Read H. D." *American Poetry Review* 12, no. 2 (1983): 29–38.

Owen, Stephen. "Omen of the World: Meaning in the Chinese Lyric." In *Chinese Aesthetics and Literature: A Reader*, 71–103. Albany: SUNY Press, 2004.

———. *Readings in Chinese Literary Thought.* Cambridge, MA: Council on East Asian Studies, Harvard University Press, 1992.

———. Review of *Chinese Poetry: Major Modes and Genres*, by Wai-lim Yip. *Journal of Asian Studies* 37, no. 1 (November 1977): 100–102.

———. *Traditional Chinese Poetry and Poetics: Omen of the World.* Madison: University of Wisconsin Press, 1985.

Palmer, Martin. *T'ung Shu: The Ancient Chinese Almanac.* Boston: Shambhala, 1986.

Palumbo-Liu, David. *The Poetics of Appropriation: The Literary Theory and Practice of Huang Tingjian.* Stanford, CA: Stanford University Press, 1993.

Park, Jin Y. "The Logic of Nothing and A-Metaphysics." In *Buddhism and Postmodernity: Zen, Huayan, and the Possibility of Buddhist Postmodern Ethics.* Lanham, MD: Lexington Books, 2008.

Park, Josephine Nock-Hee. "What of the Partition": *Dictée's* Boundaries and the American Epic." *Contemporary Literature* 46, no. 2 (2005): 213–42.

Parkinson, Thomas. "The Poetry of Gary Snyder." *Southern Review* 4 (Summer 1968): 616–32.

Patke, Rajeev S. Response to "Gary Snyder, Dōgen, and 'The Canyon Wren.'" *Connotations* 8, no. 2 (1998/99): 261–67.

Perelman, Bob. "Poetry in Theory." *Diacritics* 26, nos. 3–4 (1996): 158–75.

Perloff, Marjorie. *The Dance of the Intellect: Studies in the Poetry of the Pound Tradition.* Cambridge: Cambridge University Press, 1986.

———. *The Poetics of Indeterminacy: Rimbaud to Cage.* Princeton, NJ: Princeton University Press, 1981.

Pound, Ezra. *ABC of Reading.* Norfolk, CT: New Directions, 1951.

———. *The Cantos.* New York: New Directions, 1970.

———. *Cathay.* London: E. Mathews, 1915.

———. *The Classic Anthology Defined by Confucius.* Cambridge, MA: Harvard University Press, 1954.

———. *Confucius: The Great Digest, the Unwobbling Pivot, and the Analects.* New York: New Directions, 1969, 1951.

———. "A Few Dont's by an Imagiste." *Poetry* 1 (March 1913): 200–206.

―――. *Literary Essays of Ezra Pound*. Edited with an introduction by T. S. Eliot. Norfolk, CT: J. Laughlin, 1954.

―――. *Pavannes and Divagations*. New York: Knopf, 1918.

―――. *The Selected Letters of Ezra Pound, 1907–1941*. Edited by D. D. Paige. New York: New Directions, 1971.

―――. *Selected Poems*. New York: New Directions, 1949.

―――. "Vorticism." In *Gudier-Brzeska: A Memoir*, 81–94. New York: New Directions, 1970.

Pruning the Bodhi Tree: The Storm over Critical Buddhism. Edited by Jamie Huggard and Paul Swanson. Honolulu: University of Hawai'i Press, 1997.

Pyle, Kenneth. *The New Generation in Meiji Japan: Problems of Cultural Identity, 1885–1895*. Stanford, CA: Stanford University Press, 1969.

Qian, Zhaoming. *Orientalism and Modernism: The Legacy of China in Pound and Williams*. Durham, NC: Duke University Press, 1995.

Quasha, George, and Jerome Rothenberg, eds. *America, a Prophecy: A New Reading of American Poetry from Pre-Columbian Times to the Present*. New York: Random House, 1973.

Richardson, Brenda. *Brice Marden: Cold Mountain*. New Haven, CT: Yale University Press, 2007.

Rickett, Adele Austin. *Chinese Approaches to Literature from Confucius to Liang Ch'i-ch'ao*. Princeton, NJ: Princeton University Press, 1978.

Rinder, Lawrence. "The Plurality of Entrances, the Opening of Networks, the Infinity of Languages." In *The Dream of the Audience: Theresa Hak Kyung Cha (1951–1982)*, by Constance Lewallen, with essays by Lawrence R. Rinder and Trihn T. Min-ha, 15–31. Berkeley: University of California Berkeley Art Museum and University of California Press, 2001.

Robertson, Maureen. " . . . To Convey What Is Precious: Ssu-k'ung Tu's Poetics and the *Erh-shih-ssu Shi P'in*." In *Translation and Permanence: A Festschrift in Honor of Dr. Hsiao Kung-ch'uan*, edited by David C. Buxbaum and Frederick W. Mote, 323–57. Hong Kong: Cathay Press, 1972.

Robinet, Isabelle. *Taoism: Growth of a Religion*. Stanford, CA: Stanford University Press, 1992.

Russell, George. *The Candle of Vision*. London: Macmillan, 1918.

Said, Edward. *Orientalism*. New York: Vintage, 1979.

Sang-hun, Choe. "Shamanism Enjoys Revival in Techno-Savvy South Korea." *New York Times*, July 7, 2007.

Sapir, Edward. *Selected Writings of Edward Sapir in Language, Culture, and Personality*. Edited by David G. Mandelbaum. University of California Press, 1989, 1949.

Sarra, Edith. "Whistling in the Bughouse: Notes on the Process of Pound's Confucian Odes." *Paideuma* 16, no. 1 (1987): 7–31.

Saso, Michael. *Blue Dragon, White Tiger: Taoist Rites of Passage*. Honolulu: University of Hawai'i Press, 1990.

———. *Teachings of Master Chuang.* New Haven, CT: Yale University Press, 1978.

Saussy, Haun. "Fenollosa Compounded: A Discrimination." Introduction to *The Chinese Written Character as a Medium for Poetry: A Critical Edition,* 1–40. New York: Fordham University Press, 2008.

———. *Great Walls of Discourse and Other Adventures in Cultural China.* Cambridge, MA: Harvard University Press, 2001.

———. *The Problem of a Chinese Aesthetic.* Stanford, CA: Stanford University Press, 1993.

Scalapino, Leslie. Introduction to *Overtime,* by Philip Whalen. New York: Penguin Poets, 1999.

Scharfstein, Ben-Ami. "Zen: The Tactics of Emptiness." Introduction to *The Sound of the One Hand: 281 Zen Koans with Answers,* by Hau Hōō; translated, with a commentary by Yoel Hoffmann; foreword by Zen Master Hirano Sōjō. New York: Basic Books, 1975.

Schelling, Andrew, ed. *The Wisdom Anthology of North American Buddhist Poetry.* Boston: Wisdom Publications, 2005.

Schipper, Kristofer. *The Taoist Body,* translated by Karen C. Duval. Berkeley: University of California Press, 1993.

Schipper, Kristofer, and Franciscus Verellen. "Quanzhen Texts: An Introduction." In *The Taoist Canon,* edited by Kristofer Schipper and Franciscus Verellen. Chicago: University of Chicago Press, 2005.

Schleifer, Ron. "The Poetics of Tourette Syndrome: Language, Neurobiology, and Poetry." *New Literary History* 32, no. 3 (2001): 563–84.

Sharf, Robert H. "The Zen of Japanese Nationalism." In *Curators of the Buddha: The Study of Buddhism under Colonialism,* edited by Donald S. Lopez. Chicago: University of Chicago Press, 1995.

———. "Who's Zen: Zen Nationalism Revisited." In *Rude Awakenings: Zen, the Kyoto School, & Zen Nationalism,* edited by James W. Heisig and John C. Maraldo. Honolulu: University of Hawai'i Press, 1995.

Shen Yue. "Xie Lingyun zhuanlun" [Biography of Xie Lingyun]. In *Song Shu* [History of the Song dynasty]. Beijing: Zhonghua Shuju, 1974.

Shigematsu, Soiku. *A Zen Forrest.* New York: Weatherhill, 1981.

Shih, Shu-mei. "Nationalism and Korean American Women's Writing: Theresa Hak Kyung Cha's *Dictée.*" In *Speaking the Other Self: American Women Writers,* edited by Jeanne Campbell Reesman, 144–62. Athens: University of Georgia Press, 1997.

Shirō, Matsumoto. "The Doctrine of *Thatāgata-garbha* Is Not Buddhist." In *Pruning the Bodhi Tree,* edited by Jamie Hubbard and Paul Swanson, 165–73. Honolulu: University of Hawai'i Press, 1997.

Snodgrass, Judith. *Presenting Japanese Buddhism to the West.* Chapel Hill: University of North Carolina Press, 2003.

Snyder, Gary. *Axe Handles.* San Francisco: North Point Press, 1983.

———. *The Back Country.* New York: New Directions, 1968.

———. *Earth House Hold: Technical Notes & Queries for Fellow Dharma Revolutionaries.* New York: New Directions, 1969.

———. Foreword to *A Zen Forest, Sayings of the Masters,* compiled and translated, with an introduction by Soiku Shigematsu. New York: Weatherhill, 1981.

———. *The Fudo Trilogy.* Berkeley, CA: Shaman Drum, 1973.

———. *The Gary Snyder Reader: Prose, Poetry, and Translations, 1952–1998.* Washington, DC: Counterpoint, 1999.

———. *He Who Hunted Birds in His Father's Village: The Dimensions of a Haida Myth.* Bolinas, CA: Grey Fox, 1979.

———. *Left Out in the Rain: New Poems, 1947–1985.* San Francisco: North Point Press, 1986.

———. *Manzanita.* Bolinas, CA: Four Seasons Foundation, 1972.

———. *Mountains and Rivers without End.* Washington, DC: Counterpoint, 1996.

———. *Myths & Texts.* New York: Totem Press/Corinth Books, 1960.

———. *No Nature: New and Selected Poems.* New York: Pantheon, 1992.

———. *North Pacific Lands & Waters: A Further Six Sections.* Waldron Island, WA: Brooding Heron Press, 1993.

———. *The Old Ways: Six Essays,* San Francisco: City Lights, 1977.

———. *A Place in Space: Ethics, Aesthetics, and Watersheds: New and Selected Prose.* Washington, DC: Counterpoint, 1995.

———. *The Practice of the Wild.* San Francisco: North Point Press, 1990.

———. *A Range of Poems.* London: Fulcrum Press, 1966.

———. *The Real Work: Interviews & Talks, 1964–1979.* Edited by William Scott McLean. New York: New Directions, 1980.

———. "Reflections on My Translations of the T'ang Poet Han Shan." In *The Poem behind the Poem,* 233–38. Honolulu: University of Hawai'i Press, 2004.

———. *Regarding Wave.* London: Fulcrum Press, 1972.

———. *Riprap.* Kyoto, Japan: Origin Press, 1959.

———. *Riprap & Cold Mountain Poems.* San Francisco: Four Seasons Foundation, 1965.

———. *Turtle Island.* New York: New Directions, 1974.

Soothill, W. E., and Lewis Hodous, comps. *A Dictionary of Chinese Buddhist Terms.* Livingston, NJ: Orient Book Distributors, 1977. Available online at http://www.acmuller.net/soothill/soothill-hodous.html.

Spahr, Juliana. *Everybody's Autonomy.* Tuscaloosa: University of Alabama Press, 2001.

———. "Postmodernism, Readers, and Theresa Hak Kyung Cha's *Dictée.*" *College Literature* 23, no. 3 (October 1996): 23–43.

Staggs, Kathleen M. "In Defence of Japanese Buddhism: Essays from the Meiji Period by Inoue Enryō and Murakami Shenshō." Ph.D. diss., Princeton University, 1979.

———. "'Defend the Nation and Love the Truth': Inoue Enryō and the Revival of Meiji Buddhism." *Monumenta Nipponica* 38, no. 3 (1983): 251–81.

Stalling, Jonathan. "Five Variations of a Poem by Li Yu." *Chain* 10 (2003): 96–109.

Stambaugh, John. *Impermanence Is Buddha-Nature: Dogen's Understanding of Temporality.* Honolulu: University of Hawai'i Press, 1990.

Stimson, Hugh M. "The Sound of a Tarng Poem: 'Grieving about Greenslope,' by Duh-Fuu." *Journal of the American Oriental Society* 89, no. 1 (1969): 59–67.

Stomberg, John. *Looking East: Brice Marden, Michael Mazur, Pat Steir.* Seattle: University of Washington Press, 2002.

Storhoff, Gary. *Understanding Charles Johnson.* Columbia: University of South Carolina Press, 2004.

Storhoff, Gary, and John Whalen-Bridge, eds. *American Buddhism as a Way of Life.* Buddhism and American Culture Series. Albany: SUNY Press, 2010.

Stutley, Margaret. *Shamanism, an Introduction.* London: Routledge, 2003.

Sun, Cecile Chu-chin. *Pearl from the Dragon's Mouth: Evocation of Scene and Feeling in Chinese Poetry.* Ann Arbor: Center for Chinese Studies, University of Michigan, 1995.

Surette, Leon. *Pound in Purgatory: From Economic Radicalism to Anti-Semitism.* Champaign: University of Illinois Press, 1999.

Suzuki, Daisetz Teitaro. *The Lankavatara Sutra: One of the Most Important Texts of Mahayana Buddhism, in Which Almost All Its Principal Tenets are Presented, Including the Teaching of Zen.* Boulder, CO: Prajña Press, 1978.

The Svatantrika-Prasangika Distinction: What Difference Does a Difference Make? Edited by Georges B. J. Dryfus and Sara L. McClintock. Boston: Wisdom Publications, 2003.

Swanson, Paul L. *Foundations of T'ien-T'ai Philosophy: The Flowering of the Two Truths in Chinese Buddhism.* Berkeley, CA: Asian Humanities Press, 1989.

Taccheri, Umberto. "Louis Althusser's 'Ideology and Ideological State Apparatuses.'" 1998. Available online at http://www.english.upenn.edu/~jenglish/Courses/taccheri2.html.

Tedlock, Dennis. *Breath on the Mirror: Mythic Voices and Visions of the Living Maya.* Albuquerque: University of New Mexico Press, 1997.

———. *Finding the Center: The Art of the Zuni Storyteller.* Lincoln: University of Nebraska Press, 1999.

———. *The Spoken Word and the Work of Interpretation.* Philadelphia: University of Pennsylvania Press, 1983.

Translating Chinese Literature. Edited by Eugene Chen Eoyang and Yao-fu Lin. Bloomington: Indiana University Press, 1995.

Trigilio, Tony. *Allen Ginsberg's Buddhist Poetics.* Carbondale: Southern Illinois University Press, 2007.

Tweed, Thomas. *The American Encounter with Buddhism, 1844–1912: Victorian*

Culture & the Limits of Dissent. Chapel Hill: University of North Carolina Press, 2000.

Twelbeck, Kirsten. "'Elle venait de loin': Re-reading *Dictée.*" In *Holding Their Own: Perspectives on the Multi-Ethnic Literatures of the United States,* edited by Dorothea Fischer-Hornung and Heike Raphael-Hernandez, 227–40. Tübingen: Stauffenburg, 2000.

Ueda, Makoto. *Zeami, Bashō, Yeats, Pound: A Study in Japanese and English Poetics.* The Hague: Mouton, 1965.

Varsano, Paula. "Transformation and Imitation: The Poetry of Li Bai." Ph.D. diss., Princeton University, 1988.

Venuti, Lawrence. *The Translator's Invisibility: A History of Translation.* London: Routledge, 1995.

Victoria, Brian (Daizen) A. *Zen at War.* New York: Weatherhill, 1997.

———. *Zen War Stories.* London: Routledge Curzon, 2002.

Wainwright, Bodman Richard. "Poetics and Prosody in Early Mediaeval China: A Study and Translation of Kukai's 'Bunkyo Hifuron.'" Ph.D. diss., Cornell University, 1978.

Waldron, William S. *The Buddhist Unconscious: The Alaya-vijnana in the Context of Indian Thought.* London: Routledge, 2003.

Walsh, Alexander. *Roots of Lyric: Primitive Poetry and Modern Poetics.* Princeton, NJ: Princeton University Press, 1978.

Wang, Robin R. "Zhou Dunyi's Diagram of the Supreme Ultimate Explained (Taijitu shuo): A Construction of the Confucian Metaphysics." *Journal of the History of Ideas* 66, no. 3 (2005): 307–23.

Wang, Wei Wang. *Youcheng ji jian zhu* 王右丞集箋注 [The annotated poetry of Wang Wei, Minister of Works]. Edited by Zhao Diancheng. Shanghai: Guji, 1984.

Waters, Geoff. "Some Notes on Translating Classical Chinese Poetry." *Cipher-Journal's Forum on Chinese Poetry Translation,* http://www.cipherjournal.com/html/waters_forum.html.

Watts, Alan. *Tao: The Watercourse Way.* Edited by Al Huang. New York: Pantheon, 1975.

Whalen-Bridge, John. "Gary Snyder, Dôgen, and 'The Canyon Wren.'" *Connotations* 8, no. 1 (1998–99): 112–26.

———. "My Poet Is Better than Your Poet: A Response to Rajeev Patke." *Connotations* 9, no. 2 (1999–2000): 167–73.

———. "The Sexual Politics of Divine Femininity: Tārā in Transition in Gary Snyder's Poetry." *Partial Answers* 5, no. 2 (2007): 219–44.

Whalen-Bridge, John, and Gary Storhoff, eds. *The Emergence of Buddhist American Literature.* Buddhism and American Culture Series. Albany: SUNY Press, 2009.

Whorf, Benjamin. *Language, Reality, Thought.* Cambridge, MA: MIT Press, 1956.

Wilhelm, James J. *Ezra Pound: The Tragic Years, 1925–1972*. University Park: Pennsylvania State University Press, 1994.

Williams, Rowan. "Insubstantial Evil." In *Augustine and His Critics: Essays in Honour of Gerald Bonner*, edited by Robert Dodaro and George Lawless, 106–23. London: Routledge, 2000.

Wilson, Rob. *Inside Out*. Lanham, MD: Rowman and Littlefield, 1999.

———. *Reimagining the American Pacific*. Durham, NC: Duke University Press, 2000.

Wong, Eva. *Cultivating Stillness: A Taoist Manual for Transforming Body and Mind*. Boston: Shambala, 1992.

———. *The Zen Canon*. Oxford: Oxford University Press, 2004.

Wong, Tak-wai. *East-West Comparative Literature: Cross-Cultural Discourse*. Hong Kong: Department of Comparative Literature, University of Hong Kong, 1993.

Wright, Dale. *Philosophical Meditations on Zen Buddhism*. Cambridge: Cambridge University Press, 1998.

———. *The Zen Canon*. Oxford: Oxford University Press, 2004.

Yamaguchi, Seiichi. *Fenollosa: Nippon bunka no sen'yō ni sasageta isshō* [Ernest Francisco Fenollosa: A life devoted to the advocacy of Japanese culture]. Tokyo: Sansaidō, 1982.

Yampolsky, Phillip, trans. *The Platform Sutra of the Sixth Patriarch*. New York: Columbia University Press, 1967.

Yang, Vincent. *Nature and Self: A Study of the Poetry of Su Dongpo, with Comparisons to the Poetry of William Wordsworth*. New York: Peter Lang, 1989.

Yeats, William Butler. "Where There Is Nothing, There Is God." In *The Collected Works in Verse and Prose of William Butler Yeats*. Stratford-on-Avon: Shakespeare Head Press, 1908.

Yeh, Michelle. "The Chinese Poem: The Visible and the Invisible in Chinese Poetry." In *The Poem Behind the Poem: Translating Asian Poetry*, edited by Frank Stewart, 251–64. Port Townsend, WA: Copper Canyon Press, 2004.

Yip, Wai-lim. "Aesthetic Consciousness of Landscape in Chinese and Anglo-American Poetry." In Yip, *Diffusion of Distances*, 100–137.

———. *Chinese Poetry: An Anthology of Major Modes and Genres*. Durham, NC: Duke University Press, 1997.

———. *The Complete Works of Wai-lim Yip*. Hefei, China: Anhui Education Publishing House, 2002.

———. *Diffusion of Distances: Dialogues Between Chinese and Western Poetics*. Berkeley: University of California Press, 1992.

———. "Language and the Real-Life World." In Yip, *Diffusion of Distances*, 63–99.

———. *Modern Chinese Poetry: Twenty Poets from the Republic of China, 1955–1965*. Iowa City: University of Iowa Press, 1970.

————. *Pound and the Eight Views of Xiao Xiang.* Taipei: National Taiwan University Press, 2009.

————. "Syntax and Horizon of Representation in Classical Chinese and Modern American Poetry." In Yip, *Diffusion of Distances*, 29–62.

————. "The Taoist Aesthetic: Wu-yen tu-hua, the Unspeaking, Self-generating, Self-conditioning, Self-tranforming, Self-complete Nature." *New Asia Academic Bulletin* 1 (1978): 17–32.

————. "The Use of 'Models' in East–West Comparative Literature." In Yip, *Diffusion of Distances*, 8–28.

————. *Zhongguo shi xue* [Chinese poetics]. Beijing: Sanlian, 1992. [An expanded edition of this title was published by Renmin Wenxue Chubanse in 2006.]

Yip, Wai-lim, and Ezra Pound. *Ezra Pound's Cathay.* Princeton, NJ: Princeton University Press, 1969.

Yu, Pauline. *The Poetry of Wang Wei: New Translations and Commentary.* Bloomington: Indiana University Press, 1980.

————. *The Reading of Imagery in the Chinese Tradition.* Princeton, NJ: Princeton University Press, 1987.

————. "Ssu-k'ung T'u's *Shih-p'in*: Poetic Thoery in Poetic Form." In *Studies in Chinese Poetry and Poetics,* edited by Ronald Miao, 81–103. San Francisco: Chinese Materials Center, 1978.

A Zen Forest, Sayings of the Masters. Compiled and translated, with an introduction by Soiku Shigematsu; foreword by Gary Snyder. New York: Weatherhill, 1981.

Zhang, Longxi. "The Challenge of East-West Comparative Literature." In *China in a Polycentric World: Essays in Chinese Comparative Literature*, edited by Yingjin Zhang. Stanford, CA: Stanford University Press, 1998.

————. *Mighty Opposites: From Dichotomies to Differences in the Comparative Study of China.* Stanford, CA: Stanford University Press, 1998.

————. *The Tao and the Logos: Literary Hermeneutics, East and West.* Durham, NC: Duke University Press, 1992.

Ziporyn, Brook. *The Penumbra Unbound: The Neo-Taoist Philosophy of Guo Xiang.* Albany, NY: SUNY Press, 2003.

Žižek, Slavoj. *The Ticklish Subject: An Essay in Political Ontology.* New York: Verso, 1999.

Index